VISITATION

VISITATION

THE CONJURE WORK OF BLACK FEMINIST AVANT-GARDE CINEMA

Jennifer DeClue

Duke University Press   *Durham and London*   2022

© 2022 Duke University Press. All rights reserved
Designed by Courtney Leigh Richardson
Typeset in Portrait by Copperline Book Services

Library of Congress Cataloging-in-Publication Data
Names: DeClue, Jennifer, [date] author.
Title: Visitation : the conjure work of black feminist avant-garde cinema / Jennifer DeClue. Description: Durham : Duke University Press, 2022. | Includes bibliographical references and index.
Identifiers: LCCN 2022026536 (print)
LCCN 2022026537 (ebook)
ISBN 9781478016526 (hardcover)
ISBN 9781478019169 (paperback)
ISBN 9781478023791 (ebook)
Subjects: LSCH: Womanism—United States. | Feminism and motion pictures—United States. | Experimental films—United States. | African American women motion picture producers and directors. | African American feminists. | Women, Black, in motion pictures. | Feminist film criticism. | BISAC: SOCIAL SCIENCE / Ethnic Studies / American / African American & Black Studies | SOCIAL SCIENCE / Feminism & Feminist Theory
Classification: LCC HQ1197.D435 2022 (print) | LCC HQ1197 (ebook) | DDC 305.48/896073—dc23/eng/20220714
LC record available at https://lccn.loc.gov/2022026536
LC ebook record available at https://lccn.loc.gov/2022026537

Publication of this book is supported by Duke University Press's Scholars of Color First Book Fund.

Cover art: *Six Miles from Springfield on the Franklin Road*, film still, 2009. © Kara Walker. Courtesy of Sikkema Jenkins & Co., New York, and Sprüth Magers, Berlin.

For Miles Violet

Contents

Acknowledgments ix

Introduction. Visitation 1

1 **THE ARCHIVE AND THE SILHOUETTE**
   Framing Black Feminist Avant-Garde Cinema 29

2 **RECKONING AT THE BRIDGE**
   SAVED and the Archive of Laura Nelson 65

3 **CARRYING THE KNOWLEDGE /
   PERFORMING THE ARCHIVE**
   An Afternoon with Marsha P. Johnson 99

4 **ECSTASY AND THE ARCHIVE**
   A Black Feminist Phenomenology of Freedom 143

Coda. On Tenderness 183

Notes 187
Bibliography 211
Index 221

Acknowledgments

I write these acknowledgments from a place quite different from the one I called home for so many years, where the first inklings of this project appeared to me. Some foundational ideas that course through this book emerged while I was a graduate student in the Department of American Studies and Ethnicity (ASE) at the University of Southern California. Now, after seven years in western Massachusetts, this book has come to completion. I have been accompanied by *Visitation*, which found its name nearer the end than the beginning of this process, for so long that it is hard to let go—but it is time to share. As you read and engage with these pages, I hope that you are also able to tap into the frequency that has kept me company for all these years. It is with great pleasure, my deepest honor, and heartfelt gratitude that I share this work with you. I am excited to acknowledge everyone who has been with me and supported me during this chapter of my life. If I missed you, the oversight is entirely unintentional; please know that my gratitude extends to you as well. I have been the grateful recipient of generous support, advice, care, and love from my family and dear friends, treasured scholarly mentors, my fellow grad students and faculty advisors in ASE, archivists, readers, my editors at Duke University Press, and my colleagues here at Smith College.

As a PhD student in ASE, I had the joy of working alongside brilliant fellow graduate scholars Treva Ellison, Jih-Fei Cheng, Sriya Shrestha, Marshall Green, Analena Hope, Jessi Quizar, Rox Samer, Ren-yo Hwang, Deb Al-Najjar, Freda Fair, and Umayyah Cable, who helped me learn to study and express myself as a scholar. I am honored to have worked with, and am still in awe of, our stellar ASE faculty. Ruthie Gilmore, you taught me that power is power and introduced our cohort to the field of American studies and ethnicity by reading, among other vital volumes, W. E. B. Du Bois's *Black Reconstruction in America*, which has impacted me and my work in ways I could not have imagined upon that first reading. Jack Halberstam, you taught me the many dimensions and shapes that a queer form can take and let me sit in on a legendary class way before I joined ASE. Macarena Gómez-Barris, Diana Williams, Lanita Jacobs, and Nayan Shah, you gave me incredible support without question. I was truly given a great gift when Kara Keeling agreed to be my advisor. You taught me how to write about film and how to write about blackness. Kara, you modeled for me just how to be a Black cinema studies professor, and I am forever grateful.

I have also had the great benefit of learning from scholars outside my graduate school experience. The late Kelly Madison introduced me to Stuart Hall, one of the best gifts of a lifetime. Talia Bettcher has been from the start a confidant, an inspiration, and a brilliant teacher, and I am lucky to call her a friend. Alex Juhasz invited me to publish my very first scholarly essay and has been a guiding presence in my academic life since then. You all have given me the foundation, the support, and the courage to become the scholar that I am today. Thank you.

I have been helped, mentored, and academically cared for by Kevin Quashie, Jayna Brown, Amber Musser, E. Patrick Johnson, Arlene Keizer, Daphne Brooks, Jacqueline Najuma Stewart, Jordy Rosenberg, Jasbir Puar, and Roderick Ferguson. Each of you at different moments in time have given me your careful attention, shared your wisdom, and helped me enter into and thrive in academia in ways that every new scholar needs. Thank you.

I have made some of the most exciting and intellectually curious scholarly friends. Our conversations over the years have helped me think about my work and also find comfort in this academic life. Ronak Kapadia, Uri McMillan, Darius Bost, Sybil Cooksey, J. T. Roane, Fumi Okiji: you are brilliant, fun, warm, and kind. You have given me bright lovely memories when our paths have converged, for far too brief but exquisite moments nonetheless.

My lifelong friends supported me during graduate school, before, and beyond. I could not have done what I did without you. Tirien Steinbach, my sister, you inspire me. You make life legendary and I am so thankful that our paths crossed on that fortuitous night in NOLA. Karla Zombro, friend, auntie, road trudger, you keep me sharp and honest. Sally White, you accompanied me to The Kitchen that unforgettable afternoon, thank you for being my STL road dog in NYC. Jian Neo Chen, you helped me understand what academia is, and you've been a friend from the first moment we met. Vick Quezada, you listened, shared your thoughts and style, and helped keep me motivated as I wrote this book. Joaquin Lazo, you were my first art critic co-conspirator. Our explorations of film, art, and music over these many years have helped me hone my aesthetic sensibility, always with good humor and exquisite timing. My friends at the Tropical Cafe, the morning lot and beyond, you keep me here. Thank you. My east coast people, my western Massachusetts confidants Serena Kabat-Zinn, Tommy Claire, Sam Ace, Jasper Gardner, and Jamecia Estes, thank you for bringing joy and clarity and sweet friendship to my life here. Thank you all for becoming my family.

My colleagues at Smith College are amazing and brilliant, warm and dynamic. Lisa Armstrong and Carrie Baker are impeccable models of full professorship; they lead the Program for the Study of Women and Gender in ever-expanding ways. I am as excited about working alongside you as I was on the day that I got the most wondrous phone call letting me know that I was to be Smith's first tenure-track queer studies hire. I am quite fortunate to have wonderful colleagues at Smith: Mehammed Mack, Andrea Moore, Liz Pryor, Jennifer Guglielmo, Daphne Lamothe, Alex Keller, Darcy Buerkle, Kim Kono, Ginetta Candelario, Loretta Ross, Jina Kim, and Candice Price, thank you for making this work fantastic.

I was the recipient of two national fellowships while writing this book, the American Association of University Women Fellowship and the Schomburg Center for Research in Black Culture Scholars-in-Residence Fellowship. I was also awarded funding for my research for this book by Smith College through two Jean Picker Fellowships. The generous support that I received helped me research, write, and complete this manuscript during my sabbatical leave in the 2019–20 academic year. The Schomburg Fellowship was a rich and meaningful experience made possible by the steady leadership and mentorship of the program director, Brent Edwards. I was part of a very special cohort and was able to share work, learning with and from Tashima Thomas, Jarvis McInnis, Tobi Haslett, Jaime Coan, Cord Whitaker, Selena Doss, Maya Harakawa, Laura Helton, Isma'il Kushkush, and Neil Clarke. We all were buttressed by the outstanding work of our research assistants, Margaret Odette and Naomi Lorrain, and graced by the presence of Sister Aisha Al-Adawiya. An extra bonus of my experience at the Schomburg was being able to work with my former ASE colleague, Michelle Commander.

The dedicated archivists at the Schomburg helped me enormously, as did archivists at the New York Public Library, National Archives and Records Administration, and Smith College.

The Dark Room has been a source of camaraderie, deep thinking, and joy. I want to thank Kimberly Juanita Brown for her invitation to join this brilliant group of Black feminist thinkers and for being a fearless, undaunted leader in our pursuit of studying Black visual culture.

I would like to thank the artists whose work I study and discuss in this book: Kara Walker, Kara Lynch, Tourmaline and Sasha Wortzel, Ja'Tovia Gary, Cheryl Dunye, and Julie Dash; your vision inspires as it helps us all see differently. Each of you is devastatingly brilliant, and I am so fortunate to have found your work when I did. It has helped me grow as a scholar and as a Black feminist. You are all incredibly courageous, you make me more courageous, and I hope that what I have written makes you feel seen.

The manuscript was read at various stages of production by brilliant friends and colleagues who gave me kind, honest, clarifying, and incisive feedback. Thank you, Jih-Fei Cheng, Talia Bettcher, Tashima Thomas, Iyko Day, Lisa Armstrong, and Lester Tome; this book would not be what it is without your glorious minds. Because of Kevin Quashie's simple yet provocative question, the book found its beginning. Thank you.

My editor at Duke University Press, Courtney Baker, supported me and this project through its many iterations and through every stage of the process. The whole team of editors and designers at Duke is marvelous—you bring out the best in a writer. Thank you for believing in me and this book.

My family has been with me, supporting me through my years of graduate school and now in my life in western Massachusetts. I would not be here were it not for their kindness, love, and generosity. My mother, Faye; my sister, Julia; my daughter, Miles: you are my rocks and you make life so sweet. Miles, you saw me "on my quals" and loved me through it. I'm so, I'm so, I'm so proud of you! Ray, you came as a surprise in my life during a global pandemic, and now I can't imagine a life without you or your beautiful Young clan. What a whirlwind we've had. I am overjoyed to be on this road with you, and I'm looking forward to all the many seasons of life and crops and books to come. I love you all, and I love how you love me. To all of my DeClues in the Lou—Frank B., Jeff, Rici, Temika, Maria, Cheryl Lynn (sweetheart in heaven)—I love you and thank you for loving me. Ruth DeClue, Nana, you showed us all how to be strong and graceful. You taught us that education is something that no one can take away. I thank you for that lesson. YOU have given me the life that I have today. I miss you every day.

Thank you all for helping me become, helping me belong, helping me be.

INTRODUCTION

Visitation

And besides, contrary to what you may have heard or learned, the past is not done and it is not over, it's still in process, which is another way of saying that when it's critiqued, analyzed, it yields new information about itself. The past is already changing as it is being reexamined, as it is being listened to for deeper resonances. Actually, it can be more liberating than any imagined future if you are willing to identify its evasions, its distortions, its lies, and are willing to unleash its secrets. —TONI MORRISON, "Be Your Own Story"

I am concerned with embodied power, with power derived from the will to domination, I am simultaneously concerned with the power of the disembodied and the stories that those who forcibly undertook the middle passage are still yearning to tell, five centuries later. —M. JACQUI ALEXANDER, *Pedagogies of Crossing*

Disembodied. This is a most exquisite way of describing the quality of existing without, or outside of, or despite not having a body. I, like M. Jacqui Alexander, am concerned with embodied power especially as it relates to storytelling that counters domination and connects with the disembodied. The disembodied can be traced by following Toni Morrison's direction in her "Be Your Own Story" commencement address. Not only does Morrison's speech assure us that the past reveals information about itself upon reexamination, but it also beckons an intrepid archival explorer toward a liberatory path that enlivens dormant temporal connections. Morrison's instigation unleashes the past from ideological conventions that foreclose possibility, an instigation that resonates with Alexander's invocation of the disembodied. In *Pedagogies of Crossing*, from which this epigraph is drawn, Alexander describes the way that dominant time, as it is bound up with secular power, cements the boundary between the embodied and the disembodied, rendering the latter void and silent and imbuing the former with value through its proximity to whiteness, manhood, wealth, and western ideals of progress. The multiplicity of time, the presence of the past in the present, and the impact of the disembodied on the here and now are actively and persistently nullified by "dominant corporate, linear time."[1] Time, as Alexander describes, "becomes a moment, an instant, experienced in the now, but also a space crammed with moments of wisdom about an event or series of events already having inhabited different moments, or with the intention of inhabiting them, while all occurring simultaneously in this instant, in this space, as well as in other instants and spaces of which we are not immediately aware."[2] Black feminist temporal interventions, like those made by Morrison and Alexander, ask us to reexamine a past full of activity and possibility. They remind us of what we already know, that the past is a woefully incomplete story and that the disembodied have crucial perspectives to share.

In *Visitation: The Conjure Work of Black Feminist Avant-Garde Cinema*, I argue that Black feminist avant-garde films use the cinematic medium to conjure visitations that defy dominant impositions of temporality. Following Morrison's challenge to consider the prospect of an unfixed past, I employ the liberatory power of listening for and parsing out the lies, distortions, and evasions that have been embedded within a past presumed unyielding, immutable, complete. In the chapters that follow, I discuss the ways that Black feminist avant-garde filmmakers push the cinematic medium to register encounters with those who once lived and who left behind a record of their time on earth. My attention to conjure work in *Visitation* reveals the ways that Black feminist artists channel stories of the disembodied and in so doing act as mediums who identify evasions, distortions, and lies while they unleash secrets from the past. The filmmakers whose pieces I have brought together in *Visitation* use their conjure work to bend the medium of film into the shape of Black feminist avant-garde cinema. Through their approach to cinema, which I read as a methodology of tenderness, Black feminist avant-garde filmmakers interrupt the force of archival violence that distorts the image of Black women. These are artists who listen deeply for what happened and intervene in the violence that is bound up in an archival document, collection, or repository through cinematic pieces that contribute something back to that very archive.

By following the lead of Black feminist avant-garde filmmakers who grapple with the shifting ground of many pasts, I became immersed in the place where the embodied and disembodied meet. I not only recognized the practice of listening for deeper resonances taking place in Black feminist avant-garde film, but I noticed that I was also participating in this practice. As a scholar tracking this cinematic-archival relationship, I became moved by the current of tenderness in my analysis of archival documentation and the films that incorporate them. From this tender, open place I was able to tap into the frequency that eludes dominant corporate, linear time to better study the conjure work of these Black feminist avant-garde filmmakers, a process that usurps a temporally imposed order that is legitimated through archival collections, assembly, and retrieval and that has no traction or authority in this realm. Through this process, I realized that the archival study, the close readings, and the critical analysis that I share throughout the pages of this book comprise some conjure work of my own. The practice of studying the visitations that unfold in each film demands that I invite the unknown, brace for horrifying details, and listen for that which exceeds sound, time, and bodies. The process of opening to the pain that presents itself plainly in the archive, of being aware of generational suffering that can only be witnessed and not prevented, of seeing, studying, and writing from that vulnerable spot, without reproducing the violence held within an archive but rather mobilizing a love that travels back in time, this is a methodology of tenderness—a practice that allows for an experience of engaging with visitations.

The films that I discuss in Visitation contend with an array of pivotal and exceedingly violent moments in US history, moments in which Black women find themselves marked as targets, as people whose humanity has been evacuated from them, as people who have suffered differently yet persistently from state-sanctioned terror because of their gender, sexuality, and blackness from the time of chattel slavery and reconstruction, through jim crow segregation and the civil rights era, on through the eras of the Stonewall rebellion, the Black Power movement, and now in the age of #BlackLivesMatter.[3] While all Black feminist avant-garde films are not necessarily tied to archival documentation and imperatives, the films that I study here are all immersed therein. These artists use their avant-garde films and videos to channel the stories of disembodied Black women who have moments of their lives, albeit some of the most terrifying ones, recorded and preserved. Though these records exist in the margins of archival collections and are often dispersed across many collections, they do have places in archival repositories and can be found if the one who searches is resolute and a concerted effort is made. The filmmakers whose work I study in this book each harness resolute attention in their transfer of archival documentation into cinematic unfolding.[4]

Visitation examines the relationship between experimental cinematic visualization and the archival documentation, occlusion, and erasure with which these Black feminist avant-garde films contend. I study ways that this work uses cinematic space to respond to documented acts of violence without reproducing the horror of those acts of violence. I discuss how regimes of knowledge, which establish and maintain epistemologies of Black womanhood, are disrupted through Black feminist avant-garde approaches to cinema. The cinematic analysis that I offer over the course of this book demonstrates the ways that these filmmakers, through their use of the short avant-garde film form, exhume Black women in national archives of violence and, I argue, set about to change the past with their visual treatment. The visitations conjured and documented in the films that I discuss are informed by historical documentation of the deaths, sometimes the lives, and most certainly the suffering of the Black women who occupy these filmmakers' cinematic spaces. Together, the Black women who lived and the Black women filmmakers who capture the archival connection, direct the medium of film to magnetize stories and images and register the fact of Black, queer, trans women being, meeting, and being seen through the medium. The past does change when these filmmakers tell the stories of disembodied Black women and tenderness is the methodological key that enables visitations to occur through the conjure work of Black feminist avant-garde cinema.

It is important to note that I am writing about Black womanhood and Black feminist avant-garde cinema as a cisgender Black queer feminist who recognizes that Black womanhood is not tied to biological definitions of womanhood. While I do discuss reproductivity throughout this volume, I am not suggesting that womanhood is defined by one's ability or desire to reproduce. I am interested in tracking the ways that oppression has circulated through the apparatus of Black women's reproductive capacity during slavery and in its afterlife. I believe that *womanhood* is a limiting and oppressive category that actively excludes Black trans women, Black women who are not trans, and trans women who are not Black; in fact, it depends on our exclusion to secure its meaning.[5] In my analysis, I use the term *woman* and I push beyond its limitations to unequivocally address anyone who identifies as a Black woman, and anyone who connects with the experiences of life, subjugation, exclusion, and resistance that I am outlining here. I recognize that we have a wide range of journeys in, to, and through Black womanhood and my use of this term includes people who identify as trans, transsexual, transgender, cis, or non-trans women. If none of these terms works, if the language of gender is too constricting, I hope that the work I am doing here to describe an experience can still reach you despite the limitations that encumber it.

Visitation: Haunting and Conjure Work

The term *visitation* has a host of meanings that range from the pietistic to the apparitional; though the pressure of the former undergirds structures of power that exert themselves on the lives of the women with whom this book is concerned, the latter is the more generative description for this study. The concept of visitation provides a framework with which to discuss an elusive experience of nonnormative time and the sensations that Black feminist avant-garde films materialize. My attraction to the term *visitation*, and the spectral quality that it invokes, is informed by Avery Gordon's foundational book *Ghostly Matters: Haunting and the Sociological Imagination*. In *Ghostly Matters*, Gordon describes haunting with some incisive specificity that bears within it a host of necessarily inexplicable details. In the introduction to the new edition of *Ghostly Matters*, Gordon reveals with alacrity what she meant by haunting in the first edition of her influential volume.

> What's distinctive about haunting is that it is an animated state in which a repressed or unresolved social violence is making itself known, sometimes very directly, sometimes more obliquely. I used the term *haunting* to describe those singular yet repetitive instances when home becomes unfamiliar, when your bearings on the world lose direction, when the over-and-done-with comes alive, when what's been in your blind spot comes into view. Haunting raises specters, and it alters the experience of being in time, the way we separate the past, the present, and the future. These specters or ghosts appear when the trouble they represent and symptomize is no longer being contained or repressed or blocked from view. The ghost, as I understand it, is not the invisible or some ineffable excess. The whole essence, if you can use that word, of a ghost is that it has a real presence and demands its due, your attention. Haunting and the appearance of specters or ghosts is one way, I tried to suggest, we are notified that what's been concealed is very much alive and present, interfering precisely with those always incomplete forms of containment and repression ceaselessly directed toward us.[6]

Visitations revealed through the Black feminist avant-garde films that I discuss in this book chart out pathways through the phenomenon of haunting that Gordon is describing, yet these ghosts have names. The violence that they experienced happened in very specific places at very specific moments in time. The horrific acts suffered were captured in photographs, detailed in sworn testimony, and documented in videos; those records were then stored in physical repositories or in digital archives. The unresolved social violence that occurred was made legible, visible, and certain through the records kept about the specific acts of violence that took place. The conjure work of Black feminist avant-garde film involves this archival documentation; these filmmakers use the records left behind as springboards into pasts where unresolved acts of violence took place. From those cinematic places, they listen for deeper resonances, they let the disembodied tell the stories of their suffering and deaths, and out of this conjure work come visitations.

The films that capture my attention in this book are made by Black women who use the medium to convey cinematically what the archive reports while centering Black women in visual treatments of archival material. I argue that these films, this conjure work, contributes to, as it intervenes in, archival collections. These filmmakers use the short-film form to produce avant-garde cinematic experiences that enable ways of seeing Black women and do not reproduce hypervisibility or become pornotropic.[7] Their films refuse dominant readings of archival material and see beyond evasions and inside distortions by cinematically intervening into archival processes that have left some Black women cruelly overexposed, others obscured in archival repositories, and still others rendered dormant in or absent from archival records entirely. Black feminist avant-garde filmmakers use cinematic techniques of disruption and resistance to call attention to the process of perceiving Black women. Through their cinematic approaches to contending with archival material, these filmmakers unveil systems of knowledge production that collude to create abject epistemologies of Black womanhood; their conjure work creates the space for visitations to unfold before the camera.

Visitation searches the past, through the films that appear in it, for ways that the past can reveal new information about itself; I am compelled by the notion that liberation can be attained by searching the past for evasions and distortions as a means to see anew. I am equally as preoccupied by cinematic pieces that work and rework visual terrain and in so doing expose perversions that are embedded in archival material. Some secrets of the past hide in plain sight in archival documents, while others are scrubbed from the record or withheld entirely. No matter the state of the archival document, attention to the past—in particular attention to Black women in archival collections—unearths deeper resonances and with it lies, secrets, and revelations. My analysis of the visitations that occur through each filmmaker's conjure work studies the way these films do not simply recognize and reproduce images that serve as evidence of Black women's presences in history and in archival collections but rather invite the presence of historical figures to mount the cinematic stage and reveal history from their point of view. Visitations open up an exchange between historical figures and the filmmakers who encounter that subject's archival presence, filmmakers who then find ways to communicate, through the cinematic medium, something fundamental and otherwise occluded about that subject's experience. In this way, Black feminist avant-garde filmmakers are the intrepid souls who become conduits to the past through cinematic conjure work that clears the terrain needed to visualize visitations unleashed by their archival investigations.

On the Avant-Garde

My use of the term *avant-garde* is not employed in opposition to the term *experimental* but rather incorporates that term in its understanding of the work that *avant-garde* does. In their embrace of avant-garde cinematic techniques, these filmmakers use tactics such as etching on celluloid, blurring and stuttering images, startling juxtaposition and repetition, disjointed and nonsequential editing, the presences of puppets, reenactment and performance, the abstraction of sound and image, and temporal contortions and expansions. In fact, the short-film form itself is an instigation that frees filmmakers from the expectations of mainstream film marketing and demands.[8] In the absence of the kinds of restraints and conventions that cleave to feature-length films, Black feminist avant-garde short films are able to innovate through the use of boundary-pushing aesthetics while also using the form to dislodge entrenched understandings of Black womanhood.

I am drawn to the cinematic category of the avant-garde because of the political resistance in which the genre is immersed, and because of the commitment to using the cinematic form to interrogate vision.[9] Though the definition of avant-garde film defies strict categorization, the innovative use of aesthetics to disrupt normative modes of perception may be the most obvious defining feature of films that fall into this category. Avant-garde filmmakers who are credited with creating the genre convey cinematic feelings through their uses of light and color, repetition and duration, overexposure and shadow play, scratching and puncturing the celluloid, voice-over and silence, shock and the mundane.[10] Avant-garde films tend to resist narrative conventions and mainstream appeal while using abstract imagery to trouble visuality, shift perspective, and demand new ways of seeing.

Black feminist avant-garde films use these kinds of aesthetic cinematic practices to instigate their multivalent disruptions. Feminist avant-garde filmmakers—

this is coded as a white feminist mode of visuality—have employed avant-garde aesthetics and techniques to evoke the quiet horror of mundane domesticity.[11] White feminist avant-garde films demand room for lesbian sensuality in the cultural imaginary of women's liberation and produce images that disrupt the male gaze—all of which interrupt mainstream appeal.[12] The Black feminist avant-garde corpus is related to white feminist avant-garde cinematic imperatives in their disturbance of the pleasure derived from watching women's bodies on screen.[13] Like films that are regarded as foundational to avant-garde cinema, Black feminist avant-garde films recalibrate and repurpose visual grammar but focus their disruption of normative conventions on images of Black womanhood, which are as instantiated as normative conventions of cinema.[14] Although mainstream cinematic representations have abstracted Black womanhood to the point of absurdity, Black feminist avant-garde films use the cinematic form to destabilize and upend outmoded tropes while elaborating on narrative conventions and interrupting pervasive depictions of Black womanhood.

Because of their disruption of the film form and their resistance to the expectation that representations of Black womanhood follow the well-worn groove of hypersexuality, criminality, or abject motherhood, these films find their audiences in art galleries, museums, and film festivals, and they produce experiences of witnessing that are decidedly not designed for the uncomplicated pleasure of the viewer. The films that I discuss are in service of Black women who lived, who were violated, who died, who are due. This body of work agitates the codified impossibility of Black women's survival; they break up and then shake loose shards from the fractured concretization of Black womanhood. Black feminist avant-garde cinema can provide a reckoning as it clears space for the complicated act of witnessing—with specificity and without spectacle—acts of violence and violation that have been overlooked or discarded or occluded or overexposed.

The discussion of Black feminist avant-garde cinema forwarded in *Visitation* fills a lacuna in cinema studies, as it relates to both avant-garde and Black film, and addresses a gap in African American analyses of the avant-garde. The field of avant-garde cinema has paid exiguous attention to Black feminist film, and analyses of feminist avant-garde cinema rarely contend with Black women, but when Black women filmmakers are recognized as avant-garde, two filmmakers emerge: Cheryl Dunye and Julie Dash.[15] Unlike the prominent feminist avant-garde filmmakers whose work resists, or disregards, or is indifferent to mainstream appeal, Dunye and Dash are included in the annals of avant-garde feminist film *because* their work has garnered a measure of mainstream success. Dash and Dunye were able to make short and feature-length films that defy cinematic convention, center Black womanhood, embrace avant-garde aesthetics and techniques, and achieve award-winning acclaim.[16] The blackness of these avant-garde feminist filmmakers demanded that they reach a wide audience if they were going to be seen at all, yet they existed on the periphery of the feminist avant-garde cinematic intervention that was taking place throughout the mid to late twentieth century.[17]

While the discourse of the Black avant-garde spans a wide range of artistic mediums and is alive with debates surrounding the essentializing effects of locating a Black aesthetic, discussions of the avant-garde in Black culture have been concerned primarily with literature, visual art, theater, and musical traditions. Black abstract and revolutionary sentiments of the twentieth century that usurped imposed conceptions of Black identity and pushed conventional generic boundaries in poetry, visual art, stage plays, and musical arrangements constitute the preeminent understanding of the Black avant-garde. For example, the insurgent spirit of Black avant-garde approaches to artistic expressions of Amiri Baraka, Jayne Cortez, Sonia Sanchez, and Nikki Giovanni are linked to the Black Power movement through the Black Arts movement of the 1960s and 1970s but can be followed back to the New Negro movement through the work of Langston Hughes, Romare Bearden, Jean Toomer, James Van Der Zee, and Marita Bonner.[18]

Filmmakers from the L.A. Rebellion film movement (1960–80) were creating short and feature-length films about Black experiences that pushed cinematic convention, yet this body of work is not readily described as avant-garde; the blackness of an artist or the subject matter represented within becomes the most indelible descriptor of the work.[19] The form, the resistance to form, the interrogation of seeing and being that is issued forth by Black filmmakers, even if it is consistent with avant-garde aesthetics and imperatives, is not often read as such. Films that bend cinematic convention and produce aesthetics of resistance cohere within the rubric of avant-garde cinema, yet the subject of blackness—in form or maker—precludes Black films that share these same characteristics from being read as works of avant-garde cinema. Consider L.A. Rebellion School filmmakers such as Zeinabu irene Davis, Julie Dash, Barbara McCullough, and Charles Burnett, who made films that could be read as avant-garde but are not recognized by cinema history as filmmakers foundational to the genre.[20] Chantal Akerman, Stan Brakhage, Maya Deren, Jack Smith, Yvonne Rainer, and Su Friedrich are a few of the filmmakers whose work is regarded as foundational to avant-garde cinema; the obvious non-Blackness of this group of filmmakers produces the canon of avant-garde film as that which is distinctly white. To be clear, I read Black feminist avant-garde films as expanding and complicating and provoking the category; I am not making an argument for acceptance or inclusion but remarking on the way that whiteness is embedded in the understanding of avant-garde cinema.

In his reading of Duke Ellington's sound in *In the Break: The Aesthetics of the Black Radical Tradition*, Fred Moten discusses the relationship between blackness and the avant-garde. He draws out the meanings of each category to examine how they have been produced as incommensurate. Moten insists:

> What I've been specifically interested in here is how the idea of a black avant-garde exists, as it were, oxymoronically—as if black, on the one hand, and avant-garde, on the other hand, each depends for its coherence upon the exclusion of the other. Now this is probably an overstatement of the case. Yet it's all but justified by a vast interdisciplinary text representative not only of a problematically positivist conclusion that the avant-garde has been exclusively Euro-American, but of a deeper, perhaps unconscious, formulation of the avant-garde as necessarily not black. Part of what I'm after now is this: an assertion that the avant-garde is a black thing . . . and an assertion that blackness is an avant-garde thing.[21]

Moten recognizes that *Black* and *avant-garde* appear to exist in a contradistinction to one another that shapes the definition of each; the avant-garde is regarded as distinctly that which is not Black—the robust Black avant-garde multigenerational, multigeneric artistic evidence notwithstanding. Despite the polarization between these terms, and the common reading of the avant-garde as a white mode of art, Moten contends that the avant-garde is a Black thing. The point that Moten makes about the avant-garde, which is invaluably germane to my analysis, is the provocation found in the second half of his framework— "that blackness is an avant-garde thing." My notion of Black feminist avant-garde cinema is as committed to recognizing the avant-garde aesthetics and imperatives at work in the films that I discuss as it is to deepening the meaning of this category by studying the ways that blackness itself is an avant-garde thing.

In *Embodied Avatars: Genealogies of Black Feminist Art and Performance*, Uri McMillan discusses the paradox of the avant-garde for Black women performance artists. McMillan explicates that while performance art has proven to be a launching point for artists to explore the range and depth of their practice, situating performance art as the exemplary avant-garde practice among other art practices, Black women have been categorically excluded from avant-garde performance. In the realm of performance, McMillan brings to our attention that although Black women performance artists "share qualities often attributed to the avant-garde—cutting edge, marginal, seamless moves across disciplines—

their relationship to it is deeply vexed."[22] Whether the artistic arena is performative or cinematic, Black women artists who are making work that has all of the qualities of the avant-garde are consistently excluded from the category. The value of embracing Black avant-garde cinema lies in the intervention into the genre that such a move makes as well as the dimensions that it adds to the category of blackness. Black feminist avant-garde films visualize the avant-garde of blackness while using avant-garde approaches to cinema to express this fact of blackness. What has become clear through my study of these films is not only that Black is an avant-garde thing but that Black feminism is an avant-garde thing; the films that I have brought together here visualize the multivalent dimensions of this fact.

Cinematic Tenderness and Aesthetics of Resistance

Black feminist avant-garde films share a visual integrity that balances the representation of historic acts of racialized sexual violence within the visual field by cultivating tenderness. Through their cultivation of a cinematic tenderness, these films mobilize *aesthetics of resistance* that counter archival violence; tenderness and aesthetics of resistance are integral components of the films I discuss in *Visitation*. While I focus on short films made in the twenty-first century in the chapters of this book, I look to Julie Dash's *Daughters of the Dust* (1991) to lay the foundation for this rubric, as Dash's film—the first feature film directed by a US-based Black woman to have a national theatrical release—is an exemplar of aesthetics of resistance and the mode of cinematic tenderness that I am working to describe.[23] Set in 1902 in the South Carolina Sea Islands, *Daughters of the Dust* tells the story of the fracture of the Peazant family of Ibo Landing. An unborn child narrates the languid tale of this Gullah family. Some members of the Peazant family are moving to the mainland and others will remain on the island. The matriarch, Nana Peazant, works desperately to impart familial knowledge to those leaving. It is a sorrowful day, yet one that will be celebrated with a bountiful feast on the shore. In most visual treatments of Black women who lived through slavery and then experienced emancipation, there is an inevitable reveal of a whip-scarred back or poorly healed broken bones, but Dash makes a different choice, one consistent with an aesthetic palate that produces cinematic tenderness—a tenderness that is underscored by resistance.

In an interview with bell hooks that was included in Dash's 1994 book about the film, Dash talks about the scars of slavery and how she wanted to create a new kind of iconography, one that did not reproduce the images of whelped skin and fields of scars on the backs of people treated like chattel.[24] She chose to use the stain of indigo on the hands of women who were forced to work in poisonous indigo-processing plants. Dash's historical advisor told her that these stains would not have remained in perpetuity on the hands of elders who were once enslaved, but Dash was not concerned with historical accuracy; the scars of slavery are made of indigo in this world, and whip marks and chains do not have a place in this film, in this memory, in this cinematic record.[25] The aesthetics in *Daughters of the Dust* disrupt dominant ways of remembering a past that we have never seen with our own eyes. This is resistance. Dash is looking to the past with this film, examining what she finds there and yielding new information from it. *Daughters of the Dust* visualizes the act of looking back and trusting in the place that exists between the grave and the womb, where ancestors share memories and tell stories, where myths are made. The record of this spectral place is written in feelings rather than ink; the archival material is spoken and sensed rather than coded and cataloged. Dash's willingness to dispense with historical accuracy is an exemplification of the point of this film; this is not a documentary or an ethnographic film but a work of cinema that uses the visual and the aural to communicate something beyond paper and ink, beyond microfilm, even beyond celluloid and light, and certainly beyond historical accuracy. She is offering something beyond this world that beckons our attention. Through the visual grammar, the tone, and the quiet of the film, Dash produces images of blackness that add something wholly unusual to the archive of cinematic representation of Black womanhood; these are qualities that produce aesthetics of resistance, qualities that appear in the short films I discuss in the chapters that follow. This is cinematic tenderness.

In the conversation between hooks and Dash, the filmmaker shares another story—there was a scene that she shot but cut from the final edit of the film.[26] This scene is a flashback to Nana Peazant's mother, who cut off a lock of her hair and sewed it into Nana Peazant's baby quilt just before Nana was sold away from her. Nana Peazant's mother still had breasts full of mother's milk, and rather than have Nana Peazant's mother break down and wail when her baby was sold away, Dash has her breasts cry tears of milk. This scene, with only Dash's description as a guide, is evocative and perhaps produces an even greater sense of loss through its absence in the film. It exists in my mind now: I can see the milk teardrops; I can imagine the feeling, the burden, the sorrow, and the resistance to crying in the face of such a brutal, cruel, unconscionable theft. The scars of indigo and tears of milk are generational suffering, ancestral sorrow made visible, made known without chains, or the crack of a whip, or a scene of rape—these are the tender aesthetics of resistance at work in Dash's cinematic field.

I am captivated by this lost scene of milk tears because of its vivid imagery but also because it becomes a part of an imagined archive, yet not my own imagination. This scene moves into the spectral realm, the space of the disembodied, where the unborn and the no longer living commune. This scene does not exist in an official record, it is not a part of the story that we can see, the strips of celluloid that capture this scene do not live in the space of the film, and yet I see it. The cinematic poetry of *Daughters of the Dust* becomes more tragic and beautiful with the knowledge that this scene exists but is unviewable. In my scene, I see a woman with her head bowed: the day is ending; her dress is a faded indigo blue, dingy with soil and sweat; pools of wetness collect at her bosom. But somehow, I am able to see the drops of milk as they drip beneath her dress onto her belly, slow drops turning faster as the pressure builds. A mother too defiant, too willing to survive to let tears fall from her eyes, so her milk gives her the release.

This scene held next to another mother's story captured in *Daughters of the Dust*, that of Yellow Mary, shows a relationship if not a continuum between women through reproductive violence. Yellow Mary tells a story of fixing the titty when she was in Cuba with the family that kept her, as a prisoner of sorts, to be their wet nurse. Yellow Mary begins by sharing that her baby was born dead. At that time, she worked for a family who kept her; wherever they went, she went. She fed their baby with her dead baby's milk. Even though Yellow Mary was experiencing the world in the generation after slavery was abolished in the United States, she was still experiencing bondage to a family. She mutilated herself so that she could be of no use to them. She took her freedom. She found release. She gave herself a different future at the cost of her own body. As the women on the island observed, Yellow Mary is a different kind of woman. She is called *ruint* by pious women in the family and a new kind of woman by the young women who could imagine a future that their mothers could not. Yellow Mary was a sex worker on the mainland and she traveled from the mainland to Ibo Landing with her lover, Trula. Pointedly, Trula is quiet in this film. We hear her laughter with Yellow Mary, but she speaks only once during the film, when she is describing what she wants from the wish book, also known as a catalog, probably Sears and Roebuck. She imagines owning the plush bed pictured in the wish book. Rest and comfort and a safe place for lovemaking are Black feminist visions of freedom imagined through the wish book. The new kind of woman that Yellow Mary is, is not married, is not in need of a man. She makes her own money and she is not ashamed of how she makes it. She remains impervious to those who mock her. When she returned to Ibo Landing that day, it was not clear that she would stay, but there she remained with Nana Peazant while her lover, Trula, along with most of the Peazant family, crossed over back to the mainland.

Trula is an interesting name in this cosmology—one character's name is Iona, which calls to mind "I own her," and another name is Myown. The name Trula in this sonic space sounds like true love. Is this Yellow Mary's true love? The presence of this intimacy and love between women, between Trula and Yellow Mary, weaves into this narrative a refusal of shame for one's own history, for one's own desires, for one's own path, while also producing aesthetics of resistance. Throughout the film, Trula, Yellow Mary, and a central character in this story, Eula, are on the periphery. The island is full and active on this day. Baskets are teeming with corn, bread, and sweet treats; pots of gumbo are cooking; children are playing; stories are being told; photographs are being made; and on the outskirts of all this activity are Trula, Eula, and Yellow Mary. Eula is pregnant with the baby who narrates this film—Unborn Child. Unborn Child moves in spirit and is sensed by the family members, if they are open and aware. Unborn Child cannot be felt by those who are shut down by self-righteousness, like one of the pious mothers who pushes Yellow Mary to the periphery. But still on the line between family and shame, between love and rejection, sits this trio. Eula was raped before she became pregnant; we do not see this violation but are living in the aftermath of it. Unborn Child is the future of this family and is mending hearts in that place between—where the ancestor and the womb are the same. The tenderness and acceptance that these three women cultivate, on the eve of this crossing, shore each other up until they break from the periphery and breach the center, where they shed some light, dispel some lies, melt some ire, and let some love happen. These scenes that brim over with lush hues of indigo and golden light, delicious seaside feasts, bountiful oak trees, and flowing white eyelet dresses utilize aesthetics to resist dominant ways of seeing Black women and produce alternative pasts that liberate Black women from the confines of outmoded tropes and limits of archival documentation.

Archives of Violence / Violence of the Archives

The films that I study here are intimately invested in archival matters; in particular, they attend to the violence that circulates in archival documents and through archival practices. The archives of violence that *Visitation* is concerned with are the records that document acts of violence perpetrated against Black women. The violence of the archive takes place through archival processes that devalue, occlude, or extract Black women from the record. A film that depicts the treacherous landscape of archives of documented acts of violence and the violence embedded in the archival repository is another landmark Black feminist avant-garde feature, Cheryl Dunye's *The Watermelon Woman* (1996). The first feature-length film to be directed by an out Black United States–based lesbian filmmaker, *The Watermelon Woman* is a cinematic interrogation of the archive in which the director also plays the lead character, Cheryl. The protagonist happens to be a Black lesbian filmmaker who is in search of the archival trace of an actress who is listed in the credits of the films she stars in only as "The Watermelon Woman." With *The Watermelon Woman*, Dunye, the filmmaker, visualizes the frustration of archival obfuscation that has been historically leveraged against Black women, sending Cheryl, the character, on an archival research quest. Dunye, the filmmaker, cinematically renders the humiliation and dismissal experienced by the Black lesbian protagonist that unfolds in part because of who she is and in part because of the subject of her study. The character Cheryl uncovers virtually nothing about the Watermelon Woman in public archives; a bit of archival documentation is found in a lesbian archive but it is treated with careless disregard. Cheryl discovers that the records of the Watermelon Woman are not found in national repositories or lesbian collections but have actually been kept and collected by those who knew and loved the Watermelon Woman, whose name we learn was Fae Richards. Not only is evidence of this seemingly unknown Black woman's film career found, but the evidence determines that Fae Richards was a lesbian as well. Dunye's cinematic point was made even more salient by audience responses to early screenings of the film in which they believed that Dunye's fake documentary film was an actual recounting of the life of an actress called the Watermelon Woman; this confusion epitomizes the central premise of the film.[27] The archive of Fae Richards that Cheryl discovered in the film did not exist before this film was made; it was fabricated. This cinematic choice agitates the impacted archival sediment and creates a disruption of the violence of the archive. *The Watermelon Woman* is a cinematic act of resistance to the violent erasure and obfuscation of Black women from cinema history. The invention of "The Watermelon Woman," which is at the heart of Dunye's film, demands an examination of the production of knowledge about Black women and sexuality. Dunye is offering a provocation and issuing a reminder that knowledge is produced and that the archival process is subjective, incomplete, and unreliable. Through Dunye's avant-garde techniques of archival invention and the production of a fake documentary, the filmmaker produces a trickster archive that combats the violence of the archive itself.

In addition to this epistemological jolt, the act of seeing the archive—repositories, boxes, file folders, shelves, and all—in Dunye's film makes visible something that often eludes the cinematic landscape. Seeing an archival question form, and then watching a confounding excursion unfurl that exposes the Black lesbian filmmaker and her project to dismissal, manages to make legible the covert and elusive pain of the interlocking mechanisms of racism, sexism, and homophobia that are often quite difficult to pinpoint and describe. The process of disregard for the Black lesbian filmmaker in the repositories themselves and the archival omission of "The Watermelon Woman" therein exemplifies the archival violence that takes place through delegitimization and expulsion. There is a dominant understanding that Black women do not have an archival presence at all; the audience's nearly unilateral belief in Cheryl Dunye's invention of her titular character is testament to this fact. Like *The Watermelon Woman* and *Daughters of the Dust*, the short films I discuss in *Visitation* use aesthetics of resistance to contend with the archival documentation of violent acts suffered by Black women as well as the violence of the archive itself and the violence endured by Black women researchers who enter an archival location. By reckoning with the violence of epistemological dislocations and the horror of hypervisibility, Black feminist avant-garde films make palpable Black women's archival presences, without visually reproducing the violence recorded in the documents that place them there.

The compound violence of the archive is expertly addressed by Saidiya Hartman in her stirring article "Venus in Two Acts," in which she returns to her discussion of Venus's murder and archival presence, first addressed in her monograph *Lose Your Mother*. In the article, Hartman attends to the way Venus's life and death have been obscured in the scant record of her horrifying murder and expresses her trepidation over reading more into the archive of Venus than the record has to offer. She wrestles with examining a slave ship's ledger that references an enslaved girl, called Venus, who was viciously and sadistically tortured and killed during her journey through the Middle Passage.[28] The slim, gruesome archival impression in the shape of Venus is the only evidence of her experience. Hartman refuses to ameliorate the sense of loss that surrounds Venus in the archive and is careful not to infer or create into the absence of the archive. No matter how tempting it is to imagine into the record some semblance of resistance or triumph, Hartman resists. She does not want to make an archival romance out of this young enslaved Black girl's rape and murder.[29] For Hartman, the archive of Venus is a "death sentence."[30] In "Venus in Two Acts," Hartman revisits and extends the query she poses in *Lose Your Mother*. She asks: "If 'to read the archive is to enter a mortuary; it permits one final viewing and allows for a last glimpse of persons about to disappear into the slave hold,' then to what end does one open the casket and look into the face of death? Why risk the contamination involved in restating the maledictions, obscenities, columns of losses and gains, and measures of value by which captive lives were inscribed and extinguished? Why subject the dead to new dangers and to a second order of violence?"[31]

Venus becomes legible in the archive through a record of her torture, which exemplifies an archival reality for Black women—the archive may be a death sentence or it may be a torture chamber, as following Black women into the archive so often leads to torture, rape, and murder. Hartman does not let the absence, the occlusion, seal the record. She returns to the past, she allows the disembodied to speak, she makes room for the past to reveal itself. Hartman forwards a theory of critical fabulation that enables her to fashion a narrative that is based on, as it critiques, archival documentation of enslaved women's experiences of violence and death.[32] Hartman explains the value and impetus for her use of critical fabulation in re-presenting what happened to Venus:

> By throwing into crisis "what happened when" and by exploiting the "transparency of sources" as fictions of history, I wanted to make visible the production of disposable lives (in the Atlantic slave trade and, as well, in the discipline of history), to describe "the resistance of the object," if only by first imagining it, and to listen for the mutters and oaths and cries of the commodity. By flattening the levels of narrative discourse and confusing narrator and speakers, I hoped to illuminate the contested character of history, narrative, event, and fact, to topple the hierarchy of discourse, and to engulf authorized speech in the clash of voices.[33]

Critical fabulation, reading the past for distortions, hearing the voices of the disembodied: these are Black feminist strategies for contending with the violence of the archive; these are the strategies that I see working in the films I have brought together in *Visitation*. As Hartman details in "Venus in Two Acts" and *Lose Your Mother*, Black women's archival legibility is achieved through a record of violence that holds them in abeyance. I, like Hartman and the filmmakers present in *Visitation*, am compelled by entering into the epistemological void that grows up around Black women, subsuming them yet rendering them through violence. This void is a field animated by the indeterminate friction between life and death, knowledge and disregard, visibility and nothingness.

Here, in what Hartman has described as the afterlife of slavery, a reckoning through visuality is quite a satisfying prospect—but a reckoning does not produce recovery from the archive.[34] As Hartman acknowledges, the archive will always be bereft, full of violence and disappointment. To recover from an archive of slavery imagines that the violence of that time is over, but as we know, it persists. As I read them, Black feminist avant-garde films are not invested in recovering knowledge from the archive, or in recuperating from the deepest, most immense losses. Rather, these films channel spirits that linger in repositories, appear in documents, and haunt collections. Archival traces are incomplete and to attempt recovery out of such fragile and violated places is asking too much. Rather than recovery or recuperation, I contend that reckoning and witnessing is what takes place through Black feminist avant-garde cinema.

Black Womanhood and Distortion of Vision

The paradox of concomitant visibility and invisibility, a human/other/object status that ferments in this void, has been carefully and tenderly examined by Saidiya Hartman as it has been by Hortense Spillers in her paradigm-shifting essay on New World captivity and Black women's sexuality, "Mama's Baby, Papa's Maybe: An American Grammar Book." Here, Spillers begins to build the grammar with which to discuss the meaning of Black womanhood and the violence that shrouds Black women's sexuality and foments Black women's condition of abjection. Spillers asserts:

> First of all, their New-World, diasporic plight marked a *theft of the body*—a willful and violent (and unimaginable from this distance) severing of the captive body from its motive will, its active desire. Under these conditions, we lose at least *gender* difference *in the outcome*, and the female body and the male body become a territory of cultural and political maneuver, not at all gender-related, gender-specific. But this body, at least from the point of view of the captive community, focuses a private and particular space, at which point of convergence biological, sexual, social, cultural, linguistic, ritualistic, and psychological fortunes join. This profound intimacy of interlocking detail is disrupted, however, by externally imposed meanings and uses: 1) the captive body becomes the source of an irresistible, destructive sensuality; 2) at the same time—in stunning contradiction—the captive body reduces to a thing, becoming *being for* the captor; 3) in this absence *from* a subject position, the captured sexualities provide a physical and biological expression of "otherness"; 4) as a category of "otherness," the captive body translates into a potential for pornotroping and embodies sheer physical powerlessness that slides into a more general "powerlessness," resonating through various centers of human and social meaning.[35]

The reduction of Black women into things meant only for use by the captor during slavery begets the otherness that impedes Black women's ability to be; the powerlessness of Black women's captured sexualities imposes on the meaning of Black womanhood in slavery's afterlife. As Spillers elucidates, the pleasure derived from eliciting or watching Black pain, or pornotroping, is intricately intertwined with Black women's sexuality and desire. Pornotroping, and the violence that encumbers Black women's sexuality, contributes to the impossibility that haunts Black womanhood. Though the enslaved reproductive woman was imagined by enslavers as existing without humanity, her human body reproduced human bodies into slavery. The epistemology of Black womanhood that produced her captive Black body as nonhuman under chattel slavery remains in every calculation of Black womanhood that emerges after the abolition of slavery. The machinations and contortions of logic that had to be executed in order to refute the humanity of an enslaved woman whose reproductive capacity was being exploited during chattel slavery to reproduce more enslaved people, Black people, not-recognized-as-human people, chattel, are particularly confounding.

Evelynn Hammonds, a Black feminist scholar of the history of science, draws upon her background in physics to begin to untangle the knot of impossibility, the visual paradox, that obscures Black women's sexuality. Hammonds uses the astrophysics of black holes to conceptualize the silence and invisibility that contort Black women's desire.[36] She produces a theory of the "black (w)hole" as a metaphor that can index the paradox of visibility that at once overdetermines Black women as pathologically overly sexual, while also diminishing the ability to see Black women's capacity for knowledge production. Hammonds contends:

> The existence of the black hole is inferred from the fact that the visible star is in orbit and its shape is distorted in some way or it is detected by the energy emanating from the region in space around the visible star that could not be produced by the visible star alone. Therefore, the identification of a black hole requires the use of sensitive detectors of energy and distortion. In the case of black female sexualities, this implies that we need to develop reading strategies that allow us to make visible the distorting and productive effects these sexualities produce in relation to more visible sexualities.[37]

Looking at what seems like absence yet recognizing that the space is in fact full and dynamic is a reading strategy that can be applied to searching for Black women's presences in archival collections. The animated absence becomes detectable because of the effect that it has on the space around it. The places in archival repositories where Black women have been overlooked or redacted or discarded distort the space around them by indexing the terror perpetrated by white domination through organizational control, legislative manipulation, wealth building, imagined moral superiority, and coercive power. This is a distortion that has been read as lack or inability or pathology or ignorance or ineptitude. If the space around Black women is read for their presence rather than their deficiency, then the growth of crops, the health of families, the practice of insurgent survival, the invention of surreptitious communication—the fact that enslaved people survived at all—points to the genius of Black womanhood. This genius cannot be overlooked or disregarded even though archival records may not directly reflect this; the knowing through seeing what is missing—the distortion of space—must be counted as knowledge.

In "The Transformation of Silence into Language and Action," Audre Lorde contends that "within this country where racial difference creates a constant, if unspoken, distortion of vision, Black women have on one hand always been highly visible, and so, on the other hand, have been rendered invisible through the depersonalization of racism. Even within the women's movement, we have had to fight, and still do, for that very visibility which also renders us most vulnerable, our Blackness. For to survive in the mouth of this dragon we call america, we have had to learn this first and most vital lesson—that we were never meant to survive. Not as human beings."[38] Lorde speaks to the "distortion of vision" that produces the impossibility of Black womanhood as both overexposed and disregarded. If the distortion of vision that obscures Black women's place in archival collections can be perceived by the impact it has on the space around it, and if secrets are unleashed when what appears to be an absence is recognized as opaque yet populated, then an archive becomes a repository of redaction as much as it is a storehouse of information. Hammonds and Lorde are asking us to contend with the void through which the meaning of Black womanhood is deployed and consider how it operates on the visual register—a visuality that includes occlusion.[39] Black women are obscured in archival processes by the combination of epistemological redaction and ontological splaying that codifies the void, the distortion of vision, that makes abject Black womanhood. The apparitions that animate this volume emerge out of the persistent distortion of vision to which Lorde directs our attention, what Hammonds theorizes, and what Morrison culls for new information.

A short film that eloquently captures the archival dimensions, historical stakes, and cinematic interrogation of Black feminist avant-garde cinema is an earlier work of Julie Dash, *Illusions* (1982). Beautifully rendered in 16mm black-and-white celluloid, and set in 1942 during World War II, *Illusions* follows Mignon Dupree, a Black woman film executive who is passing as white. On this particular day at the office, Mignon's Black identity is discovered while she is working to solve a problem with a film that is in postproduction. Mignon's fortitude is confirmed when she refuses to be intimidated by the white man in the office who learns that she is Black, but a deeper issue, one that takes us into the void, unfolds through her solution to the problem with the film.

Dash sends us behind the scenes into a postproduction suite where older white men are currently stumped by an issue with the sound of the film. On a screen in that production suite, the executives roll a scene from the film in which a white actress is draped across a chaise lounge. The image is in focus, no bothersome shadows are being cast, not a hair is out of place on the actress's head, but her singing has been thrown irrevocably out of sync. The actress's mouth does not move in time with the sound of her voice. Because film is captured by a motion picture camera without sync sound, the sound is recorded with external audio equipment, and the picture and sound have to be brought into sync in a postproduction process. Something went terribly awry in the editing process and now the image and sound do not match. The original actress is unavailable to come in to the studio to sing the song in rhythm to her own lips' movements on the screen, so Mignon hires a young Black actress, Esther, to sing and match her singing with the white actress on screen.[40]

Through Mignon's passing and Esther's beautiful voice being lent to a white woman's cinematic performance, two kinds of occlusion are being visualized. Clearly Mignon is a brilliant executive, but if she were to be out as a Black woman when she applied for the position, she would have never been seriously considered, let alone hired by the film studio. Esther has the beauty and the talent to be a Hollywood star but because she is Black, she cannot be seen on screen as the protagonist of a Hollywood film; she can only have a cinematic presence that is subsumed within the body of the white actress who is center stage. When Mignon buries her blackness at work in order to have a career that she is clearly well suited for, she enters the void. When industry standards relegate a capable and gifted young Black actress to the margins of film production and the recesses of cinematic representation, she is forced into the black (w)hole to which Hammonds directs our attention. The fact that Julie Dash is not a household name is a machination of this distortion of vision, one that obfuscates the brilliance of a foundational Black woman filmmaker.

Black feminist avant-garde films bring attention to the impact that the cinematic medium, its portrayals and occlusions of Black women, have had on *seeing* Black women. In *Seeing through Race*, W. J. T. Mitchell argues that race is a medium, and not simply the object of study in visual culture but a framework through which seeing happens. Mitchell contends that the medium of race is a vehicle of illusion and reality that "can both obstruct and facilitate communication; [can be] a cause of misunderstanding and blindness, or conversely, a mechanism of 'second sight'; a prosthesis that produces invisibility and hypervisibility simultaneously."[41] Mitchell's contention that race is a medium of illusion calls up the work that Julie Dash has done in her short film by that name and offers a complement to Morrison's excavation of distortions and lies that become recognizable by examining the past and finding new information. Race, paradoxically, produces an invisibility that becomes endemic to visual culture and is a production of distortions and lies that are then embedded in archival documents, processes, and subsequent archival exploration. If, as Barbara Jeanne Fields argues in "Slavery, Race, and Ideology in the United States of America," the concept of race was invented to produce, support, and solidify the master/slave relationship during US chattel slavery, and race really is meant to signal blackness, then the medium of race is measured by its proximity to or immersion within blackness.[42] With this rubric of race and visuality as a core tenet, *Visitation* tracks the ways that seeing, recognition, disregard, overexposure, occlusion, and erasure work in concert to produce knowledge about Black womanhood in visual culture through cinematic representation in repositories, through viewing archival documents, and—in quotidian dynamics of power—through the medium of race.

The idea that race is itself a medium implies that seeing through race is a creative process and serves as a mode of communicating and exchanging information. I regard Black feminist avant-garde cinema as a medium; I use *medium* with an eye toward Mitchell's conception of race as a medium, while holding onto *medium* as an artistic form, and going further to include the concept of *medium* as an intermediary figure who acts as a channel between apparitional and corporeal entities. My analysis of spectral archival avant-garde visualizations in *Visitation* is given shape and dimension through these multiple meanings of medium. By understanding race as a medium through which seeing happens, and using the medium of cinema as the object of my analysis, I recognize Black feminist avant-garde filmmakers as mediums who channel otherworldly presences, who conjure up visitations and then present them to us on the screen.

Visitation *and Black Feminist Theory*

Visitation is an intervention into archival study and avant-garde cinema that builds on analyses of haunting, pornotropy, and Black being and contributes to Black feminist theories of visuality, cinema, and knowledge production. My understanding of Black feminism emerges out of foundational Black lesbian feminist theory forwarded by the Combahee River Collective, which recognizes the inherent value of Black womanhood, contends with the specificity of oppressive forces that impose themselves through vectors of blackness and womanhood, and holds fast to the conviction that when the most vulnerable are free, only then can any sense of collective freedom be claimed.[43] The imperatives of Black feminism that undergird my understanding of this critical intervention are exemplified by Audre Lorde's crystalline reading of white feminist racism in "The Master's Tools Will Never Dismantle the Master's House"; Hortense Spillers's foundational essays, most notably "Mama's Baby, Papa's Maybe"; the disruptive work of Black women historians like Deborah Gray White, Angela Davis, bell hooks, Saidiya Hartman, and Jennifer L. Morgan whose scholarship exposes the horrors of slavery experienced through the particular location of Black womanhood; and the Black queer feminist power that has coalesced in #BlackLivesMatter and propelled our contemporary movement for Black liberation.[44] My engagement with Black feminism is fortified by C. Riley Snorton and Marquis Bey's Black trans theories of fungibility and fugitivity that explore the ungendering process, first noted by Spillers, that is imposed through Black womanhood. My conception of Black feminism is shored up by the interventions of Alexis Pauline Gumbs, Jennifer Nash, Christina Sharpe, Daphne Brooks, and Jayna Brown, whose theories of being, sensuality, performance, and power counter knowledge production that erases and devalues Black womanhood.[45] Queer-of-color critique as an intervention, a body of scholarship, and a direct descendant of Black feminist theory is fundamental to my theoretical framework. Roderick Ferguson's *Aberrations in Black: Toward a Queer of Color Critique* has shaped my thinking about the prescience of Black feminist thought on queer theory and the relationship between blackness, heteronormativity, and queerness. Kara Keeling's cinematic analysis of Black lesbian representation in *The Witch's Flight: The Cinematic, the Black Femme, and the Image of Common Sense* and her analysis of Black trans legibility, queer temporality, and the politics of representation in "Looking for M—: Queer Temporality, Black Political Possibility, and Poetry from the Future" have grounded my understanding of Black feminism, and pushed my thinking about Black queerness, possibility, temporality, and cinema.

These Black feminist, queer, trans theorists have fortified my understanding of the breadth and depth of Black feminist criticism and its bountiful legacies. This collective contributes heavily to my understanding of Black feminist thought as a critical intervention into power structures that impose meaning and delimit value through the vectors of blackness and the definitions of womanhood. Black feminist theory upends dominant ways of knowing by centering Black women; by eschewing white supremacist stratifications of race, gender, class, sexuality, and national belonging; and by insisting that the liberation of any of us depends on the liberation of all of us. Black feminist analyses of power and conceptions of knowing and being defy boundaries of genre and discipline. They refute strictures of form, as those epistemological expectations impede the critiques, reversals, and inventions that expose the exclusions, erasures, and systemic violence inherent in white supremacist taxonomies of knowing, being, and creating. Black feminist thought carves out voluptuous space from a place of imposed negation. This body of work activates bounty as it allows us to luxuriate in our sensuality, grieve the inconsolable, name the violations, rebuff the intolerable, host an invocation of our names in a resounding chorus that builds, in defiance of slaughter, an amplification that makes undeniable the power we possess, and where together we can marvel at and imbibe the exquisite prowess of our creativity. My conception of Black feminist avant-garde cinema is imbued by all these understandings of Black feminist critique. From this place, with this understanding of Black feminism, I study the work of Black feminist avant-garde filmmakers.

The Chapters

Even as the short films and installation pieces that I focus on in each chapter of *Visitation* turn to the past through their examination and incorporation of archival documentation, the chapters themselves progress in a kind of chronological order that includes gaps, lapses, retreads, and overlaps. I open the chapters with an exploration of the mobilization of archival documentation that unfolds through Kara Walker's use of avant-garde cinematic techniques in the installation piece *National Archives Microfilm Publication M999 Roll 34: Bureau of Refugees, Freedmen and Abandoned Lands: Six Miles from Springfield on the Franklin Road*. This chapter lays theoretical groundwork for my discussion of archives of violence and the violence of the archive and their relationship to visuality. Kara Walker is arguably the most well-known artist whose work I will engage in *Visitation*.[46] The 2007 exhibition *Kara Walker: My Complement, My Enemy, My Oppressor, My Love* brought Walker to prominence as a visual artist who has the ability to tap into the national unconscious with panoramic pastoral silhouettes that spell out ghastly nightmarish scenes of antebellum life. Walker's *Bureau of Refugees* series, of which the short film *Six Miles from Springfield on the Franklin Road* is a part, makes the archive endemic to the project by taking the titles of each piece directly from testimony given to the Freedmen's Bureau in 1866. In *Six Miles from Springfield on the Franklin Road*, Walker throws her signature silhouettes into motion as they reenact a grisly scene of white vigilantism in which an adolescent Black girl is raped and her family's house set on fire. The archival document being visualized in Walker's film is the testimony given to the Freedmen's Bureau by this young girl. I discuss the way that Walker uses avant-garde cinematic techniques to visualize the interior world of a young Black girl who suffered unspeakable terror and managed to register this act of violence in the Freedmen's Bureau archive. In my analysis, I examine how Walker's Black feminist avant-garde film reframes a documented act of violence waged against a newly emancipated family during the era of Reconstruction, and, I argue, through the visual field Walker reveals an affective dimension of this archival record.[47] While Walker's work does use hyperbolic imagery as an entry point into her visual historical interrogations, I contend that within the terrifying landscape of *Six Miles from Springfield on the Franklin Road*, the artist carves out tender cinematic space for the perspective of a young Black victim of rape to enter the record.

Chapter 2 builds upon the theoretical and historical ground covered in the first chapter's analysis of Walker's visualization of Reconstruction-era white supremacist vigilante violence by examining a video that takes a lynching photograph as its impetus. This chapter explores the haunting aspects of visitation and the cinematic. My discussion of Kara Lynch's video installation *SAVED :: video postcard* moves the chapters forward in time, from Reconstruction to the jim crow era, and also reflects a progression in the technology of visual culture from the silhouette to the photograph. Kara Lynch is a video artist, insurgent archivist, and sound collector who makes time-based visual and sonic pieces that interrogate blackness, gender, and class.[48] With *SAVED :: video postcard*, Lynch offers a cinematic study of the only known lynching photograph of a Black woman, Laura Nelson, who was raped and lynched in 1911 in Okemah, Oklahoma. Lynch's treatment of this photograph manages not to make a spectacle out of the horror of this image but rather stirs up the sensation of an otherworldly visitation that ushers in a reckoning across time and space. There are ghosts that linger on the periphery of reason and being, subsumed within records of American life and value whose resurgence unearths a past rife with the rape of Black women by white men; I call these presences specters of miscegenation, and they emerge in the archive of Laura Nelson's lynching and in Kara Lynch's cinematic treatment of the photographic evidence of the terror that Nelson suffered.

While half a century elapses between the jim crow–era violence examined in chapter 2 and the era of the Stonewall rebellion in which chapter 3 is situated, that temporal gap is attended to in the fourth and final chapter. In the third chapter, I discuss Tourmaline and Sasha Wortzel's *Happy Birthday, Marsha!*, which visualizes a pivotal moment in the life of legendary trans activist Marsha P. Johnson. The film pairs archival documentation with historical dramatization to produce a vibrant cinematic vehicle that reverses the subsumption of Marsha P. Johnson's role in the struggle for gay liberation in Stonewall-era New York City. My discussion of *Happy Birthday, Marsha!* examines the filmmakers' use of archival footage, poetry, performance, and historical dramatization to mobilize their liberatory production. In order to contextualize the activism that surrounded the Stonewall rebellion, in which Marsha P. Johnson and Sylvia Rivera were major actors, I offer a brief history of post–civil rights Left social movements. This chapter recognizes the archival labor of the filmmaker Tourmaline, a Black trans woman whose years of research and publication have been fundamental in bringing the legacies of Marsha P. Johnson and Sylvia Rivera into contemporary conversations about trans, queer, LGBTQ activism. *Happy Birthday, Marsha!* was included in the Brooklyn Museum's 2019 exhibit *Nobody Promised You Tomorrow*, which commemorated the fiftieth anniversary of the Stonewall rebellion.[49] My analysis of *Happy Birthday, Marsha!* was initially focused on the cinematic landscape and historical context of the film, but after attending a 2018 screening in which the film was woven into a theatrical performance launched by the filmmakers, I expanded the scope of my discussion. That theatrical cinematic experience opened up the analytic field and enabled me to incorporate theories of performance into my analysis of this work of avant-garde Black feminist cinema. My discussion of *Happy Birthday, Marsha!* brings together performance studies, social movement history, and archive theory to examine the way this piece cinematically reimagines the past and carries a reconstituted archive into the proscenium.

The final chapter offers a reading of Ja'Tovia Gary's *An Ecstatic Experience*. Gary's body of cinematic work is both experimental and archival, historic and personal. She uses the cinematic medium to crack open entrenched ways of knowing and seeing blackness, while capturing and visualizing an affective experience of Black womanhood—something that eludes most mediums and modes of communication.[50] In this chapter, I study the way Gary visualizes archival specters with her etchings onto black-and-white footage of a young Ruby Dee delivering a monologue from the point of view of an enslaved daughter witnessing her mother being savagely beaten. Juxtaposed with Dee's monologue is stuttering archival footage of civil rights–era Black worship, a flurry of colorful microbial abstractions, an interview with Assata Shakur in the mid-1980s, and contemporary digital video recordings of police violence and radical Black resistance. This film calls up chattel slavery with Dee's monologue, which was filmed at the apex of the civil rights movement in 1965, then moves through the twentieth century and into the twenty-first with scenes of violence, resistance, and escape that are juxtaposed. The theme of freedom courses through Gary's cinematic intervention that connects the terror of slavery with scenes of racial violence that persist in its afterlife. Gary's *An Ecstatic Experience* catalyzes my concept of Black feminist phenomenology, which I construct through an assembly of Black feminist theory, poetry, essays, and lyrics that describe what it feels like to be a Black woman. Through the analysis and theorization that I forward in this chapter, I argue that Gary's film becomes an archive of Black resistance that activates a phenomenology of freedom for Black women.

The films and artists who appear in *Visitation* are representative of a lineage of Black feminist avant-garde filmmaking. The short films that I discuss in each chapter center Black womanhood, interrogate gender, visualize desire, and produce a sensibility that captivates as it instigates. With their cinematic contributions, Walker, Lynch, Tourmaline and Wortzel, and Gary participate in as they produce a tradition of Black feminist avant-garde cinema. Their films are integral to the lineage of this category of cinema but are certainly not exhaustive. Kathleen Collins's *Losing Ground* (1982), Barbara McCullough's *Water Ritual #1: An Urban Rite of Purification* (1979), Cauleen Smith's *Dark Matter and the Postcard* (2006) and *Sojourner* (2018), and Zeinabu irene Davis's *Compensation* (1999), for example, each contribute to the category of Black feminist avant-garde cinema.[51] The films that I have selected to discuss in *Visitation* have a place in this volume because of their particular approach to archival visualization and experimental inventiveness, which they harness to conjure subjugated archival presences of Black women. All the short films discussed in *Visitation* break narrative conventions as they use cinematic landscapes to respond to the archival violence of devaluation, erasure, and obfuscation. Through their processes of image making, these filmmakers raise specters of those who suffered racialized sexual violence, while they disrupt the visual and epistemological void that confounds Black womanhood; these films create spaces of mourning and reckoning rather than voyeurism and pornotropy. The naming of a Black feminist avant-garde cinematic tradition fortifies a corpus out of works that have been regarded as diffuse, incidental, or disarticulated pieces of visual culture. A legacy of Black feminist filmmaking is before us, and not only is it vital to recognize the tradition that these films are contributing to and emerging from, but, I contend, it is an act of epistemological violence to disconnect them as a body, since they gather power together, they change the landscape, and they make room for us.

With *Visitation*, I am producing visual analysis that grapples with the history of violence that haunts Black womanhood and its attendant experiences of gender, desire, sexuality, and vitality. Black feminist avant-garde films transform avant-garde cinematic representation by using experimental film techniques to highlight Black women's roles in cinema history and expose a legacy of violence that gathers power through the visual. These films contribute to the archival collections that they visualize as they shore up a tradition of resistance to racialized sexual and reproductive violence buried within these collections. *Visitation* brings Black feminist theories into conversation with conceptions of haunting to address the violence of archival processes, the paradox of vision, and the epistemological trap that structures experiences of Black womanhood. With their films, Walker, Lynch, Tourmaline and Wortzel, and Gary reimagine history as they connect missing pieces of the past. These filmmakers disrupt the centralizing power of archival institutions and cinematic regimes of visuality by deploying aesthetics of resistance that reveal harm inflicted and losses sustained. The tenderness that activates the conjure work of these films enlivens documents, photographs, testimonies, interviews, archival film footage, and performances in which disembodied Black women are the guiding forces, the narrators of the harm done them, and through their spectral guidance cinematic visitations occur before us.

The narratives that unfold over the course of this book exist in spaces of the unknown, the misremembered, and the overlooked. These are historic tales that chronicle life-altering events of Black women whose stories have been written down and cataloged but undermined throughout that process. Disembodied Black women are guides through events that have been half-told, untold, or categorically misrepresented. These figures are beacons to a past that is changing, a past that is in process because we are now looking there. The disembodied direct my attention here, in these pages, just as they have found their narrators in the Black feminist avant-garde filmmakers whose sumptuous work makes visible their stories. *Visitation: The Conjure Work of Black Feminist Avant-Garde Cinema* moves with the flow of the films within it, as these pieces respond to archival surges that emanate from documented acts of unresolved racialized sexual and gender violence—a confluence of betrayals that distorts the vision of the space we are about to enter.

1

THE ARCHIVE AND THE SILHOUETTE

Framing Black Feminist Avant-Garde Cinema

On May 30, 1866, a hanging was reported. Someone, identified as mulatto, was found hung by a grapevine on the side of the road leading from Tuscaloosa to Greensboro, Alabama.[1] We know about this incident because it was reported to the Bureau of Refugees, Freedmen, and Abandoned Lands, an entity that was established through the United States War Department during the era of Reconstruction. The Freedmen's Bureau, as it was commonly called, was charged with managing the mayhem that would ensue once the Emancipation Proclamation was signed in 1863, and after the Union won the Civil War in 1865 and the Thirteenth Amendment to the Constitution was signed into law that same year.[2] This hanging is one of the documented acts of Reconstruction-era vigilante violence that Kara Walker visualizes, through still and moving imagery, in her *Bureau of Refugees* series (2007) (see figure 1.1).[3] I am drawn to the silhouettes

FIGURE 1.1 Kara Walker, *National Archives Microfilm Publication M999 Roll 34: Bureau of Refugees, Freedmen and Abandoned Lands: Six Miles from Springfield on the Franklin Road*, 2009 (film still).

and short films that Walker produced for this series, as they each reframe and provocatively interpret murderous eruptions of anti-Black animus that were boiling over in the South during the summer of 1866. Walker's *Bureau of Refugees* is immersed in archival matters. The incidents she visualizes were documented, delineated, and briefly described in a Freedmen's Bureau report that lists acts of malicious violence and murder, then categorizes each act as an "outrage," a murderous assault, or a murder.[4] Between January 1 and September 12, 1866, ten murders, seven murderous assaults, and three outrages were reported to the Bureau of Refugees in the District of Alabama (see figure 1.2). About midway through this report, a sentence fragment appears after the date "May 30." The short description records that a person described only as "mulatto" was hung by a grapevine near a roadside between Tuscaloosa and Greensboro (see figure 1.3). The slash next to this entry counts this incident as a murder. The recording of murders, murderous assaults, and outrages through chits in each column belies the heinous nature of the torture that preceded the making of those marks.

In this chapter, I explore the meaning that circulates through Kara Walker's rendering, on paper and in film, of her interpretation of documented acts

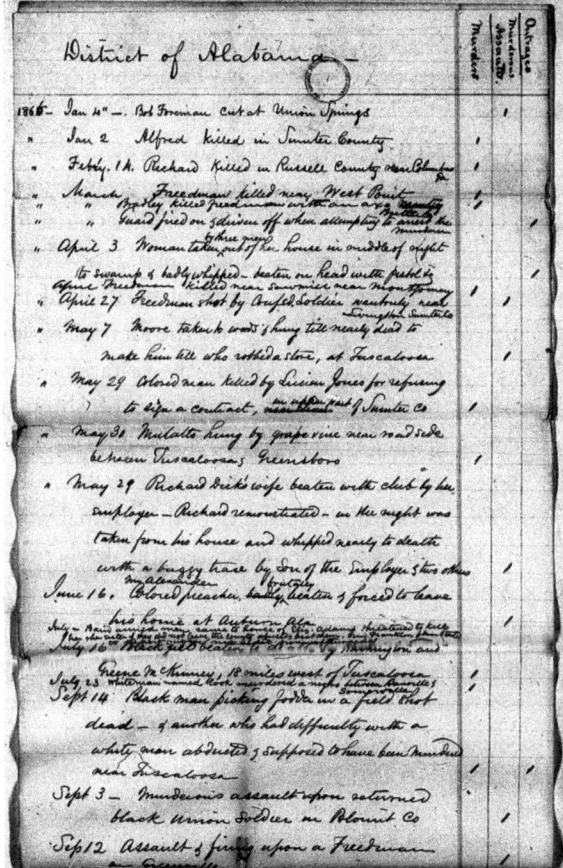

FIGURE 1.2 A single page from a list of murders in 1866 recorded by the assistant commissioner for the Bureau of Refugees, Freedmen, and Abandoned Lands for the District of Alabama. Unbound miscellaneous papers, July 1865–October 1867, District of Alabama List of Murders, Record Group 105, Roll M809, National Archives, Washington, DC.

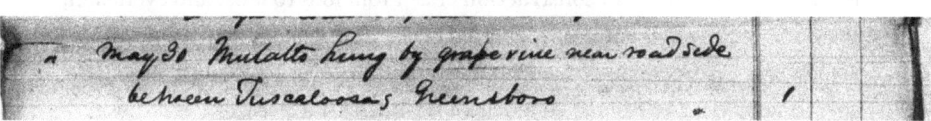

FIGURE 1.3 "May 30 Mulatto hung by grapevine near road side between Tuscaloosa & Greensboro." Unbound miscellaneous papers, July 1865–October 1867, District of Alabama List of Murders, Record Group 105, Roll M809, National Archives, Washington, DC.

of white supremacist vigilante violence. I support my analysis of Walker's *Bureau of Refugees* by studying the Freedmen's Bureau records of white supremacist depravity suffered by newly freed people, specifically women and girls, that Walker visualizes in this series. I connect my archival analysis with Black feminist interrogations of pornotropy and spectacle as well as the discourse and debates surrounding archival study, abstraction, and avant-garde image making to provide the framework with which to address the gravity of Walker's series. As I study Walker's shift from still to moving imagery in this chapter, I forward an argument that Walker's *Bureau of Refugees* contributes something valuable back to the Freedmen's Bureau archive. With this analysis, I lay the foundation for my notion of Black feminist avant-garde cinema as I follow the visitations that take shape along the archival landscape of Freedmen's Bureau records through the beacon of light and shadow, color and horror that is Kara Walker's *Bureau of Refugees*.[5]

Throughout his chapter, "Of the Dawn of Freedom," in the seminal work *The Souls of Black Folk*, W. E. B. Du Bois describes the terror that the newly freed had to contend with in the South after the Union defeated the Confederacy. The southern refusal to accept Black freedom fueled vicious acts that were designed to terrorize Black people back into abject positions of subservience, to be made perpetually vulnerable to violence and subject to white supremacist force. The postwar climate for freedwomen and men in the South was volatile, and Alabama was a particularly lethal district. The southern gall over Black freedom was registered upon the bodies and within the hearts of those who bore the blows, suffered the nooses, and died the horrific deaths during the transition from slavery to emancipation. Du Bois recounts the lawlessness of Alabama in the early days of the Reconstruction era: "From 1865 to 1868, and even later, there was for all practicable purposes over the greater part of the people of Alabama, no government at all. . . . From 1865 to 1874, government and respect for government were weakened to a degree from which it has not yet recovered. The people governed themselves extra-legally, and have not recovered from the practice."[6] The clash between vindictive white people and newly freed people created a new kind of battleground after the Civil War, one in which white supremacist violence was used to terrorize Black people back into compulsory submission. This is the context in which the hanging of the mulatto on the side of the road between Tuscaloosa and Greensboro occurred.

With *Bureau of Refugees*, Kara Walker reaches back in time to visualize the archive of violence drafted and collected by the Freedmen's Bureau. This archive has within it a record of acts of violence committed as well as the sentiments of people whose experiences are recorded in ink and parchment, recordings that implicate the institutions, aggrieved southerners, and systems of power that were attempting to wrest control in the South after the Civil War. The Bureau of Refugees archives are populated with letters sent and received by Freedmen's Bureau officers in which they summarize and delineate details of testimonies made by freedwomen and freedmen. In the collection of affidavits made by those who survived racial and sexual violence are also the sworn testimonies of those who witnessed murders, found bodies, and identified perpetrators. These letters explicate some of the worst moments in newly freed people's lives; their descriptions of the horrors suffered during this era of complete societal, geographic, political, and racial upheaval make palpable the extent to which their lives were in danger. Walker's incorporation of archival material into her work in this series makes salient the precarity of Reconstruction for those recently freed from the bondage of slavery.

Walker produced two short films and rendered twenty-eight colorful silhouettes for her *Bureau of Refugees* series, which abstractly depicts incidents recorded by the assistant commissioner for the Bureau of Refugees, Freedmen, and Abandoned Lands for the District of Alabama in 1866.[7] In her introduction to the catalog of the exhibition, Walker writes that this project developed out of a frustration that she was having about painting and postmodernism, which she expressed first in written form. Walker snipped and reconstructed elements of the admittedly "heavy handed letter writing" and created a set of internet searches with reconstituted phrases such as "a Black man is a painting" and "a hollowed out-construct."[8] This act of random internet searching led Walker to the National Archives database, specifically "The Bureau of Refugees, Freedmen, and Abandoned Lands—Records, 'Miscellaneous Papers' National Archives M809 Roll 23." This particular National Archives publication roll contains the District of Alabama list of murders as well as descriptions of the riots and outrages inflicted on freedwomen and freedmen by white supremacist mobs and individual assailants.

Walker raises questions about the archival process with the colorful still silhouettes and short films that she produced for this series, work that departs from the towering Black silhouettes placed against white walls that capture the grotesque violence of the antebellum era for which the artist is most widely known.[9] While the focus of my analysis in *Visitation* centers on avant-garde short films, I am launching the discussion from a place of stillness. By beginning this examination of Walker's *Bureau of Refugees* with a reading of her colorful silhouette *Mulatto hung by a grapevine near road side between Tuscaloosa and Greensboro*, then moving to an analysis of her short film *National Archives Microfilm Publication M999 Roll 34: Bureau of Refugees, Freedmen and Abandoned Lands: Six Miles from Springfield on the Franklin Road*, I am laying the historical and analytic groundwork to grapple with the visual terrain that she is covering in this series. Walker's direct reference to the archival record made with each piece instigates an archival challenge that I take up and follow into the repository. For the silhouetted paintings, which measure between two and three feet tall and about a foot and a half wide, Walker moves away from entirely Black silhouettes and integrates colorful hues of gauche. With *Mulatto hung by a grapevine near road side between Tuscaloosa and Greensboro*, Walker uses a palette of rust and emerald and coal to visualize a body racially and figuratively bifurcated. Her interpretation of this Reconstruction-era act of violence, and the poetics used to describe the murder, is delicate yet rough, amorphous yet detailed. Walker's contradiction in form mirrors the oddity of short phrases and slashes on a page that document the murders of Black people in the aftermath of the abolition of chattel slavery. With the two short films in this series, each less than fourteen minutes long, Walker and her crew stage scenes using her silhouettes as puppets to reenact horrifying events reported to the Bureau of Refugees in the summer of 1866. The musical accompaniments in these films serve as ominous sonic backdrops to the fray.[10]

Of the list of murders that Walker discovered on a roll of archival film titled "National Archives Microfilm Publication M999 Roll 34," Walker writes: "The writing style is blunt, suggesting that brevity was in the service of progress. However, the short tenure of the Freedmen's Bureau and the long years of Black Codes and Jim Crow segregation attest to the political failure of this progressive legislation. For me, however, the endgame of Southern reconstruction reads like short-form poetry. For this reason, 'The Bureau of Refugees' takes the form of simple cut-outs, responding solely to the economy of this descriptive language."[11]

The tension between the stilted language and the grisly incidents they record is made evident in Walker's *Mulatto hung by a grapevine near road side between Tuscaloosa and Greensboro*, in which the artist freezes in time two halves of a figure's whole—a genteel silhouette of a proper lady made of deep-forest green with perfectly coiffed hair rests atop a grapevine that is crafted out of a combination of the lush green and sharp black (see figure 1.4). The lady's silhouetted bodice tapers off into an emerald misshapen figure that mimics a languid body, which twists down and lightly caresses a woman's splayed corpus painted in burnt orange. The unkempt, wild, short hair of the woman hanging upside down, naked and exposed, signifies blackness, yet she is painted with a ruddy ochre hue. Black roots entangle the head and chest of the lifeless woman's body that hovers above the ground, her right leg lifted above her head by a thick piece of the vine that rises up to the proper lady's bodice. The angular, poised, carefully crafted bodice indexes a refinement associated with western

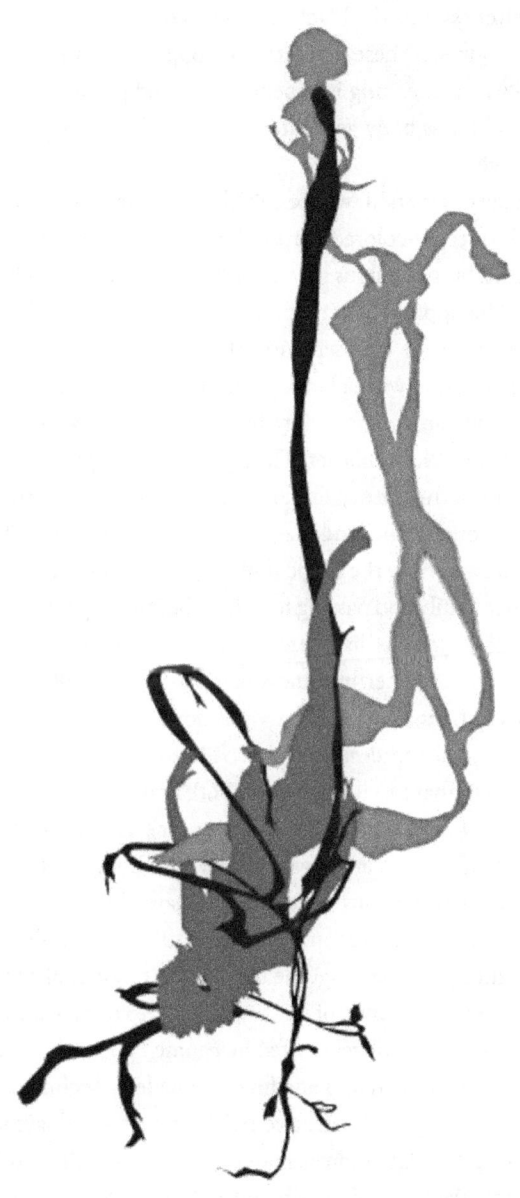

FIGURE 1.4 Kara Walker, *Bureau of Refugees: Mulatto hung by a grapevine near road side between Tuscaloosa and Greensboro*, 2007.

ideals of beauty and whiteness, but the black root reaches her, creating a spine along her backside that connects these diametrically opposed figures—the abject and the exemplar—whose meaning is dependent on and productive of the other. The abject figure's lifeless body generates the exemplar, who appears to triumph over the wreckage.

The elevated lady made of emerald, whose solid black spine is firmly affixed behind her, and the forlorn rusty-colored corpse that is engulfed by the gaggle of black spikes are tethered by a nebulous green body. This ghostly form haunts the silhouetted bodice. The apparition stretches out, trying to mimic the human figure, filling the white space that separates these women yet joins them by their roots. The emerald figure with a black spine calls up the tragic mulatta trope, a comely woman who can pass for white but has "dark roots" or a "dark past" that manacles her to her Black mother. The figure of the tragic mulatto in nineteenth- and early twentieth-century literary melodramas exposed the sanguine entanglements that bound white and Black people to the same bloodline.[12] As she appears in literature and film, the tragic mulatto figure tries to escape her Black blood by denying her family and passing for white, but she inevitably meets a disastrous end when her blackness is discovered. The tragic mulatto's happiness is always stymied by the threat of her blackness being exposed. Nella Larsen's *Quicksand* (1928) and *Passing* (1929) are quintessential novels of this genre. William Wells Brown's *Clotel; or, The President's Daughter: A Narrative of Slave Life in the United States* (1853), Emma Dunham Kelley's *Megda* (1891), Frances E. W. Harper's *Iola Leroy; or, Shadows Uplifted* (1892), and Charles Chesnutt's *The Marrow of Tradition* (1901) preceded Larsen's novels and weave narratives about the secrets of sexual violence and the hypocrisy of anti-miscegenation laws.[13] While films like Oscar Micheaux's *Within Our Gates* (1920) and Elia Kazan's *Pinky* (1949) deal with rape, miscegenation violence, and the sanguine bind of the tragic mulatto, *Imitation of Life* may be the most well known of the tragic mulatto tales. *Imitation of Life* first entered popular culture as a novel written by Fannie Hurst in 1933; it was adapted for the screen by John Stahl in 1934 and finally remade in Technicolor by Douglas Sirk in 1959.[14] Through grand narrative twists or subtle dialogic innuendo, tales in which the tragic mulatto appears point to a shadow culture during chattel slavery and its immediate afterlife in which Black women were routinely raped by white men and bore "mulatto" children as a result.

As Walker's *Mulatto hung* unleashes in paper and gauche, the tragic mulatto figure can hide her blackness behind her or within her, but her lineage, her life and her death, are forever tied to the blackness of her mother and the Black blood that courses through her veins. This piece, in response to the archival documentation of this Reconstruction-era murder, brings our attention to the pathological contradiction of miscegenation that permeated US chattel slavery. This was a paradoxical horror in which white enslavers raped Black women, and owned and increased their wealth with the children born of this sexual and reproductive violence, while concomitantly developing a system of laws that criminalized miscegenation and produced racist scientific studies that professed the dangers of "mixing" white and Black blood. The matrix of rape, miscegenation, and anti-miscegenation legislation depended on a willful blindness to the rape of enslaved Black women by white men and the overlooking of mulatto children born of this violence.[15] What I am describing here is the specter of miscegenation that haunts the meaning, power, and production of race in the United States. The artist's use of green, a blend of the primary colors yellow and blue, gestures toward the mixing of "race blood" that conjoins these women in the likeness and representation of white beauty and in the depiction of Black death, as the Black woman's body, painted in burnt orange, flails in the white space.[16] The elongated, miscegenated green form stands in for the violence of miscegenation—the rapes and their systemic obfuscation—while it excretes a replica of white womanhood in the form of the silhouetted bodice, an aesthetic choice that lays bare this history of rape and traces back to a pro slavery scare tactic meant to usurp the promise of emancipation.

In his seventy-two-page, anonymously published pamphlet titled *Miscegenation: The Theory of the Blending of the Races, Applied to the American White Man and Negro*, David Goodman Croly deployed a hoax that peddled pseudoscientific explanations, extolled a twist in eugenicist logic, and issued a plea for Christian charity and equality. Croly's full-throated embrace of miscegenation was not a radical stance against anti-Black racism but a ruse designed to thwart the abolition of slavery. He declares:

> It is clear that no race can long endure without a commingling of its blood with that of other races. The condition of all human progress is miscegenation. The Anglo-Saxon should learn this in time for his own salvation. If we will not heed the demands of justice, let us, at least, respect the law of self-preservation. Providence has kindly placed on the American soil for his own wise purposes, four million of colored people. They are our brothers, our sisters. By mingling with them we become powerful, prosperous, and progressive; by refusing to do so we become feeble, unhealthy, narrow-minded, unfit for the nobler offices of freedom, and certain of early decay.[17]

The publication and dissemination of this duplicitous pamphlet was a sly attempt to undermine the imminent abolition of chattel slavery and Abraham Lincoln's reelection in 1864. Croly coined *miscegenation* in this pamphlet and defined the term as follows: "from the Latin *Miscere,* to mix, and *Genus,* race, [miscegenation] is used to denote the abstract idea of the mixture of two or more races."[18] He used his treatise to declare the Republican Party "the party of miscegenation."[19] Croly's use of eugenicist logic to unabashedly encourage and promote the commingling of Black and white blood was antebellum propaganda meant to incite outrage and defeat Lincoln's reelection in 1864.[20] By advocating so audaciously for miscegenation of the races, Croly perpetrated a hoax to alarm white voters who may have supported emancipation yet would balk at the prospect of miscegenation as the way out of the proverbial race problem in a post-emancipation United States.[21] The visually resonant language of commingling racialized blood was a visceral and surreptitious way to ensure the separation of the races and protect white supremacy.[22]

Understanding the stakes and implications of the racialization of blood and the trope of the tragic mulatto adds weight to the meaning of Walker's piece, but the archive from which Walker works can offer even more clarity about this particular incident. Walker's visualization of the Freedmen's Bureau record of a mulatto woman hung by a grapevine between Tuscaloosa and Greensboro has within it the annihilation of an enslaved Black mother, the systemic rape of Black women upon which chattel slavery depended, and the symbolics of blood that protect categories of race and engineer the tragedy that ensnares the tragic mulatto. While the visual record of lynching in this country evidences the hideous torture and murder of Black men, the hanging of a woman at this time demonstrates another level of violence that Black women suffered.

Freedmen's Bureau: An Archive of Violence

Following Kara Walker into the Freedmen's Bureau archive led me to the very repository that housed the documents that she reenacts with her films and illustrates with each colorful silhouette. I wanted to learn more about the circumstances of the death, and perhaps the life, of the mulatto hung. I knew that the list of murders was just that, a list—a consolidation of a spate of crimes onto a single page. The occurrences of these murders, riots, assaults, and outrages must have been communicated to the Bureau of Refugees somehow. Since the hanging was on this list, I believed that the original report should exist. If I could find the letter that was written to the Bureau of Refugees to alert them about the mulatto woman's hanging, I would be able to gather more details about the incident. So little public discourse exists about the lynching of Black women that I needed to learn more about the circumstances of this murder. I wanted to know more about the person who found her, perhaps learn why she was killed, and who was left to mourn her. With this task firmly set in my mind, I traveled from Los Angeles, where I was living at that time, to the National Archives in Washington, DC, to recover all that I could about the woman hung by a grapevine on a roadside between Tuscaloosa and Greensboro.

Upon entry into the National Archives, I was greeted by the smiling photograph of President Barack Obama, whose framed portrait hung on the wall of the atrium where security guards checked our bags and validated our identification. After passing inspection, I worked my way into the dark modest space, which was smaller than I expected; I hoped that what I was looking for could be found. The size of the room was deceptive; what amounts to miles of records on microfilm has been economically cataloged in long filing cabinets by date, year, and region. I sat at one of the workstations where I would learn how to load the film and copy the pages that were pertinent to my research. In my exploration of the records, I found letters written to the Freedmen's Bureau that reported crimes or requested help as well as reports drafted by the assistant commissioner that recounted incidents of violence perpetrated by southern white men upon newly freed people, sometimes causing serious injury and other times ending in murder. As an archival collection is bound to do, it pulled me in.

On my search for anything that could point me to the circumstances surrounding the hanging of the mulatto on that stretch of road between Greensboro and Tuscaloosa, I combed through publication rolls of letters sent and received by military officials who were posted in the district of Alabama in 1866. I became comfortable with the microfilm and began to sink into a rhythm that enabled me to tune in to another time. I was transported back to the post–Civil War South. I began to understand the position of the Bureau of Refugees officials, military men whose authority in the South was met with hostility by southern whites who resentfully sought out the assistance of northern troops cum aid workers. These were the refugees, I would learn: southern whites who were destitute, landless, losers of the Civil War who had to now depend on their victors for support—the animosity lingers in the afterlife of chattel slavery.[23] The landlessness, the poverty, and the equality between the formerly enslaved and enslaver stoked the white fury that abounded in the South at this time. The formerly enslaved were free and trying to find a way to survive alongside former enslavers, and those who would have owned slaves if they could have afforded it, and this leveling out of circumstance wrought by the Confederate loss infuriated white supremacists in the South. Those who had just been released from bondage encountered a familiar threat with a different mission, ruthless white men who needed to reassert their dominance outside the confines of chattel slavery; vigilante violence replaced slave codes.

As I worked to decode the flourish of nineteenth-century handwriting, I began to hear the cadences of the writers. The details of post–Civil War tumult became clearer with each letter that I read. Through each instance of rape, hanging, whipping, arson, bludgeoning, and stabbing, white men tried to assert their place as superior to Black people in the wake of the abolition of slavery. Postbellum legislation that reinforced white superiority through jim crow segregation worked to reinstitute this racial hierarchy, but at the time of Reconstruction, vigilante violence was used to force Black people to relinquish the freedom they had just won. After several days spent deciphering the handwriting of assistant commissioners and generals in the US Army stationed in the district of Alabama, I had an invaluable archival encounter. In the National Archives, cataloged among a collection of letters received, I found a letter dated June 4, 1866, written by Assistant Superintendent Captain W. M. H. H. Peck, that reports an incident from the Tuscaloosa, Alabama, field office (see figures 1.5 and 1.6).

The letter reads:

Tuskaloosa Ala. June 4th 1866-

Major O. D. Kinsman
Asst. Adjt General
R. Y. & A. L. Ala.

Major:

I have the honor to submit the following statements. The affairs of the Office are being prosecuted in a reasonably successful manner.

The call upon the Commissary Dept. is still great—and the number of destitute people—especially white—is gradually increasing—

Today a resident of this city—stated to me, that last Wednesday 30th (wtt,) while coming home on a by-road about thirty miles from here to the left going on the Greensboro road, between Greene and Perry Counties, he saw a mulatto man of ordinary size hung to a tree by a grapevine. The body, he said appeared to have been in this position five or six days—It was off the road in the woods and several miles from a house—None of the people living near knew of the circumstances connected with the case.

Gen, Major
Very Respectfully
Your (Abdt. Sesst)
W. M. H. H. Peck
Capt. Asst. Sutd
R. F & A. L

I was surprised by the contents of this archival find. Not only do the spare details in this letter starkly capture the quotidian horror of emancipation life for newly freed people, but the letter also indicates that the mulatto hung by a grapevine was not a woman, as depicted in Walker's silhouette; the "mulatto hung" was in fact a man. After drawing myself back from the scene, I realized that the evidence provided by this document had upended my hypothesis. Then as I sat with this letter, I began to wonder what it meant that Walker illustrated this line on a Reconstruction-era list of murders with a Black woman as the lynched figure. What does this artistic/archival friction produce? What is she making visible about Black women and the archive of Reconstruction? Walker uses the language from the Bureau of Refugees description of this hanging as the title of the silhouette but diverges from the historical record in her visualization in a way that makes salient the violence that freedwomen suffered during this volatile era in US history. The mulatto man who was actually hung from a grapevine, the passerby who reported the murder, and the hung man's mother are all specters in Walker's *Mulatto hung by a grapevine near road side between Tuscaloosa and Greensboro*. Whether or not Walker had knowledge beyond the information given on the list of murders is not necessarily relevant when considering this piece as a work of art and not a historic rendering. Historical inspiration, not historical accuracy, is being demonstrated with Walker's *Mulatto hung*.

Walker's choice to illustrate this account of a lynching through the vector of womanhood forces attention to be paid to Black women during this era. She visualizes what Toni Morrison was working to bring our attention to with her contention that the past begins to change with inspection, with provocation, with our attention.[24] Walker's piece visualizes the index that Black women who have been subsumed by an archive of violence carved into being. She makes material Evelynn Hammonds's theory of the black (w)hole with a painting that cuts through the opacity of the archive to find the Black women who exist therein while illuminating Lorde's analysis of the persistent distortion of vision that encumbers Black women who "have on one hand always been highly visible, and so, on the other hand, have been rendered invisible through the depersonalization of racism."[25] With the artistic choice of making the "mulatto hung" a woman, Walker is making a Black feminist archival intervention that brings attention to the reproductive violence of miscegenation that permeated US chattel slavery, and Black women's experiences of violence and death during the terrifying era of Reconstruction. Walker's silhouette of a Black woman's body sprawled, exposed and defiled, invokes the enslaved mother who was raped and gave birth to the mulatto man who was hung. Enslaved women who were terrorized and raped as well as the white men and women of the slavehold-

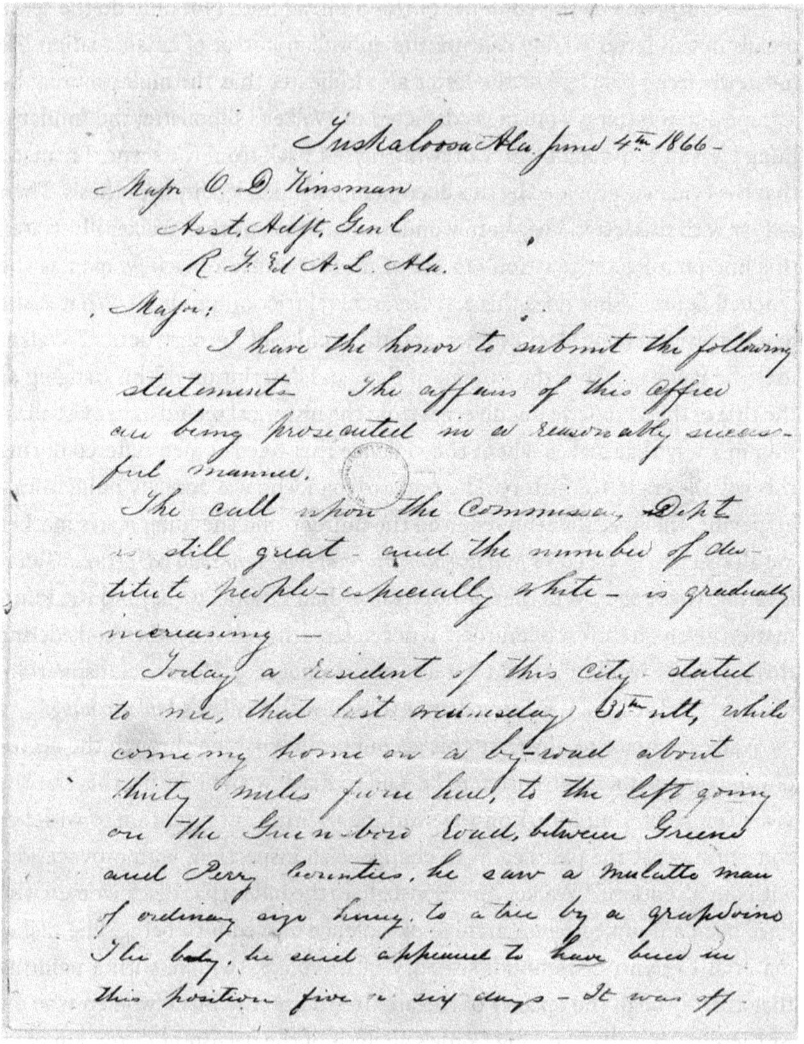

> Tuskaloosa Ala June 4th 1866 —
>
> Major O. D. Kinsman
> Asst. Adjt. Genl
> R. F. & A. L. Ala.
>
> Major:
>
> I have the honor to submit the following statements. The affairs of this office are being prosecuted in a reasonably successful manner.
>
> The call upon the Commissary Dept is still great — and the number of destitute people — especially white — is gradually increasing.
>
> Today a resident of this city stated to me, that last Wednesday 30th ult, while coming home on a by-road about thirty miles from here, to the left going on the Greensboro Road, between Greene and Perry Counties, he saw a mulatto man of ordinary size hung to a tree by a grapevine. The body, he said, appeared to have been in this position five or six days — It was off

FIGURES 1.5 AND 1.6 Letter from W. M. H. H. Peck, Capt. Asst. Sutd, to Major O. D. Kinsman, Alabama, June 4, 1866. Letters Received, July 1865–October 1867, Record Group 105, Roll M809, National Archives, Washington, DC.

the road in the woods and several miles from a house — none of the people living near, knew of the circumstances connected with the case.

I am, Major,
Very Respectfully
Your Obt Svt
W. H. H. Peck
Capt Asst Sup't.
R. F. & A. L.

ing class who committed acts of racial and sexual terror all haunt Walker's visualization of this archival entry. Walker's rendering of this document makes visible the terror of Reconstruction and the reality of white supremacist vigilante violence suffered by Black women.

Miscellany and Bureau of Refugees

Though Black women's experiences are present in the Freedmen's Bureau archives, the way they are presented, represented, and understood is through acts of violence and death. Walker's *Bureau of Refugees* makes this strikingly clear. The fact of this man's mulatto-ness points to the rape of his mother during slavery and the system of racialized sexual violence that Black enslaved women suffered under the regime of slavery. The Black mother who lost her son becomes legible in Walker's *Mulatto hung* as the ghastly Black figure suspended by a grapevine that was used to hang her child, but whose life and loss are obfuscated in the archival record; only through Walker's imagery does she appear in the record. The specter of that violence emerges from the void of life that the man hung suffered, and it exposes the pathological, willful blindness that erases the systemic rape of Black women. The history of the systemic rape of Black women during slavery, which has been categorically redacted from the cultural imaginary of slavery, is made vividly apparent in Walker's visualization of this Reconstruction-era archival document.[26]

Walker's *Bureau of Refugees* draws Black women out of the miscellany with her attention to the archival material stored on "The Bureau of Refugees, Freedmen, and Abandoned Lands—Records, 'Miscellaneous Papers' National Archives M809 Roll 23." This roll of microfilm holds the last pages on the last roll of microfilm in the Alabama 1866 publications in the National Archive; the relegation of these vicious crimes to a miscellaneous roll of microfilm points to the dislocation of Black suffering. The placement of archives that document the murders, lynchings, rapes, and torture of newly freed women, children, and men among the miscellaneous, as the miscellaneous, is emblematic of the space Black women occupy in this archive. The classification of records of Black death as miscellaneous reveals both a value system of the archival process as well as the role of the Freedmen's Bureau in the immediate post–Civil War years. The miscellaneous archival classification signals that the Freedmen's Bureau's specified purpose was not protecting newly freed people; it is almost as if the white supremacist attacks and murders were a surprise to the assistant commissioners who were tasked with providing supplies to the newly freed people and destitute white refugees. The institution may hold the record, but the power lies with the historian, the archivist, the intrepid researcher, and the artist to call a particular record forward. Reconstruction-era records hold traces of untold or under-told history that, if attended to, would amplify the voices and experiences of Black women during this period of time. The unaccessed archive, though recorded, becomes an epistemological tomb for newly freed people whose stories remain buried in the stacks and rolls of archival film.[27] My analysis of the miscellaneous publication rolls that Walker has brought to light—brought to life—with this series risks the contamination of which Saidiya Hartman is wary when she opens the archive of Venus's murder. In her article "Venus in Two Acts," Hartman asks, "Why subject the dead to new dangers and to a second order of violence?"[28] My engagement with Walker's *Bureau of Refugees* and the Reconstruction-era documents that account for the voices of emancipated human beings does choose to open up the archival casket, but instead of issuing a second order of violence, I am arguing that Black feminist avant-garde filmmakers enter into the archive, wade through the miscellany, and invite visitations through their visualization of historic acts of violence.

Walker's archival retrieval and visualization in *Bureau of Refugees* throw into question the construction of history and the role that cataloging, preserving, and classification play in our understanding of this pivotal moment in US history. Unlike the archival records of US chattel slavery found in ship manifests, slave logs, plantation inventories, insurance claims, and the very rare court transcript, all of which elide the perspective of human beings captured, transported, and sold as chattel, Freedmen's Bureau records hold the testimonies of people who were once enslaved.[29] While the record of the testimonies made by formerly enslaved people abound in the Freedmen's Bureau archive, Walker's retrieval of the documents is imbued by systems of power that assign value and enable access. In *Silencing the Past: Power and the Production of History*, Michel-Rolph Trouillot describes three tenets of historical production, beginning with the fact that inequalities present at the time of an event, or the recording of that event, privilege some voices and silence others. What is lost, what is made absent in the production of history, also constitutes the production of history.[30] Trouillot makes a distinction between the moment of an event and the moment when that event enters the archive, to exemplify the unevenness of power with which historical events are treated when they are excluded from or given a place in an archival collection. The second tenet brings our attention to the assembly of the archive itself and the different kinds of institutions that together generate mechanisms of inclusion, cataloging, ranking, accessibility, and of course exclusion. The third aspect of this paradigm has to do with the retrieval of archival documents from repositories. The use of the archive to produce history is inflected with what Trouillot calls archival power. As the story of an event, or a period of time, or a person's life is narrated into history, choices are being made, silences are being produced, and archival power is being exerted.[31] Trouillot's analysis of archival power and silence, and their role in the production of history, provides a way to understand the occlusion that distorts Black women's archival presences.

Reconstruction-era affidavits held at the National Archives convey some details about incidents of violence that newly freed women, children, and men suffered in the aftermath of the Civil War, from the perspective of those newly freed people. These documents register the presence of Black women and girls in this archive, presences made legible through devastating acts of violence described in testimonies and affidavits submitted to the Freedmen's Bureau. In order to give a sense of the kind of violence that Black women suffered after emancipation, I will share a few letters received by the Freedmen's Bureau. In August 1866 an outraged citizen in Garland, Alabama, N. B. Markley, reported that a man by the name of James Pryor arrested a woman, Winni, because he suspected her of stealing some meat from him (see figure 1.7).

As this letter details, "Pryor Hanged her until nearly dead in order to make her confess the crime, failing in this, the woman professing her innocence, he then tied her up and gave her some 2 or 300 lashes, the woman's husband, he Knocked in the head with his gun injuring him severely if not fatally." A month before Winni was whipped savagely and hanged nearly to death by James Pryor, a Black girl named Eliza was beaten to death. The murder was reported in a correspondence between Captain Assistant Superintendent W. M. H. H. Peck and the assistant adjutant general, Major O. B. Kinsman (see figure 1.8)[32]:

> Bureau Refugees Freedmen & A. L.
> Tuskaloosa. Ala July 16. 1866-
>
> SGT. Major O. D. Kinsman
> Asst. Adjt-Gen'l
> District
>
> Major:
> I have the honor to call your attention to the fact—that about a month since Washington and Greene McKinny living near eighteen |18| miles west of town /white men/ are reported to have beaten a Black girl /Eliza/ to death for a trivial offense or supposed offense—

I cannot learn that any steps have been taken by the civil authorities in the matter—
[unintelligble]

> Very Respectfully
> W. M. H. Peck
> Capt. Asst. Sutd

Reports like this of unchecked violence are testament to the lawlessness and ungoverned extralegal conditions in which vulnerable newly emancipated women and girls had to try to survive. The preservation of these letters in the National Archives provides a resting place for the documentation of vigilante violence against Black women but certainly offers no restitution. Walker's retrieval from the miscellany of the Freedmen's Bureau archive counteracts the force of archival subsumption to which this history has been relegated.

In an interview in which Kara Walker responds to a question about her use of history in her artwork, the artist recognizes her position as an instigator. Rather than holding fast to the facts, she sees her role as a kind of trickster, one who understands the construction of art as lie.

> I am kind of interested in that sort of project of getting the facts. And part of the reason that I am interested in the project of getting the facts is because so much of what art is, is like telling the lie. I got all of the facts and now I'm going to make a puppet show. And I mean, that's what I do. And, I'm trying to find that fine line between where the reality kind of catches you off, off kilter? And where the falseness, the stagecraft, or where the lighthearted quality maybe also kind of sideswipes, sideswipes you/me/us.[33]

Like the trickster archive created for Cheryl Dunye's fake documentary film, *The Watermelon Woman*, I see Walker's engagement with history not as a lie but as a provocation that asks us to interrogate the fabrication of history.[34] Both Dunye's *The Watermelon Woman* and Walker's *Bureau of Refugees* extend invitations to interrogate the construction of history not only by exposing archival gaps but by showing the production and craftwork of their cinematic pieces. Through Walker's visualization of the Freedmen's Bureau archive in *Bureau of Refugees*, the packaging and occlusions of Reconstruction-era history become apparent and force our understanding of the past to be thrown off kilter.

Walker's signature silhouettes, such as those that animated her exhibition *Kara Walker: My Complement, My Enemy, My Oppressor, My Love*, are exaggerated, bombastic figurations that mark blackness and whiteness.[35] Walker's style cap-

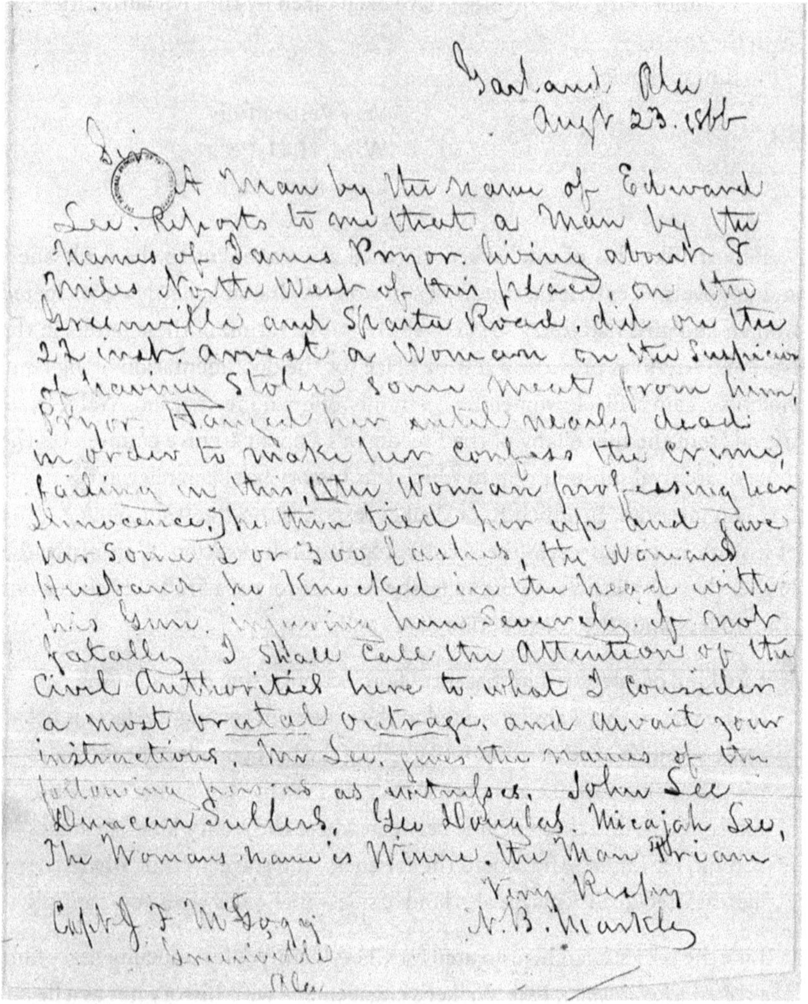

Garland, Ala
Augt 23. 1866

Sir
A Man by the name of Edward Lee. Reports to me that a Man by the Names of James Pryor. living about 8 Miles North West of this place, on the Greenville and Sparta Road. did on the 22 inst. arrest a Woman on the Suspicion of having Stolen some meat from him, Pryor. Hanged her until nearly dead in order to make her Confess the Crime, failing in this, the Woman professing her Innocence, he then tied her up and gave her some 2 or 300 lashes, the Womans Husband he Knocked in the head with his Gun. injuring him Severely. If not fatally. I shall Call the Attention of the Civil Authorities here to what I consider a most brutal outrage. and await your instructions. Mr Lee. gives the names of the following persons as witnesses. John Lee Duncan Sellers. Geo Douglas. Micajah Lee. The Womans name is Winnie. the Man Priam

Very Respy
N. B. Markley

Capt J. F. McGogy
Greenville
Ala

FIGURE 1.7 Letter from N. B. Markley, Alabama, August 23, 1866. Letters Received, July 1865–October 1867, Record Group 105, Roll M809, National Archives, Washington, DC.

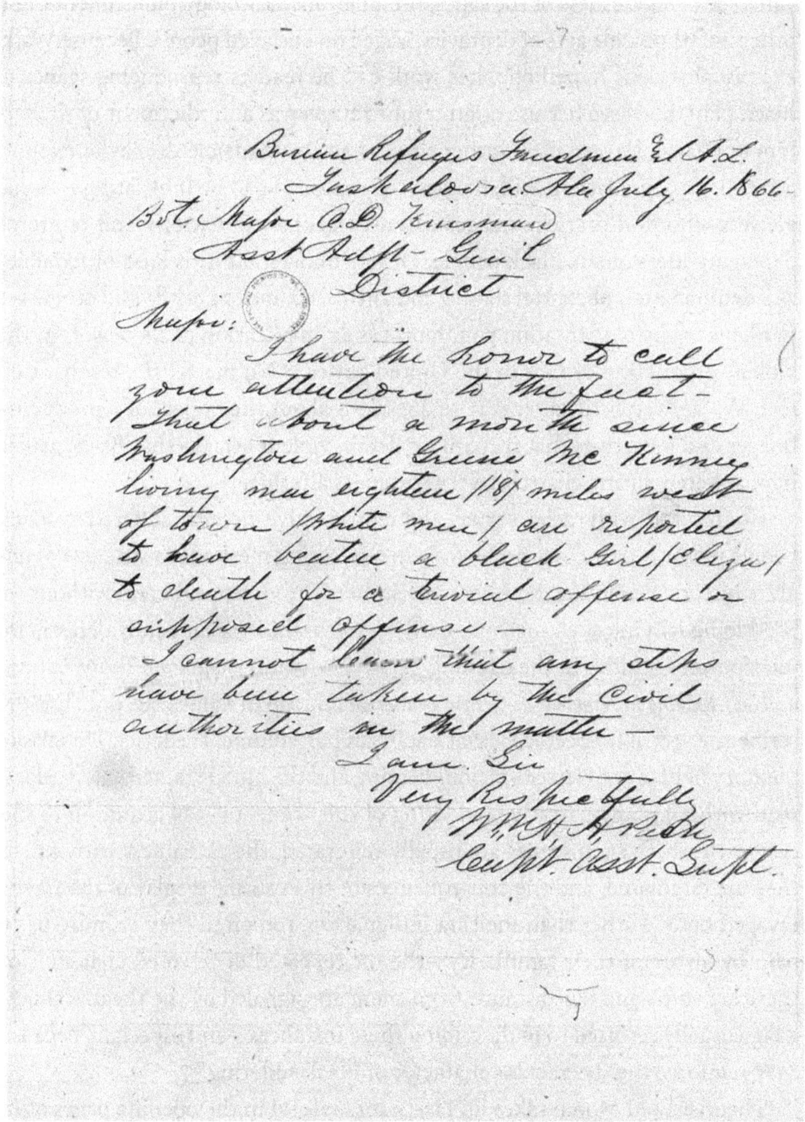

> Bureau Refugees Freedmen &A.L.
> Tuskaloosa Ala July 16, 1866
> Bvt. Major O. D. Kinsman
>   Asst Adjt Genl
>   District
> Mspi:
>   I have the honor to call your attention to the fact — That about a month since Washington and Greene McKinney (colored men) eighteen (18) miles west of town (white men) are reported to have beaten a black Girl (Eliza) to death for a trivial offense or supposed offense —
>   I cannot learn that any steps have been taken by the Civil authorities in the matter —
>   I am Sir
>   Very Respectfully
>   W. M. H. H. Peck
>   Capt. Asst. Supt.

FIGURE 1.8 Letter from W. M. H. H. Peck, Capt. Asst. Sutd, to Major O. D. Kinsman, Alabama, July 16, 1866. Letters Received, July 1865–October 1867, Record Group 105, Roll M809, National Archives, Washington, DC.

tures the egregiousness of the rapes, humiliations, scatology punishments, and other unfathomable acts of depravity waged on enslaved people. Because Walker's visual style is hyperbolic, her work can be read as reproducing scenes of Black pain, but I see her use of grotesque imagery as an indictment of the system of chattel slavery itself rather than as an irresponsible display of exploitative Black degradation. Still, her artistic approach can be infuriating to some viewers who find that the images call up blackface minstrelsy and reinforce damaging ideas about Black people. Others understand this kind of iconicity as a denunciation of chattel slavery and anti-Black racism, while still others see Walker's frightful plantation panoramas as an implication of all viewers in the violent production of race in the United States.[36] No matter the resonant effect, Walker's stylistic choices raise questions about the impact of reproducing images and narratives that recount, in detail, violent attacks that Black people have suffered during chattel slavery and in its afterlife.

Contending with racial, sexual, and reproductive violence suffered by Black people presents particular problems when selecting methods to visualize or analyze historical material; how does one address the violence therein without reproducing it? One such method, used by cultural historian Saidiya Hartman, incorporates refusal. In the opening pages of *Scenes of Subjection: Terror, Slavery, and Self-Making in Nineteenth-Century America*, Hartman names but does not describe the "terrible spectacle" that catalyzes her volume: Frederick Douglass's memory of his aunt Hester's vicious beating and the blood-stained gate.[37] Hartman withholds any narrative rendering of this scene, to "call attention to the ease with which such scenes are usually reiterated, the casualness with which they are circulated, and the consequences of this routine display of the slave's ravaged body. Rather than inciting indignation, too often they immure us to pain by virtue of their familiarity—the oft repeated or restored character of these accounts and our distance from them are signaled by the theatrical language usually resorted to in describing these instances—and especially because they reinforce the spectacular character of Black suffering."[38]

Theorist Fred Moten takes up Hartman's refusal in the opening pages of *In the Break: The Aesthetics of the Black Radical Tradition* by arguing that despite Hartman's withholding of the description of the scene at the blood-stained gate, the image of that scene persists in our imaginations.[39] If Black suffering is an inescapable referent that lingers in the history of blackness in the United States, then what measure is appropriate to contend with that suffering? Hartman's concern over recounting the details of the blood-stained gate draws attention to the distinction between what it means to witness, rather than spectate, when engaging with narratives of Black suffering. Hartman insists:

At issue here is the precariousness of empathy and the uncertain line between witness and spectator. Only more obscene than the brutality unleashed at the whipping post is the demand that this suffering be materialized and evidenced by the display of the tortured body or the endless recitations of the ghastly and the terrible. In light of this, how does one give expression to these outrages without exacerbating the indifference to suffering that is the consequence of the benumbing spectacle or contend with the narcissistic identification that obliterates the other or the prurience that too often is the response to such displays?[40]

One approach, as contradictory as it may seem, is an embrace of the image. In her visualization of Reconstruction-era Black suffering, Kara Walker does not recede from the image but moves into the visual by adding motion to her silhouettes. The reality of the myriad terrible spectacles that terrorized enslaved and formerly enslaved people, whether referred to but not described or visualized in hyperbolic detail, lingers in both of these methods of addressing the horrors of chattel slavery. Black feminist avant-garde films like Kara Walker's *Six Miles from Springfield on the Franklin Road* reimagine scenes of Black suffering yet are able to render null the pleasure of spectatorship; this nearly impossible maneuver, which I contend uses tenderness as a vector rather than spectacle, is a defining feature of Black feminist avant-garde cinema. Black feminist avant-garde filmmakers, through their encounters with Black women in an archive, conjure visitations out of archival-cinematic terrain of which we as viewers partake and concomitantly cocreate as witnesses. The unearthing of archival documentation through these films forges connections between the filmmakers, the visionaries who translate that connection through the visual field, and those of us who witness the visitations as they unfold. The spectatorial slips away as Black feminist avant-garde filmmakers disrupt the pornotropic with films that fasten connections between archival figures and those who witness the horrors they suffered.

Even though Walker's silhouettes invoke the human form, her exaggerated silhouettes communicate more about the abstraction of blackness and Black womanhood than render a figurative representation. Phillip Brian Harper's *Abstractionist Aesthetics* describes the necessary abstraction of any work of visual art. He argues that abstractionism

> entails the resolute awareness that even the most realistic representation is precisely a *representation* and that as such it necessarily exists at a distance from the social reality it is conventionally understood to reflect. In other words, abstractionist aesthetics crucially recognizes that any artwork whatsoever is definitionally *abstract* in relation to the world in

which it emerges, regardless of whether or not it features the nonreferentiality typically understood to constitute aesthetic *abstraction* per se. An *abstractionist artwork*, by extension, is one that *emphasizes* its own distance from reality by calling attention to its constructed or artificial character—even if it also enacts real-world reference.[41]

Walker's silhouettes exemplify the distance between the idea of blackness projected by white supremacist desires and anything close to the lived reality of Black people. This distance takes on another valence with Walker's transfer from the antebellum period to the Reconstruction era with *Bureau of Refugees*, along with her use of archival cataloging indices, and the interplay between still and moving silhouettes in this series. As was the case with early avant-garde filmmakers such as Man Ray, Ferdinand Léger, and Salvador Dalí, Kara Walker incorporates the cinematic medium into her full, lively, and well-established visual art practice.[42] In his essay "From Metaphors on Vision," foundational avant-garde filmmaker Stan Brakhage describes the potential depths that the cinematic medium could plumb if an interrogation of vision and perception were the catalyst for filmmaking.[43] He writes with urgency:

> To see is to retain—to behold. Elimination of all fear is in sight—which must be aimed for. Once vision may have been given—that which seems inherent in the infant's eye, an eye which reflects the loss of innocence more eloquently than any other human feature, an eye which soon learns to classify sights, an eye which mirrors the movement of the individual toward death by its increasing inability to see.
>
> But one can never go back, not even in imagination. After the loss of innocence, only the ultimate knowledge can balance the wobbling pivot. Yet I suggest that there is a pursuit of knowledge foreign to language and founded upon visual communication, demanding a development of the optical mind, and dependent upon perception in the original and deepest sense of the word.
>
> Suppose the Vision of the saint and the artist to be an increased ability to see—vision.[44]

The concept of visitation is consonant with Brakhage's supposition that an artist possesses an increased ability to see. Black feminist avant-garde filmmakers use their vision, their cinematic landscapes, to stage the connections they make with archival figures. Like Brakhage, Black feminist avant-garde filmmakers are pushing us to see beyond what we think we know and are asking us to embrace our imaginations and explore possibilities that exceed instantiated temporal boundaries. Although Brakhage used avant-garde films to produce pathways that enable us to see beyond what is readily available, these Black feminist avant-garde filmmakers are focusing that line of sight on Black women in archives of violence. While her visual art would not be located within an avant-garde art movement, I recognize Kara Walker as an artist who employs an avant-garde approach to cinema.[45] Walker's Black feminist avant-garde cinematic style disrupts the flat antebellum panoramas she is so widely known for by throwing frozen silhouettes into action and giving these figures interior lives. Walker's use of movement and dimension within a frame brings life to a set of documents previously relegated to the miscellany. The presence of the artist is not only felt but seen as she and her crew are captured moving the puppets within the frame, making the connection between artist, archive, and viewer immediate and unmistakable. With her short film *Six Miles from Springfield on the Franklin Road*, Walker deploys avant-garde cinematic aesthetics as a method of retrieval from the Freedmen's Bureau archive. The artist moves away from the colorful silhouetted figures that populated her small paintings in *Bureau of Refugees* and enlivens her Black silhouettes as puppets that play out a scene of Reconstruction-era terror. The choice to use silhouettes instead of actors to reenact this archival entry offers a measure of remove from the violence suffered by the newly freed people who gave their testimony, yet it allows the acts of terror to be made visible through the cinematic. By placing her silhouettes in motion in *Six Miles from Springfield on the Franklin Road*, Walker is able to visualize this archive of violence without inciting pleasure in the viewer; *Six Miles from Springfield on the Franklin Road* reframes the past and forces our perspective to recalibrate as we see Black women and girls in the archive of Reconstruction. Walker's *Six Miles from Springfield on the Franklin Road* takes us into the National Archives, to Tennessee in the fall of 1866, to meet a family that suffered catastrophic acts of vigilante violence and visit with a young girl who survived a brutal rape and was able to attest to that fact and have her testimony registered with the Bureau of Refugees, Freedmen, and Abandoned Lands.

Six Miles from Springfield on the Franklin Road

In October 1866, the fall of the year in which the unnamed mulatto man was found hung by a grapevine on the roadside between Tuscaloosa and Greensboro, Alabama, a band of white vigilantes stormed a house on Franklin Road about six miles from Springfield, Tennessee. An affidavit submitted to Michal Walsh, Capt. V. R. G., Chief Superintendent in the Nashville district office of the Bureau of Refugees, Freedmen, and Abandoned Lands, documents that

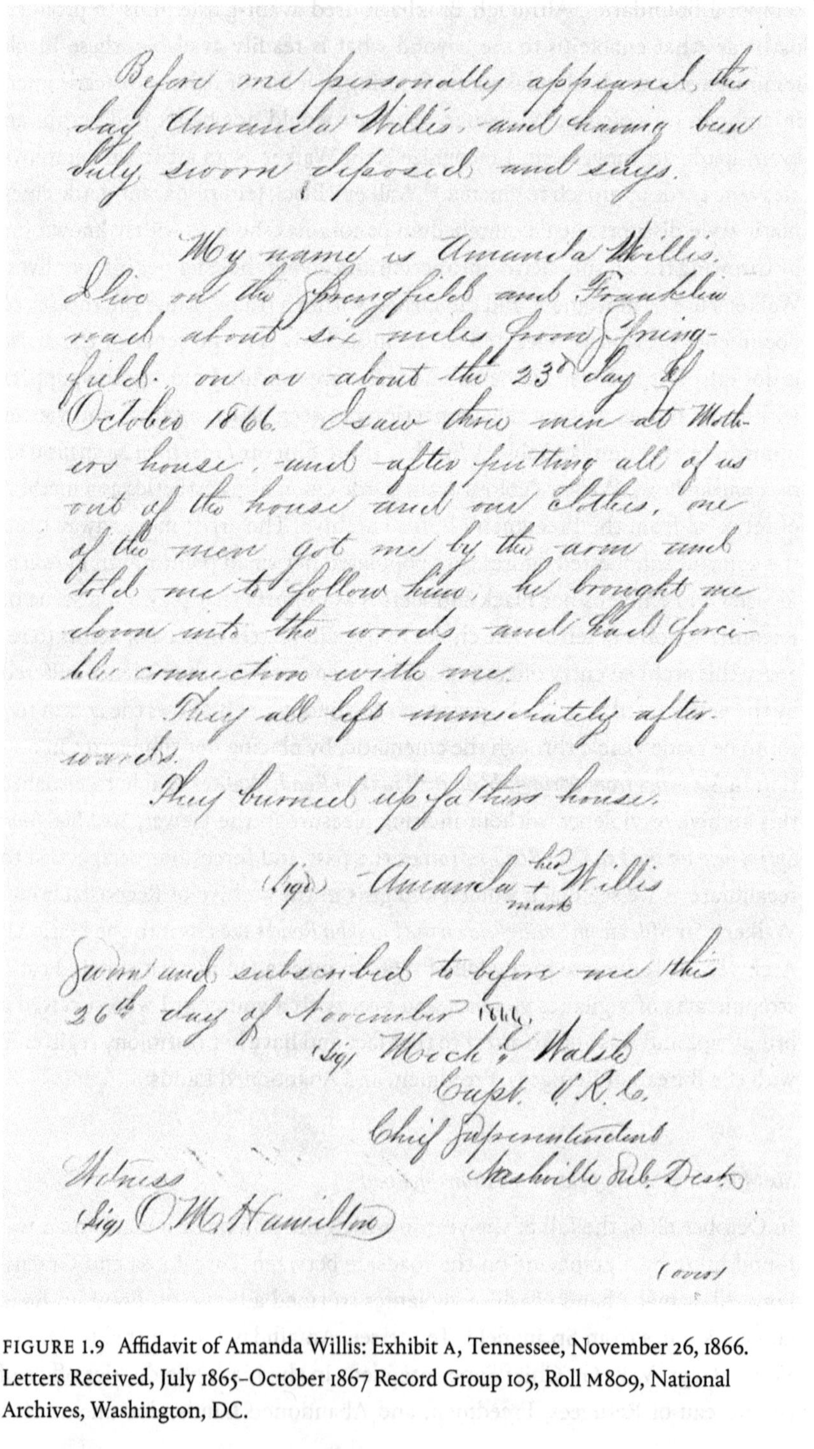

Before me personally appeared, this day Amanda Willis, and having been duly sworn deposed and says.

My name is Amanda Willis. I live on the Springfield and Franklin road about six miles from Springfield. on or about the 23d day of October 1866. I saw three men at Mothers house, and after putting all of us out of the house and our clothes, one of the men got me by the arm and told me to follow him, he brought me down into the woods and had forcible connection with me.

They all left immediately afterwards.

They burned up fathers house.

(sgd) Amanda + Willis
                   his
                   mark

Sworn and subscribed to before me this 26th day of November 1866.
Sig Mich. L. Walsh
Capt. V.R.C.
Chief Superintendent
Nashville Sub Dist.

Witness
Sig O.M. Hamilton

(over)

FIGURE 1.9 Affidavit of Amanda Willis: Exhibit A, Tennessee, November 26, 1866. Letters Received, July 1865–October 1867 Record Group 105, Roll M809, National Archives, Washington, DC.

twelve-year-old Amanda Willis "(col'd)" witnessed three white men put her family out of their house so that they could raid the place in search of money. After they ransacked this family's home, they lit it ablaze. One of the men then grabbed Amanda by the arm and forced her into the woods. The other two men followed him and the three men raped her, one after the other.[46]

The affidavit submitted to Michal Walsh (see figure 1.9) reads:

Before me personally appeared, this day Amanda Willis—and having been duly sworn, deposed and says.

My name is Amanda Willis. I live on the Springfield and Franklin road about six miles from Springfield. on or about the 23rd day of October 1866. I saw three men at Mothers house.—and after putting all of us out of the house and our clothes one of the men got me by the arm and told me to follow him. he brought me down into the woods and had forcible connection with me.

They all left immediately afterwards. They burned up fathers house.

        her
(Sign)—Amanda + Willis
        mark[47]

Sworn and subscribed to before me this 26th day of November 1866.

    (Sig) Michal Walsh
    Capt. VRG
    Chief Superintendent
    Nashville Sub Desk

    Witness
    (Sig) O M Hamilton

Kara Walker visualizes this incident in her *Bureau of Refugees* series not in watercolor but with the short film *National Archives Microfilm Publication M999 Roll 34: Bureau of Refugees, Freedmen and Abandoned Lands: Six Miles from Springfield on the Franklin Road*.[48] Walker stages the scenes described in the affidavit through the use of silhouetted puppets, colorful backdrops, and simple title cards (see figure 1.10). The title of this piece comes from the testimony of Amanda's brother, Henry Willis "(col'd)," who reports in his affidavit that he lives in "Robertson County six miles from Springfield on the Franklin road, on Thomas Willis' plantation."[49]

Six Miles from Springfield on the Franklin Road opens in silence, showing Walker and her team behind the scenes moving the puppets (see figure 1.11). The exposi-

FIGURES 1.10–1.12 Kara Walker, *National Archives Microfilm Publication M999 Roll 34: Bureau of Refugees, Freedmen and Abandoned Lands: Six Miles from Springfield on the Franklin Road*, 2009 (film stills).

tory elements of this narrative are conveyed through a tracking shot that finds a lone humble shack in the woods (see figure 1.12). We are introduced to the "characters" with title cards upon their first appearance in the film: Mother, Father, Son, and Mandy (see figures 1.13 and 1.14).

Mother sees Father and Son off to till the land. Birds fly by, clothes are drying on the line. Mother grooms Mandy, then plucks the feathers from a chicken. Soft jazz piano music accompanies this introduction to the family. The day passes; the sound of crickets chirping meets the setting sun as Father chops wood (see figure 1.15). Mandy washes a dress in the big cast-iron pot on the fire outside. The moon rises in the sky and the day is done.

The piano playing becomes erratic and sharp. The silhouettes of white men gather outside the shack (see figure 1.16). This is a mob of angry white men armed with pistols and rifles. The family wakens, terrified. They try to hide. The white men beat Father with a gun. A white man ransacks the home. Father fantasizes about chopping this white man's head off with his ax at the chopping block. The piano music is menacing. The white men force the family out of the house at gunpoint. The hands of Walker and her team can be seen moving the puppets. Father fights back. The white man shoots Father. The piano laments. Father lies in a pool of blood made of a red photographic gel. Mother, Son, and Mandy are led away from the house. The white men burn the house down. Fire

FIGURES 1.13–1.16 Kara Walker, *National Archives Microfilm Publication M999 Roll 34: Bureau of Refugees, Freedmen and Abandoned Lands: Six Miles from Springfield on the Franklin Road*, 2009 (film stills).

FIGURE 1.17 Kara Walker, *National Archives Microfilm Publication M999 Roll 34: Bureau of Refugees, Freedmen, and Abandoned Lands: Six Miles from Springfield on the Franklin Road*, 2009 (film still).

and blood are crafted out of red, orange, and yellow photographic gels. The sound of fire crackling meets the sorrowful piano. Fire blazes, burning down the shack. Son, Mother, and Mandy dash into the woods away from the fire; the mob of white men follow. The scene is filled with red and fire. Mandy gets lost in the woods. Mother and Son cannot be found. A white man with a gun grabs Mandy and snatches her into the woods. Sounds of the shack burning can be heard along with quiet, dissonant guitar strumming. Two men rape Mandy in the woods in the background. Yet Mandy is walking away in the foreground (see figure 1.17). The film ends abruptly.

The Archive and the Silhouette

The aesthetics of resistance that Walker employs in her visualization of Amanda Willis's testimony to the Freedmen's Bureau produces witnesses rather than a pleasure in viewing. Walker marshals cinematic tenderness in her rendering of a young Black girl's experience of violence, by illustrating the interiority, the humanity, of Mandy, whose rape was reported, filed away, but undoubtedly sat irreconcilably in the archive for 141 years. Walker's visual treatment of these archived statements about the horrific acts of violence committed against Mandy and her family exposes the virulence of white mob violence, reveals the handiwork of the artist, and makes salient the human tragedy suffered in the dark of night six miles from Springfield, Tennessee, in the fall of 1866. While Walker's visual style does use exaggerated characterizations, I contend that her attention to the positionality of Black women in the archive and her use of space, tone, and pacing does not produce pornotropy, but rather creates a mode of witnessing this family's suffering. The artist's avant-garde approach to visualizing this archive, with puppets and puppeteers in the frame, is a tender method of representation that focuses on Mandy and evokes emotion from her perspective. It is important to note that the only person in this film given a name is Mandy Willis; this narrative device names and thereby centers the young Black survivor of rape. Walker's insistence that we see Mandy in this archive, through this film, demands that the viewer consider the history of Reconstruction from the perspective of a young Black girl who was born into slavery, spent her first eleven years of life in bondage, and then was emancipated by Lincoln's proclamation. The horror of slavery was lifted for this young girl, only to have white supremacist vigilante violence take its place.

Walker's use of the cinematic gives spatial and affective dimension to the flat world populated by silhouetted puppets, a rickety shack, and gargantuan sycamore trees. In the closing images of the film, Mandy separates from herself in the face of horrendous trauma. She is in the foreground walking away, while she is also in the background being raped in the woods. The still frame of Mandy's dissociation demonstrates the spatial depth that Walker achieves while also visualizing Mandy's internal world and allowing the hands of the filmmaker and her crew to be seen within the frame. The puppets remind us that we are watching a representation of a rape and that knowledge of Mandy's suffering does not mean that she deserved to suffer; the absurdity of the necessity of this reminder is cacophonous. The use of puppets also reminds us that Mandy was a child and amplifies the perversity of the villainous white men who raped her. The aesthetics, the movement of Walker's silhouettes, and images of the artist herself inside the frame animating the figures destabilize and add dimension to the experience of the cinematic and the experience of the archival document—disruptions that are key components of Black feminist avant-garde cinema. With these avant-garde cinematic choices, Walker exposes the craft of the film and the construction of the archive and in so doing insists that viewers attend to the fact of their own watching.

With *Six Miles from Springfield on the Franklin Road*, the artist upends the subsumption of young Mandy's suffering and the vicious treatment of her family by demanding that this piece of history be drawn out of the miscellany. Walker brings this young girl's story out of the repository, out of 1866, and into the contemporary. This Black feminist avant-garde film enters into the Freedmen's Bureau archive, and what the artist retrieves from this repository she then transmutes into a contribution from the twenty-first century that manages to complement Mandy's Reconstruction-era affidavit. By revealing the cinematic process in this way, Walker interrupts the passive viewing of this demoralizing scene of archived violence. This approach to the archival document and the cinematic is consonant with Black feminist imperatives and produces a Black feminist avant-garde, which demands another kind of looking, another kind of representation to make visible a history of violence—with specificity and without spectacle—that has been overlooked or discarded or occluded by other records that document the history of Reconstruction.

In *The Writing of History*, Michel de Certeau contends, "The historiographer and the analyst virtually generate forms of knowledge from their continued confrontation with death, and only through this relation with death do they begin—and continue—to write."[50] Walker's visualization of documented acts of violence committed against the newly freed in her *Bureau of Refugees* series generates forms of knowledge of the past. Walker creates the cinematic space to contend with the losses, the deaths, the violence that still animate that archival space, and the unreconciled violence that bleeds into our present moment. If the archive is a storing house for loss and death—the death of the past—then the archive of Black women during Reconstruction is a holding place for violation and murder. The archive's future becomes the issue that we must contend with in the present, and Black feminist avant-garde cinematic pieces are instantiating questions of knowledge production, the violence of archival processes, and the subjugation of Black womanhood through each frame that sears the past and future together in our present as we witness and learn and know.

Amanda Willis's affidavit makes legible and undeniable the horrors that she and her family faced during Reconstruction. Through her engagement with this archival material, Kara Walker listens for deeper resonances from the past, as Morrison encourages, and stages them in *Six Miles from Springfield on the Franklin Road*. By putting her silhouettes in motion within a cinematic landscape, Walker visualizes an archival record and a record of a spectral archival encounter; this film is a visitation. What the Freedmen's Bureau record of Amanda Willis's assault does not describe, what Walker picks up through her archival encounter and what she relates through this short film, is the sense of fright and the experience of dissociation that are inevitable components of rape. In her visualization of this testimony, Walker taps into a sense and knowing that are both tender and intuitive. Walker's film places us squarely in a vantage point that offers new ways of seeing into an archival collection and witnessing the terrifying rape that is recorded therein; Walker translates the dialectical relationship that developed between Amanda/Mandy Willis and herself. With *Six Miles from Springfield on the Franklin Road*, Walker conjures a visitation with Mandy Willis that gives viewers the chance to witness, to move closer to— note that Walker calls her the more familiar Mandy rather than Amanda in this film—and grieve with this young girl, newly freed from slavery, who has suffered a terrible, vicious assault. Walker's avant-garde cinematic treatment of Willis's testimony contributes not only images to the archive of Reconstruction but also a sensual presence, a visitation with Amanda Willis. Walker's treatment of records collected during the period that immediately followed the abolition of chattel slavery—the inaugural era of what Hartman has so adroitly and resonantly called the "afterlife of slavery"—lays bare what can be accessed, what can resurface, and who can usher in a reckoning in the afterlife of this archive.[51]

Black feminist avant-garde films, like Walker's *Six Miles from Springfield on the Franklin Road*, enable artists to retrieve documents from an archive, visit with specters who surface in the process, and then visualize the encounter not simply for the sake of seeing but to engender a reckoning across time and space. In *Specters of Marx*, Jacques Derrida conceptualizes the present as something that is alive with specters, those who are no longer living and those who are not yet born but with whom we live nonetheless: "No justice . . . seems possible or thinkable without the principle of some *responsibility*, beyond all living present, within that which disjoins the living present, before the ghosts of those who are not yet born or who are already dead, be they victims of wars, political or other kinds of violence, nationalist, racist, colonialist, sexist, or other kinds of exterminations, victims of the oppressions of capitalist imperialism or any of the forms of totalitarianism."[52]

Derrida is discussing what it means to live with ghosts in such a way that the present becomes unhinged by what was, what could have been, and what may be to come, and thus time—the present—becomes multiple. Entering the archive is to traverse a field of spirits, each with their own fragment of the past to relay. With Walker's film, the ghosts of Reconstruction, the victims of racial and sexual violence, reveal themselves in visitations that unfold in the screening rooms, gallery spaces, and theaters in which they occur. The void that grows within an archive, that which subsumes Black women and girls in the aftermath of chattel slavery, becomes enlivened through Walker's silhouettes. The blank, flat spaces of the silhouettes turn into landscapes of knowledge, of affidavits, of history that had lain dormant in the repository. Walker's film exposes the lie of the archival absence of Black women during pivotal moments in US history by plunging into this epistemological obfuscation, then emerging with visualizations that place Black women in the crosshairs of Reconstruction-era terror. The archive of violence that contains the testimonies of Black women and their children throws the occlusion of Black womanhood off kilter, yet Black women surface in the archive through the violence inflicted on them. The violence of the archive takes place through erasure and also through the trajectory of inclusion that makes Black women legible in the archive of racial formation in the United States through the documentation of torturous acts of violence that they suffered.

The next chapter moves us out of the era of Reconstruction and into the early twentieth century with a Black feminist avant-garde video project that stages a public encounter at the 145th Street Bridge in Harlem, New York. The archival document at the heart of the project is an extant lynching photograph of a Black woman; the video project brings the practice of witnessing into the field as the artist gathers people together to mourn the loss of Laura Nelson more than a century after she was hung from a bridge in Okemah, Oklahoma.

2

RECKONING AT THE BRIDGE

SAVED and the Archive of Laura Nelson

Kara Lynch's video installation *SAVED :: video postcard* opens with scenes and sounds of people gathering on a grassy expanse on the bank of the Harlem River. Kids are laughing and playing, families are sitting together, and baskets of peaches and coolers of water are on hand for anyone who needs refreshments. The speed of the video slows as the camera pans up from the riverbank to catch lengths of white cloth tied to the fence along the 145th Street Bridge. Still images of people looking down from the bridge are interspersed with flashes of an abstracted sepia-toned photograph (see figure 2.1). The image, though digitally rendered by the artist to be quite distinct from the original, is the lynching photograph of Laura Nelson. What appears of the photograph in *SAVED :: video postcard* is a murky digital etching of the figure of a woman suspended in midair;

FIGURE 2.1   Kara Lynch, SAVED :: *video postcard*, 2013 (video still).

she seems to be floating (see figure 2.2). There is no rope or bridge in this image; those elements of the photograph have disappeared.

By slowly moving over cropped areas of the original photograph, the artist introduces the photographic evidence of the lynching of Laura Nelson.[1] Lynch never reproduces the two photographs of Laura Nelson's lynching in full, but draws our attention to segments: the trees, the river, the bridge, the lynch mob on the bridge looking down at her and her son, L.D., who was lynched with her. The artist discusses her interest in Laura Nelson's lynching photograph as follows:

> Laura Nelson is very specific. I am captivated by a photograph of her lynching taken by an itinerant photographer at a bridge at the edge of a town in Oklahoma in 1911. It is also a photograph of "a lynching" in that it includes a group of people on the bridge. They pose for the photograph and they have come to see an event. This photograph documents Laura and L.W.'s murder and it documents the N. Canadian River, the Old Schoolton Bridge, this group of people, and it documents this moment. It's also to my knowledge the only extant image of a woman lynched in the USA. This does not mean she was the only one, but because it's the last remaining photographic image, she stands in for all the others.[2]

FIGURE 2.2 Kara Lynch, SAVED :: *video postcard*, 2013 (video still).

Kara Lynch is an artist committed to the use of video in her practice; the feminist and interventionist uses of video to destabilize dominant power are inflected throughout her body of work. In the credits of the video, Lynch marks SAVED :: *video postcard* as a living memorial to Laura and L.D. Nelson. The title is compelling; this is a video postcard sent to enact, retroactively, the project of saving. Filmed in September 2013, this video is the third episode in Kara Lynch's long-form audio/video project INVISIBLE, which sets out to answer, through performative video art, "What if the transatlantic slave trade never happened?"[3] The video SAVED :: *video postcard* was the artist's method of mourning and honoring the centennial of Laura and L.D. Nelson's murders. As with the other audio/video work in INVISIBLE, SAVED :: *video postcard* is a collaborative project that uses visual and sonic landscapes to make indelible the connections, trajectories, and legacies of anti-Black violence and terror in the United States. From the outset, Lynch's video serves as an intervention into the archive of lynching photography and postcard circulation. Lynch's avant-garde art practice more broadly, with its commitment to video, serves as a counter to the dominant, mainstream, cinematic system of cultural production. With this video project, Kara Lynch is sending a postcard to Laura and L.D. with a message to these archival figures that they are not forgotten, that they deserve to be mourned, that they can make their way home. Lynch discusses her approach to figural representation in her work this way:

> In general I refuse traditions of the figure within my practice. This has to do with the overburden of representation that Black folks have, the hyper-representation that we experience, and that our image is overdetermined before we even put our own hands to it. In the world of art definitions my strategy is abstraction. In *INVISIBLE* this is explored through voice, embodiment, 2nd person address: YOU, duration, spatially locating time and temporally locating space i.e. installation/performance. This is my list so far, I leave the rest for curators and critics to develop.[4]

The artist brings us to the 145th Street Bridge, where people of all ages, races, and genders walk slowly and methodically across the bridge. Hums and claps and deep guttural bursts of breath ring out. The sounds of wailing and moaning grow and then transform into singing. This is a sorrow song that harmonizes and lilts. These people, dressed in white, are marching in quiet solemnity. This is a funeral procession. This movement of people wearing white calls up the 1917 NAACP Silent March in which women dressed in white silently processed down New York City's Fifth Avenue to protest the deadly mob attacks in East St. Louis, Illinois.[5] Back on the Harlem riverbank, the flow of people dressed in white reaches a small lawn beneath the 145th Street Bridge and merges with groups of participants donning bright colors. We hear snapping, singing, moaning. Voices lift in long tones that stretch and bend, not with words but with chords of grief. The scene expands, revealing more people milling, cyphers forming, and dancers moving anguish through their bodies. A choir director instructs his chorus.[6] Witnesses in procession stop and stare into the distance. People, grief stricken, enter and exit the scene. The screen cuts in half and then in quarters as blurred fragments of the lynching photograph appear and disappear. Sections of the lynching photograph come into view, revealing treetops and spectators peering down from a bridge toward the water below but never settling on the image of Laura's and L.D.'s lynched bodies.

Beneath the 145th Street Bridge, the chorus grows in sound; witnesses in white look down from the bridge to the mourners on the ground, who begin to move slowly, rhythmically back and forth, rocking, swaying, as if breathing through movement. Something is happening. Something is being stirred. A feeling or a presence is being touched. A group of young Black women swirls toward one another, moving, swaying, crying, holding up one another. They are mourning the loss of Laura and L.D. Still video images of women gathered beneath the bridge give way to moving images of young dancers who catalyze an aching sorrow with their choreography. Sorrowful harmonies crescendo, then silence. Then clapping and groans slowly fill the audioscape.

"It's like it never happened" appears on the screen above a frame of a procession of people crossing the bridge. Women are weeping and consoling one another. The phrase "and we feel it in our bones" appears in white text over a black background. Quiet. The moment has passed and people return, back to the present, to a familiar mode of being. They see each other and connect. They remain in the space together to contend with what just happened, what they witnessed, what they felt, what they stirred up together. A woman's voice is heard reflecting: "I didn't expect it to hit me like that. I don't know what I expected. Towards the end I was like oh my gosh, things just started running through my mind." Another woman adds: "I just felt that this was phenomenal. I've never experienced anything like this. It was almost as if we relived it. You could feel the energy and the elements. You felt that you were a part of it. You felt that you were there. You felt that you gave her closure. This is something that I have experienced that I will always remember." As this woman is seen remarking on her experience in one corner of the screen, a frame appears with a still image of the 145th Street Bridge with strips of white sheets tied to the fence blowing in the wind. We see a still image of the huge crowd of mourners, and then a cropped section of the lynching photograph that shows only the faces of onlookers, the murderers on the bridge looking down. Lynch layers images over one another, juxtaposes scenes, melds and distorts harmonies, breaths, and claps in a way that dynamically captures the temporal rupture and merging that just took place (see figures 2.3 to 2.10).

With this eight-minute-and-sixteen-second video, Kara Lynch sets the stage, invites the players, and produces a reckoning through a live public installation. Lynch uses performance and video to enter into this lynching archive and enact a Black feminist avant-garde intervention. Lynch is able to grapple with the heinous murder of Laura Nelson and her son through the visual register but without visually reproducing the details of the horrors that Laura and L.D. suffered. Her refusal to reproduce the totality of the photograph is a brilliant choice that uses this archive of violence without devolving into pornotropy. By focusing on the archive of Laura Nelson's and L.D. Nelson's lynchings, of which *SAVED :: video postcard* has become a part, the artist issues an archival intervention as she provides a release from the horror that snatched them from earth more than one hundred years ago at the bridge over the North Canadian River in Okemah, Oklahoma. I enter into an analysis of Lynch's work through a discussion of Laura Nelson's archive, the relationship between photography, cinema and spectrality, and Black feminist modes of knowing that defy western systems of

FIGURES 2.3–2.10 (*this page, opposite, and overleaf*) Kara Lynch, SAVED :: *video postcard*, 2013 (video stills).

knowledge production. My analysis offers a way to contend with the visceral reckoning that Lynch manages to not only produce in the field, at the 145th Street Bridge, but is able to capture with her video. Through her use of Black feminist avant-garde video production, Lynch is able to visualize and make audible a visitation with Laura and L.D. Nelson that has provided this mother and son with a measure of release. With this piece, Lynch taps into a frequency that exists in the place between here and there, between earth and the next place; this frequency enlivens the living memorial that is documented in SAVED :: video postcard. Through this video, Lynch enters into the space of Laura Nelson's archive, creates an opening for a visitation to unfold, and instigates a reckoning over visual terrain. She demonstrates the potency of the place where archival figures meet the Black feminist artists who are able to listen and produce something that can make absent archival presences palpable, while loosening the grip of archival violence that locks them into a horror for perpetuity.

Visitation: In the Space of the Erotic and the Sacred

In SAVED :: *video postcard*, it becomes clear that Lynch has awakened a visitation and that the past is here with us now. This live public installation, and the video that tracks it, cracks open the hold that is the archive of Laura Nelson. If the archive is a holding place, a mediation space between past and present, then the archival document, the lynching photograph, is the viscosity that binds archival figures in the hold. The photograph of Laura Nelson's and L.D. Nelson's lynchings submerges them in their archive, obscuring them, rendering them void. The undying image of death, that is, the lynching photograph, overdetermines any knowledge of Laura Nelson's life; this concretizes her in the space of her archive. The person, Laura Nelson, has become occluded by a set of archival documents that tether her to the void. Kara Lynch enters this space of negation with the live public installation that initiates a visitation, and Laura's presence becomes palpable through the performances staged on the 145th Street Bridge and on the banks of the Harlem River in 2013.

My notion of visitation, as it is made manifest by the spectral encounters documented in Lynch's SAVED :: *video postcard*, is buoyed by Audre Lorde's concept of the erotic. In her foundational article "Uses of the Erotic: The Erotic as Power," Lorde describes the erotic as "an assertion of the life force of women; of that creative energy empowered, the knowledge and use of which we are now reclaiming in our language, our history, our dancing, our loving, our work, our lives."[7] Lorde's concept of the erotic as an assertion of creative energy and knowledge that can be harnessed to reach back and claim a history that has been stripped away by dominant power is being visualized with Lynch's *SAVED :: video postcard*. Through the performances, the staging, and the refusals that circulate in the artist's treatment of the lynching photograph, this video is charged with the erotic power of Black feminist archival intervention, the haunting therein, and the epistemological impositions and hierarchies that dictate what serves as the official record. Later in the essay, Lorde describes the erotic as follows: "Our erotic knowledge empowers us, becomes a lens through which we scrutinize all aspects of our existence, forcing us to evaluate those aspects honestly in terms of their relative meaning within our lives. And this is a grave responsibility, projected from within each of us, not to settle for the convenient, the shoddy, the conventionally expected, nor the merely safe."[8]

Lorde's erotic offers a method of knowing that recognizes and values what is underestimated or overlooked in archival material that documents violence waged against Black women. The erotic not only names a power that exceeds dominant forms of knowledge production but also enacts that power by recognizing an interior resource as valuable and real; this in practice is an act of resistance that subverts and bypasses western modes of collecting, storing, valuing, and archiving history. This internal resource, the erotic, is being called upon by Kara Lynch as she enters the archive of Laura Nelson's lynching and sets the stage for a visitation. The erotic propels the visitation that occurs in *SAVED :: video postcard* through the artist's assembly, choreography, and documentation of performances, processions, and participants' impressions about their experiences that September afternoon at the 145th Street Bridge. A spectral encounter also occurs when *SAVED :: video postcard* is screened. As with the film discussed in chapter 1, Kara Walker's *Six Miles from Springfield on the Franklin Road*, Kara Lynch's *SAVED :: video postcard* interrupts and displaces a pleasure in watching Black women suffer. The visual and sonic language deployed in *SAVED :: video postcard* reminds us, insists really, that we are witnesses and not passive viewers.

If Lorde's concept of the erotic comes in contact with M. Jacqui Alexander's Black feminist critique of temporality in *Pedagogies of Crossing: Meditations on Feminism, Sexual Politics, Memory, and the Sacred*, an expansion of Lorde's concept of the erotic unfolds. Through her analysis of pedagogies of crossing and the sacred, Alexander interrogates dominant formulations of time, contending that in the realm of the sacred, "dominant corporate, linear time becomes existentially irrelevant. Indeed it ceases to have any currency at all."[9] Alexander encourages us to see that pedagogies of crossing disrupt time and "fit neither easily nor neatly into those domains that have been imprisoned within modernity's secularized episteme. Thus, they disturb and reassemble the inherited divides of Sacred and secular, the embodied and disembodied, for instance, pushing us to take seriously the dimensions of spiritual labor that make the sacred and the disembodied palpably tangible and, therefore, constitutive of the lived experience of millions of women and men in different parts of the world."[10]

Alexander's insistence that spiritual labor be taken seriously helps make sense of the way that Lynch's video attunes audiences to the spectral encounters that take place therein. Alexander's attention to the disembodied offers a guide to understanding the ethereal work that SAVED :: *video postcard* is doing to help Laura and L.D. achieve some release from the image of their deaths. By bringing Lorde's conception of the erotic together with Alexander's theory of the sacred, I am following their Black feminist methodological invitation to trust those forms of knowledge that cannot be seen, only felt. Their scholarly guidance offers the kind of confidence needed to move dominant knowledge aside and trust another way of being and knowing, despite its subjugated position in western epistemology.

The erotic and the sacred are portals that tunnel through dominant time and agitate archival space as they enable spectral connections that defy the constraints of each. As I gestured toward in the introduction, I am drawn to Alexander's attention to the disembodied in her concept of the sacred, and I am especially excited by the way it resonates with Avery Gordon's theory of haunting. Read together, Alexander's and Gordon's theories offer a method for considering how spectrality twists time in such a way that those who have lived are able to meet those who are living.[11] For Gordon, a haunting is distinct from trauma in that a haunting insists that there is "something-to-be-done" about violences as yet unresolved.[12] Alexander's sacred takes specters seriously, as does Gordon's haunting; they both recognize that the violence that keeps specters tethered to the earthly plane is unresolved. We, those of us who are embodied, who also take specters seriously and are committed to grappling with unresolved violences, are charged with finding the instance, the temporal eruption that ripped a hole in time, flung details to and fro, and landed specters in their archival abyss. This sense, or non-sense, or dissonance of temporality can be witnessed in Lynch's video, which positions viewers as witnesses rather than spectators and gives witnesses a chance to participate in a resolution.

Lynch activates erotic knowledge and the sacred as she connects with Laura Nelson through her engagement with the lynching photograph and through the production of SAVED :: *video postcard*. The artist carves pathways into the space of the archive where Laura's legacy has been relegated. In that space of the archive, documented acts of violence might be hypervisible, or perhaps deceptively obscured; in the case of Laura Nelson, the lynching photograph overdetermines her archival presence; she is overly visible in the archive in a way that obscures her humanity. Lynch's video offers affective information and channels sensation through the realm of the visual to present work that reveals a visitation with Laura as it occurs, while concomitantly usurping the visual overdetermination—the violence of the lynching photograph itself. The living memorial that Lynch mounts makes visible a communal foray into the void where the ghosts of Laura and L.D. Nelson emerge from the archive, where mourners consort and listen and produce something out of that encounter. With SAVED :: video postcard, Lynch shares with us the something that she did to respond to the unresolved violence that Laura and L.D. suffered at the bridge in Okemah. The something-to-be-done that Lynch has achieved with this gathering of witnesses, mourners, dancers, singers, and cameras contributes to a reckoning that sees Laura and L.D., grieves with them and for them, and tries to help them out of the archival abyss. Those who participated in the gathering at the 145th Street Bridge and those who witness a visitation as it unfolds in this video participate in that something-to-be-done.[13]

The Archive of Laura Nelson's Lynching

The archive of Laura Nelson's lynching is composed of newspaper articles, from both the colored and white press, about the crime Laura and L.D. were accused of committing, details about the horrific lynching, and the two photographs of Laura and her son hanging from the bridge—the only known photographs of a Black woman's lynching.[14] The narrative that courses through this archive is driven by the dominant white press. According to the *Okemah Ledger* and *The Independent*, sometime during the dark hours of the morning on Wednesday, May 24, 1911, Laura Nelson and her teenage son, L.D., were bound and gagged, then dragged out of the jail cells in which they were being detained in Okemah, Oklahoma. The lynch mob had quietly and quickly overpowered the sleeping jailor in order to gain access to Laura, who was being kept in a cage in the courthouse, and L.D., who was being detained in the county jail.[15] The lynch mob kidnapped this mother and son and drove them to a bridge over the North Canadian River.[16] They tied nooses around Laura's and L.D.'s necks, then threw them over the bridge, where they were hung. Their lifeless bodies languished there, suspended above the water all night and into the next day. The *Okemah Ledger* described the scene in great detail.

> The two negroes were taken west of town six miles to the Canadian river bridge in a negro settlement and were swung from the bridge. Both the woman and boy were gagged with tow sacks. The rope was half inch

hemp, and the loops were made in the regular hangman's knot. The woman's arms were swinging at her side, untied, while about twenty feet away swung the boy with his clothes partly torn off and his hands tied with a saddle string. The only marks on either body were that made by the ropes upon the necks. Gently swaying in the wind the ghastly spectacle was discovered this morning by a negro boy taking his cow to water. Hundreds of people from Okemah and the western part of the county went to view the scene. The bodies were cut down about 11:00 by order of the county commissioner and hauled to Okemah for coffins.[17]

This heinous act of mob violence was exacted as retribution for the death of Deputy Sheriff George H. Loney. According to *The Independent*, on Tuesday, May 2, Deputy Loney and his posse made of three men—Claude Littrell, Cliff Martin, and Oscar Lane—went with a search warrant to the Nelsons' home looking for evidence of Claude Littrell's stolen steer, the crime that Laura's husband and L.D.'s father, Austin Nelson, was accused of committing.[18] During the search of the Nelsons' home, the posse discovered some beef in the house as well as a shotgun hanging on the wall. Sheriff Loney had a member of the posse remove the shotgun from the wall. The article purports that Laura took exception to this and pulled out a Winchester rifle that she had stashed behind a trunk. Just then, L.W., as he is misnamed in the 1911 account, grabbed the gun from his mother's hand and it discharged during the tussle.[19] The bullet apparently went through the pant leg of Martin but did not injure him, striking Deputy Loney in the hip, then traveling up toward his abdomen; Loney made it out of the Nelsons' house and died in front of their home shortly thereafter.[20] After being taken into custody, Austin Nelson admitted to stealing the steer in order to feed his family; he was sentenced to three years in McAlester State Penitentiary for the crime of larceny of domestic animals.[21] Laura Nelson took responsibility for the shooting to protect her son and subsequently Laura and L.D. were both arrested.[22] L.D. admitted to shooting the deputy because he was afraid that Loney was going to kill his father.[23] The *Okemah Ledger*'s headline for this story is: "Deputy Sheriff Loney Murdered," and the lede clarifies "While Attempting to Search a Negro Cabin Near Paden for Stolen Meat. He was Shot Through Leg and Bled to Death. Say Negro Boy Fired Shot." Laura and L.D. were both held in the county jail without bail while they awaited their trial, which would never take place.[24]

The *Okemah Ledger* declared that the death of Deputy Loney was "one of the most cold blooded murders that has occurred in Okfuskee County."[25] The *Ledger*'s report of the events that preceded the Loney shooting is similar to *The*

Independent's, though the *Ledger* excludes the detail about the meat. The *Ledger* reported that the deputy sustained a fatal leg injury in which "both arteries in Loney's leg had been severed and the bone shattered." The article goes on to contend that a shoot-out ensued after Deputy Loney went down. In this version of events, Austin Nelson allegedly grabbed the Winchester from his son after he shot Deputy Loney, then headed outside scattering bullets after the posse. None of the other men in the posse was injured.[26]

With all the attention to detail included in the news reports of the shooting of Deputy Loney and the lynching of Laura and L.D. Nelson by the white press, that news coverage leaves out significant and damning details. Local news reports of the shooting, arrest, and lynching of Laura and L.D. do not mention that Laura had her two-year-old daughter with her, and they leave out the fact that Laura was raped before she and her son were hanged. The July 1911 issue of W. E. B. Du Bois's *The Crisis: A Record of the Darker Races* consolidates reports from the colored press, and incendiary facts emerge about the circumstances surrounding Laura's and L.D.'s lynchings.[27] *The Crisis* reveals that the Nelsons' murders would not be investigated and writes into the archive the fact that Laura was raped before she was hanged. The article shares that some news reports claim that the lynch mob was composed of Negroes and not white people at all, an assertion that can be easily disproven by looking at the photographic evidence of the lynching. Census records for 1910 show that Laura had a daughter, named Carrie, who was twelve months old at that time and a son, L.D., who was eleven years old.[28] In its report of this lynching, *The Crisis* demands that the record reflect the chilling fact that Laura Nelson had her baby daughter with her when she was held in jail, when she was raped, and when she was lynched; the colored press refuses to let these heartbreaking details be erased from the record, while the white press suppresses this incriminating information. *The Crisis* reports:

> A woman taken from her suckling babe, and a boy—a child of only fourteen years old—dragged through the streets by a howling mob of fiendish devils, the most unnameable crime committed on the helpless woman and then she and her son executed by hanging. This happened in a Christian community and where the machinery of the law was all in the hands of white men, there being no chance for escape. If the prisoners were guilty then why mob them, except to satisfy an irresistible greed and appetite for rapine and blood? The Okfuskee mob composed of white men committed the most damning and hellish crime known in the annals of crime, not excepting the burning at the stake of a number of Indians

some years ago near this same place and placed a blot on the fair name of Oklahoma that even time cannot erase.[29]

This article writes into the record, using the parlance of modesty appropriate for the time, that Laura was raped by the mob of white men while held in prison—this is "the most unnameable crime." The fact that Laura had her daughter with her, the "suckling babe," who was about two years old, was stricken from the record by the white press. It is even possible that this horrifying detail of the incidents surrounding Laura's and L.D.'s lynchings could be overlooked because of the gentility with which it is mentioned in *The Crisis* article. With this knowledge of the archive rising to the surface now, some questions arise with it: What happened to baby Carrie? Was she a witness to her mother's and brother's lynchings? These may be unanswerable questions, but the archival clues left in newsprint and census reports indicate that the entire story is not being told.

Newspaper reports of lynchings were often simply outlets for white supremacist ideology and thuggery, as the archive of Laura Nelson's lynching demonstrates. The *Okemah Ledger* describes the imprisoned Laura as being "bad" when reporting that she attempted to steal the jailor's gun when he brought a plate of food to her cell.[30] According to his report, when Laura was unable to retrieve the jailor's gun, she then tried to escape through the window but was subdued by the jailor, Lawrence Payne.[31] Given that the colored press reported that Laura Nelson had been raped, perhaps her attempt to wrestle the gun from Payne and escape through the window had more to do with trying to protect herself from being raped than being "bad." In its report of Laura's and L.D.'s lynchings, the *Okemah Ledger* reminds its readers about the shooting of Deputy Loney, the crime for which Laura and L.D. were originally arrested, an inclusion that means to justify the lynch mob's vigilantism.

> The crime for which the negro woman and boy were lynched was the murder of Deputy Sheriff Geo. Loney at their cabin about seven miles northeast of Paden some two weeks ago, while Loney and a posse were searching for stolen meat. The woman grabbed a Winchester and handed it to her son who shot Loney through the right leg. The boy's father held the posse off with the gun while Loney lay out of the door and bled to death. While Loney was dying he asked for water and was cursed by the woman. The elder Nelson plead guilty to cattle stealing last week and was taken to the pen, which probably saved his life.
>
> The woman was very small of stature, very Black, about thirty-five years old, and vicious. A few days ago she attempted to disarm Jailor

Payne and make her escape. She had to be choked into her cell and then begged to be killed.

The boy was about fourteen years old, slender and tall, yellow and ignorant. The lynching came as a complete surprise to the sheriff's forces and the people. After the prisoners had been brought out of the country where the crime was committed no further trouble was anticipated and while the general sentiment is adverse to the method, it is generally thought that the negroes got what would have been due them under due process of law.[32]

The description of Laura as vicious in this article, combined with the imagery of her cursing the deputy as he bled to death, attempts to paint Laura as a woman who does not deserve the readers' sympathy. In *Southern Horrors: Women and the Politics of Rape and Lynching*, Crystal Feimster discusses the common tactic of white newspapers reporting lynchings by couching the lynch mob's actions between descriptions of the crime for which the victim was accused. They often describe the victims of lynchings as vicious, dangerous, or monstrous. This was especially necessary in the case of women who were lynched; public opinion had to be swayed in favor of justifying this course of action. Given that the lynching of Black men was justified by accusing them of rape, there was no crime that would "justify" the lynching of a woman in many people's minds. Feimster recounts: "Between 1880 and 1930 lynch mobs murdered at least 130 Black women. Many more were tortured, mutilated, tarred and feathered, shot, burned, stabbed, dragged, whipped, or raped by angry mobs all over the south. The lynching of Black women exposes the multiple meanings behind mob violence as well as the ways in which individual women challenged or threatened the emergence of a new southern caste system. Most white southern newspapers that reported the lynchings of Black women made every effort to demonize Black womanhood and to justify the mob's brutality."[33]

Feimster describes in detail the circumstances of some of the 130 Black women who were lynched between 1880 and 1930.[34] These women were accused of murdering or assaulting a white person or destroying their property. For example, on August 18, 1886, Eliza Woods was taken from the jailhouse in Jackson, Tennessee, and hung by a mob that was reported to be as large as one thousand people. Accused of murdering the Christian woman she worked for, Mrs. J. P. Wooten, by poisoning her food, Eliza Woods was taken out of the jail cell, stripped of her clothing, hung from a tree in the yard of the courthouse, then shot five times after her death.[35] The Negro community in Jackson was outraged by Eliza's lynching and threatened to burn the town down.[36] This case garnered national attention. In the white press, Eliza Woods was described as a "Black female devil," which is akin to descriptors like "fiend" and "beast" that were used in reporting the lynchings of Black men.[37] Although no photographs of Eliza Woods have been recovered, newsprint registers her murder in the archive of black women who were lynched.

As exemplified in her pamphlet *Southern Horrors*, Ida B. Wells vehemently protested the mob violence and lynching of Black men that was considered fit punishment for being accused of raping a white woman.[38] In 1892 Wells publicly registered her outrage about a rash of lynchings in the South during the spring of that year: "Nobody in this section of the country believes the old threadbare lie that Negro men rape white women. If southern white men are not careful they will overreach themselves and public sentiment will have a reaction; a conclusion will then be reached which will be very damaging to the moral reputations of their women."[39]

Wells's indictment of white men and white women elicited the hatred of white ruffians in concert with the well-to-do gentry who denounced "the Black scoundrel" who would "utter such loathsome and repulsive calumnies."[40] The *Evening Scimitar* printed one of the threats to Wells's life: "If the negroes themselves do not apply the remedy without delay it will be the duty of those whom he has attacked to tie the wretch who utters these calumnies to a stake at the intersection of Main and Madison Sts., brand him in the forehead with a hot iron and perform upon him a surgical operation with a pair of tailor's shears."[41] Here, Wells is mistaken for a man, a mistake that may have protected her from being tied to a stake at the intersection of Main and Madison Streets. Her womanhood would not have prevented her from the noose, though I am certain that after being thwarted out of the satisfaction of performing the surgical procedure with tailor's shears, the lynch mob would have enacted an equally vicious scene of sexual violence.

Though her anti-lynching advocacy predominantly addressed the lynching of Black men, she included the lynchings of two unknown women and Mrs. Teddy Arthur in 1894 in her pamphlet *A Red Record*.[42] Wells boldly pointed out the contradiction that Black men were being lynched after being accused of rape, accusations that were most often unfounded, while white men have been raping Black women for generations with impunity.

> The editor of the *Free Speech* has no disclaimer to enter, but asserts instead that there are many white women in the South who would marry colored men if such an act would not place them at once beyond the pale of society and within the clutches of the law. The miscegnation [sic] laws of the

South only operate against the legitimate union of the races; they leave the white man free to seduce all the colored girls he can, but it is death to the colored man who yields to the force and advances of a similar attraction in white women. White men lynch the offending Afro-American, not because he is a despoiler of virtue, but because he succumbs to the smiles of white women.[43]

Laura Nelson's rape and lynching reveal the paradox, the fundamental contradiction, that white men are the perpetrators of rape and Black women are the victims, not the reverse. Wells was pointing out that accusations of rape were covers for the use of lynching as a method for white supremacists to exact their power and retain their wealth and sense of superiority. The public spectacle of lynching was meant to terrify Black citizens who were no longer enslaveable into relinquishing their rights and remaining subservient even in freedom. In *Why Is the Negro Lynched?*, published in 1895, Frederick Douglass writes of the epidemic of mob law.

Not a breeze comes to us from the late rebellious states that is not tainted and freighted with Negro blood. In its thirst for blood and its rage for vengeance, the mob has blindly, boldly and defiantly supplanted sheriffs, constables and police. It has assumed all the functions of civil authority. It laughs at legal processes, courts and juries, and its red-handed murderers range abroad unchecked and unchallenged by law or by public opinion. If the mob is in pursuit of Negroes who happen to be accused of crime, innocent or guilty, prison walls and iron bars afford no protection. Jail doors are battered down in the presence of unresisting jailors, and the accused, awaiting trial in the courts of law, are dragged out and hanged, shot, stabbed or burned to death, as the blind and irresponsible mob may elect.[44]

There was no end in sight to the mob attacks on Black men that were rampant during this post–Civil War, post-Reconstruction era.[45] The thirst for blood and vengeance that seethed through white supremacist mobs was ginned up by their loss of slave labor, even though many white southerners would not have even been able to afford owning human beings. The threat of Black equality, the denial of perpetual access to Black women's bodies, and the fear of losing power over white women to Black men comprised the charge that ignited the epidemic of mob law of which Douglass writes. Photography, and later the moving image, would play a stultifying role in threatening rights-bearing Black people with violence by circulating the hideous visual evidence of the lengths to which white supremacists would go to regain and maintain domination.

As Jacqueline Goldsby argues in *A Spectacular Secret: Lynching in American Life and Literature*, lynching was a function of modernity in America, not an aberration. Goldsby's analysis of lynching photography at the turn of the twentieth century considers how the visual components of lynching photographs—the lynch mob and onlookers, the brutalized Black body, the rope, the tree branch or bridge—all "link the deadly exercise of white supremacy to the formations of modernity's dystopia."[46] Goldsby situates lynching photography as another modern luxury of looking for the sake of looking amid modern attractions such as world's fairs, amusement parks, and skyscrapers. Another striking mark of modernity that Goldsby traces is the political impact that lynching photography imparted on freedmen. Grotesque displays of lynched Black bodies communicated the unmitigated power held by white mob rule and the inability of Black citizens to protect themselves, let alone enjoy the rights of citizenship granted by the Fourteenth Amendment to the US Constitution.

The movement to end lynching in the United States becomes apparent in the archive through news reports, pamphlets, speeches, and the photographs themselves. Leigh Raiford's *Imprisoned in a Luminous Glare: Photography and the African American Freedom Struggle* focuses on the manner in which Black liberation activists in the anti-lynching, civil rights, and Black Power movements used lynching photographs to expose the atrocities that were taking place across the jim crow South and the rest of the country.[47] These movements did not shy away from using the horror of lynching photographs to make visible the terror of anti-Black racist vigilante groups. Through analyses of visual art, Raiford contends that "the archive of lynching photography constitutes a site of struggle over the interpretation of the history of racial violence and Black citizenship in the United States."[48] To illustrate her point, Raiford discusses a collage by Emory Douglas titled *Freedom Is a Constant Struggle* that uses a photograph of the lynching of Thomas Shipp and Abram Smith, in which a large group of white men and women is entertained by the sight of the hanging men. Douglas incorporates an antebellum slave advertisement for the sale of two people, photographs of an elderly Black man, and two young Black boys not more than three years old to point to the ways that jim crow–era lynching photography recuperates the absolute domination and white supremacy of slavery for the enjoyment of the former slaveholding class, by drawing parallels between the lynching rope and hanging tree, the auction block and future generations of Black men. This collage conjures up the specter of chattel slavery on which lynching photographs produce a palimpsest. As the lynching photography that was used to terrorize Black people was repurposed by anti-lynching advocates to beat back vigilante violence, moving images of lynching scenes were used to expose the terror of white mob violence after the abolition of slavery. The burgeoning medium of motion pictures was a stage on which the struggle over the meaning of blackness and the rights of Black people took place. While D. W. Griffith's highly acclaimed *Birth of a Nation* (1915) used motion picture technology to demonize Black people during this era, Oscar Micheaux's *Within Our Gates* (1920) fought back.

Within Our Gates *as Cinematic Archive*

Oscar Micheaux's *Within Our Gates* (1920) is a narrative feature film that represents an era in US history in which lynching was routine. Micheaux, who is often hailed as the first Black independent filmmaker, was "the most successful and radical Black filmmaker of the silent-movie era."[49] Micheaux's first feature-length film, *Homesteader* (1919), was in fact the first feature film produced by a Black production company.[50] Micheaux's second feature-length film, *Within Our Gates*, has been discussed as a film that directly responds to the racist characterizations of blackness as predatory, bestial, lazy, and incompetent that abound in *Birth of a Nation*, D. W. Griffith's cinematic adaptation of Thomas Dixon's novel *The Clansman*.[51] *Birth of a Nation* is remembered as a spectacular feat of creative genius; reportedly President Woodrow Wilson remarked after screening the film at the White House, "It's like writing history with lightning. My only regret is that it is all so true."[52] *Birth of a Nation* is still celebrated by cinema scholars as having made a landmark cinematic achievement and is recognized by cinephiles as the first blockbuster film, but at the time of its release, anti-lynching activist Ida B. Wells took issue with showing this film in Chicago. In her memoir, *Crusade for Justice*, Wells wrote about her fury and the fight to remove *Birth of a Nation* from theaters. She described the process of struggling to issue an injunction to stop screening the film because of its portrayal of Black people.[53] There was a hearing about removing the film from theaters, which Wells attended each day, but the plaintiffs did not represent the case well and the injunction was subsequently lifted. Even in its nascency, Wells recognized the power of cinematic representation and wanted to deny Griffith the ability to show this film in Chicago. Philadelphia successfully boycotted *Birth of a Nation*, but the film screened across the rest of the country. Griffith's film prevailed and has since been lauded in white supremacist historical memory as a masterpiece. Micheaux, however, issued a contemporaneous cinematic rebuttal with *Within Our Gates*.

Micheaux's use of the cinematic form to expose the unmitigated terror of lynch mobs by visualizing the lynching of a family in *Within Our Gates* underscores Raiford's analysis of Black liberation movements' use of lynching photography to combat the violence of lynching.[54] *Within Our Gates* represents lynch mob violence and the violence of miscegenation suffered by Black women. Micheaux's film cinematically binds the jim crow violence of rape and lynching, by juxtaposing scenes of a "mulatta" character being sexually assaulted by a white man with the lynching and burning at the stake of a Black mother and father. Micheaux's visualization of the lynching of a Black woman in the scene of white vigilantism that serves as the climax of the film registers in the cinematic archive the reality that Black women were victims of lynch mob violence. As Cedric Robinson contends in *Forgeries of Memory and Meaning*, Micheaux was committed to rebutting characterizations of Black depravity with his films. Robinson offers a quote by Micheaux about the representation of truth in his work: "I have always tried to make my photoplays represent the truth, to lay before the race a cross section of its own life, to view the colored heart from close range. My result might have been narrow at times, due perhaps to certain limited situations which I endeavored to portray, but in those limited situations, the truth was the predominant characteristic."[55]

For contributing cinematic representations of egregious white supremacist violence alongside Black depravity at a time when images of Black buffoonery and blackface minstrelsy dominated popular culture, *Birth of a Nation* is the urtext. With *Within Our Gates*, Micheaux was inserting knowledge, albeit the truth, about white violence against Black people that was not being reported in the national newspapers or depicted cinematically.[56] In the context of the outrageously racist representation of blackness circulating in popular culture in the first decades of the twentieth century through lynching photographs, and films like *Birth of a Nation* and Thomas Edison's short comedies in which "Black" characters (white actors in blackface) were the butt of violent and humiliating jokes, Micheaux used the narrative cinematic medium to resist white supremacist justifications of Black murder, degradation, and buffoonery as well as illuminate the reality that white men, not Black men, were the chief perpetrators of rape.[57]

The scene of lynching in Micheaux's *Within Our Gates* appears in the flashback sequence that comes in the last ten minutes of the film. We learn that the protagonist, Sylvia, was raised by foster parents: a loving Black couple, Mr. and Mrs. Landry, who worked as sharecroppers. Sylvia was afforded an education, which she used to help her foster parents with accounting. One day, when looking over her parents' finances, Sylvia discovers that they had been cheated out of their income by the landowner, Mr. Gridlestone. Mr. Landry confronts Mr. Gridlestone, who threatens, hits, and kicks him out of the office. Mr. Landry

FIGURE 2.11 Oscar Micheaux, *Within Our Gates*, 1920 (film still).

complies but before he can leave the room, Mr. Gridlestone is shot and killed by a white man, another sharecropper, through the window. Somehow Mr. Landry ends up holding the gun that Mr. Gridlestone pulled on him and it looks like Mr. Landry shot Mr. Gridlestone. The Uncle Tom character, Efrem, observes this and promptly informs the townsmen that Mr. Landry killed Mr. Gridlestone. Despite his loyalty to the white supremacist landowners, Efrem is lynched by the white mob that then goes after Mr. Landry, his wife, and their young son. Sylvia is not at home when the lynch mob arrives. The lynch mob drags the family out to a field, beats them, and then ties a noose around each of their necks. The young son slips away, the mob shoots at him, but he escapes using one of the lynchers' horses. Mr. Landry and his wife are hung from a tree. This scene is one of the more abstract scenes in the film, in that Micheaux shows a wide shot of the lynch mob holding the couple with nooses around their necks, followed by a close-up of the ropes being hung over a tree branch. Then two groups of white men are seen pulling the ropes, hoisting the bodies, from opposite sides of the tree (see figure 2.11). Micheaux does not ever show Mr. and Mrs. Landry's bodies hanged. Night falls and the mob lights a bonfire in which they burn both bodies.

In the meantime, Sylvia is tracked and cornered in a home by Mr. Gridlestone's brother Armand. This scene, as Robinson notes in *Forgeries of Memory and Meaning*, mimics the rape scene in Griffith's *Birth of a Nation* in which the character Gus, a white man in blackface, attempts to rape the white maiden Flora, who jumps from a cliff to her death. Micheaux's depiction of Sylvia fighting off the rapist, Armand Gridlestone, is a cinematic technique that refutes the characterization of Black men as rapists and exposes the history of miscegenation violence in which white men, not Black men, are the systemic perpetrators of rape. Robinson contends that *Within Our Gates* has the trappings of a melodrama, the style of literary and cinematic narrative popular at the time, but this film is actually a social drama that works to expose the deep white supremacist violence that was rampant in the South.[58] As a social drama, I argue, this reversal, in which the white man is the predator and the "colored" girl is the victim of rape, records, in the cinematic archive, the long-overlooked history of white men raping Black women.[59] In a quite prolonged rape scene, Armand Gridlestone attacks Sylvia (see figure 2.12). She fights him off but he is intent on raping her. Armand rips Sylvia's blouse and discovers a scar on her chest. From this scar, Armand knows that this woman is his daughter. Micheaux communicates this discovery through the use of an intertitle (see figure 2.13).

The inclusion of Sylvia being Gridlestone's "legitimate daughter" through this intertitle seems incongruous. The melodramatic paternal plot twist seems highly unlikely, as it suggests that the kind of man who would violently rape a woman because she is Black and presumably rape-able would risk his social standing by marrying her Black mother. In *Migrating to the Movies: Cinema and Black Urban Modernity*, Jacqueline Najuma Stewart raises questions about whether this intertitle was in Micheaux's original film or if it was added later. The film print that is currently available to view was recovered in Spain, and Stewart suggests that this intertitle was added for Spanish audiences. Stewart contends that given that the publicity and press about the film mentions "concubinage," it is more likely that the narrative is conveying that Sylvia's mother was raped by Armand Gridlestone and not married legitimately.[60] Taking into consideration the history of white men raping Black women during chattel slavery and in its afterlife, and the anti-miscegenation laws that made a marriage between Gridlestone and Sylvia's mother illegal, the expository claim of legitimate birth is preposterous. As a social film that focuses on white supremacist violence against Black women, *Within Our Gates* becomes a cinematic archival document that records a rebuttal to Griffith's film, represents the sinister white mob's ruthlessness, and reveals the deep historic contradiction wherein the justification for lynching is based on the mere accusation that a Black man

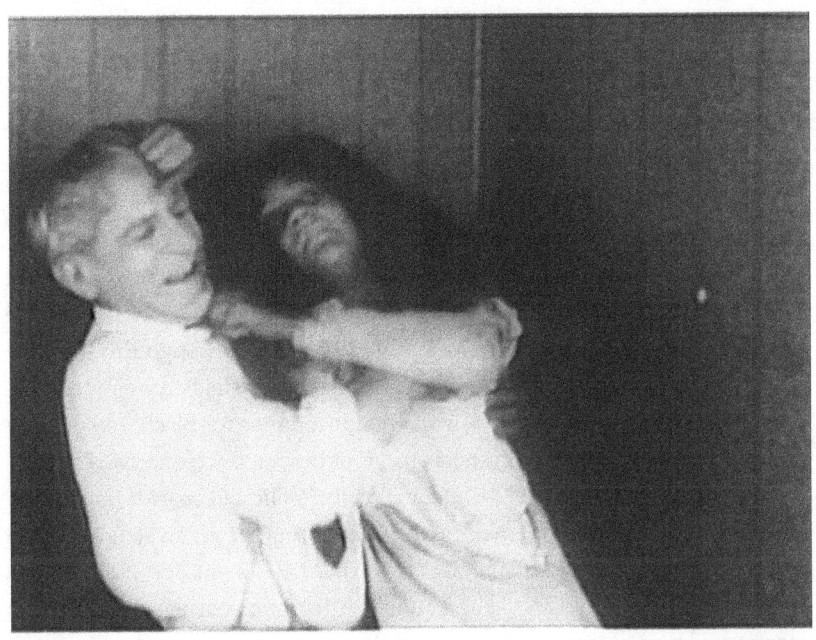

FIGURES 2.12 AND 2.13 Oscar Micheaux, *Within Our Gates*, 1920 (film stills).

raped a white woman. Even though Black men were the most highly targeted lynch mob victims, Black women were lynched, and Micheaux represents that fact with this film that produces a visual correction to the record.

Oscar Micheaux's *Within Our Gates* documents the jim crow-era violence faced by Black women with these two scenes that depict the reality of the sexual violence that Black women suffered at the hands of white men and the hideousness of lynch mob terror. With this film, Micheaux intervenes in the cinematic dissemination of Black depravity issued by filmmakers like Griffith and Edison. Micheaux contributes a critique of lynching and rape to the archive of violence that is lynching photography, and registers, through this film, the fact that Black women were victims of lynching. As Crystal Feimster made evident in her book *Southern Horrors*, it was not uncommon for Black women to be lynched for crimes that their fathers or sons or husbands were accused of committing, crimes in which they were not actually implicated apart from their relationship with the Black men accused.[61] If we bring the archival figure Laura Nelson back into this discussion, it is clear that Laura's murder in 1911 haunts Micheaux's lynching scene of the Landrys. Micheaux's narrative feature film represented twin horrors that permeated the lives of Black women, white lynch mobs and white rapists, from whom there was no protection. Laura Nelson's lynching is made evident in the archive of violence that records this crime, but the rape she suffered while held in a jail cell was buried in the archive.

The crisis of white supremacy that materialized as violence inflicted on Black women's bodies after emancipation is a reflection of the loss of capital that enslavers sustained when they were no longer able to increase their wealth by raping Black women and enslaving their children.[62] The systemic rape of Black women by white men during chattel slavery persists in its afterlife; this is the specter of miscegenation that is made apparent by studying the lynching of Laura Nelson. No longer enslaved, no longer increasing white wealth through reproductive violence, yet still able to be raped without recourse, Black women were bearing the burden of the loss of white access to their bodies and their reproductive lives. The lynching photographs of Laura and L.D. are visible evidence of the specter of miscegenation. Someone in that photograph, a man or men on that bridge, raped Laura. The fact that L.D. is described as being "yellow" in the news reports of his murder raises the specter of rape and miscegenation as well. L.D.'s "yellowness" could be an index of a previous rape that Laura survived or another reproductive reminder of the systemic rape of Black women during slavery that would give Laura a "yellow" son; either L.D.'s father was a white perpetrator who raped his mother or the lineage of systemic rape is made evident through L.D.'s "yellowness." The specter of miscegenation is buried in these archival documents that record the violence that Laura Nelson suffered. The lynching photographs carry the unknown and the unknowable chasm rendered in grayscale; the specter of miscegenation and the unresolved violence of rape are absent presences within this photograph. The archive holds figures like Laura Nelson in between life and death, where they cannot rest because of the torturous nature of the last moments of their lives. From this place, they make themselves known in the present because the injustice to which they had succumbed remains unresolved. Kara Lynch enters into that place, into the void suspended through the archive, and brings with her those who participated in and those who witness her work of Black feminist avant-garde cinema, SAVED :: video postcard.

Laura Nelson's archive is an archive of violence that inflicts and reinflicts the terror that Laura and L.D. suffered. The lynching photograph overdetermines any engagement with the memory of Laura and L.D. Nelson; in fact, they become legible in the archive because of their violent murders. The social violence, the fact of lynching, and the fact of these particular lynchings proliferate in digital space. An internet search of Laura Nelson's name calls up the image of her lynched body. The circulation of this lynching photograph is a dissemination of archival violence; her gruesome murder is likely the only thing most people will ever know about her. Questions remain: What other information about the circumstances of this lynching has been twisted or erased from newspaper reports? What happened to baby Carrie? The photograph shows that L.D.'s clothes are ripped to shreds. What happened to him? The fact that they were so hungry that Austin Nelson had to steal a steer so that his family would not starve is a violence that is submerged in this archive. The answers to these questions may reside in the realm of specters, but Kara Lynch recognizes with SAVED :: video postcard that rather than pore over the photograph for more information, an alternate vantage point is necessary, one in which another way of knowing can be accessed.

Lynching Photography and Death-Defying Moving Images

When considering the spectral qualities of Kara Lynch's visual treatment of Laura Nelson's lynching photograph in SAVED :: *video postcard*, I am drawn to examining the haunted, technological roots of photography and cinema. The practice of photographing lynched, burned, shot, mutilated bodies had been occurring since the abolition of slavery; the daguerreotype was invented in 1839 and the first Kodak camera was introduced in 1888. As Goldsby and Raiford confirm in their volumes, the relationship between the development of the photograph and lynching is no mere coincidence; they are tied together in the project of modernity and white supremacy that each depend on the abjection of Black life and subjugation of Black people.[63] At the time of Laura and L.D.'s capture, lynching photographs were held as keepsakes by white southerners to memorialize the Black suffering that served as white supremacist retribution for an alleged crime, but more appositely, the image of a lynched Black body, most often a Black man's body, was used as evidence of the punishment waged on the unenslavable rights-bearing Black people who threatened white supremacy. Photographs of lynchings were circulated to reinforce the degradation and dehumanization of Black people who had won the franchise and were in the position to capitalize on their freedom.[64] Apparently an attempt to circulate Laura Nelson's lynching photograph was made through the US mail, as the word *unmailable* was etched onto the image that exists in the archive.[65] Among white supremacists, and even in the tone of putative objectivity used in news reports of lynchings, these heinous murders were characterized as necessary acts that protected white womanhood and the southern way of life. Those who carried out lynchings were often pictured in the foreground of these photographs, numbering from a handful to hundreds of people gathered to conspire in the hanging. As Goldsby points out in *A Spectacular Secret*, that the photographed crowds generally appear well composed and calm, in contrast to the brutalized, mutilated, lifeless body hanging from a tree or a bridge or a pole, confoundingly produces a mirage of white civility in a scene of white supremacist barbarity.[66] When a lynching photograph is read as a scene of white barbarity rather than Black abjection, the photographic evidence of these ghastly public spectacles undermines rather than reinforces the logic of white composure, modern sophistication, and superiority.

The white supremacist terror that was spread through the circulation of lynching photographs haunts the medium of photography. The white supremacist glee depicted in scenes of Black suffering makes the terrifying wraiths in these lynching photographs not the victims themselves but the perpetrators of these murders who so proudly posed for their picture. There are specters and then there are ghouls; my focus is on the former, the victims who are trapped in the image, and not the ghouls who bound them there. My attention to the real-world horror of lynching and the haunted quality of photography and cinema is not meant to make a metaphor out of suffering but rather to contend with the ability that photography, cinema, and video have to reach specters through the visual and set about upon a reckoning. The image of Laura and L.D. has the potential to exist in perpetuity; always somewhere they will be dying.[67] The lynching photograph was meant to memorialize the slaughter of Laura and

L.D. Nelson, but what is also forever captured are the faces of the fiends who tortured them to death.[68] What becomes embalmed in this photographic image is the act of torture and white supremacy that congealed into the lynch mob made of men who raped her, then killed her and her son and left her daughter abandoned or killed as well. The lynching photograph is a talisman of murder shared among perpetrators while implicating the broader audiences who take pleasure in Black suffering. The unresolved social violence represented in the frame gives Laura and L.D. no rest; they are made ghosts of visual culture who do not relent, who are unable to find a way out of the frame, out of the perpetual image of dying.

Roland Barthes's analysis of the photograph in *Camera Lucida* shows us that the photograph cannot escape its referent, but the referent in a lynching photograph is not simply the body suspended or the murderers who gawk at lifeless bodies.[69] All of the events that led to this moment—the post-abolition, post-Reconstruction white supremacist regime that left Laura Nelson and her family vulnerable, unable to earn enough money to feed themselves—are referents in this photograph. In his analysis of the relationship between painting, photography, and sculpture, André Bazin discusses the way that photography usurped painting as the most effective method of depicting a moment of reality through the plastic arts. Bazin contends that photography is a way to embalm the dead, preserve a life that was lost; to be sure photography, film, and video are able to capture moments that time steals away.[70] Following Barthes, who was concerned with the mortality of the photograph—the paper disintegrates and the image eventually fades away—I ask, will the lynching photograph that now lives in digital space ever disappear? Will lynching photographs forever haunt the medium of photography and by extension cinematography?

From Civil War–era spirit photography to the entire horror film genre, the desire to bring absent presences out of the ether and into the visual field has been tethered to photographic and cinematographic technology.[71] The cinematic image is a photograph repeated twenty-four frames a second to create the illusion of movement.[72] Laura Mulvey takes up the question of this visual phenomenon as it relates to death, particularly the potential for the moving image to defy it. Mulvey suggests that the cinematic medium enables those who have been captured on film to deny the grip of death, the caveat being that they forever repeat the moments from their lives that happened to be recorded on film.[73] Early viewers of Lumière's cinematograph saw the potential of the moving image to defy death by emblazoning the darkness with light, shadow, and movement and ultimately resurrect the dead; this contributes to the understanding of cinema as a haunted medium. As spiritual photographers and modern-day ghost hunters proclaim, photography and cinema are tools that can be used to catch glimpses of the ghosts who escape human perception, or more relevant for this discussion, still and moving images capture in time those who have died and open up the possibility for visitations to occur in cinematic space. Lynch's SAVED :: video postcard does not produce an image of Laura and L.D. as ghostly figures; that was not the aim. This video project, through performance and intention, conjured the presences of Laura and L.D., presences that were felt, not seen. The connection made between Laura, L.D., and the participants in the live public installation at the 145th Street Bridge was visceral and palpable, as was made evident by the remarks included in Lynch's video.

Though the moving image may lock a body in repetitive motion, as Mulvey suggests, I argue that it also has the potential to release a body. Lynch's SAVED :: video postcard is the mechanism that begins to resolve the perpetual state of archival violence in which Laura and L.D. are frozen. Every time the lynching photograph of Laura Nelson is called up, the murder is relived, and the mortal photographic paper becomes immortal in digital space. The archive into which Laura Nelson has been plunged is fortified by the lynching photograph and the news reports that depict her as monstrous. With SAVED :: video postcard, the artist enters that archival space with Laura and L.D. and is able to combat the horror of Laura and L.D.'s perpetual dying by offering them a reckoning through the live performances that were staged at the 145th Street Bridge and in the visual field of the video itself. The accessibility of viewing a time-based installation piece like this is often limited to viewing within a gallery space. The artist has allowed SAVED :: video postcard to remain available online; it is free and accessible through an internet search.[74] The collaboration, performance, and freedom that surround this video project all contribute to loosening the archival grip that binds Laura and L.D. Nelson. Through the digital treatment of the lynching photograph, Kara Lynch erases the noose and performs a letting go, a disappearance, a relenting of the image. The persistent terror of the white supremacist lynch mob looming on the bridge fades away and is overtaken by the gathering of witnesses and mourners who come together to let Laura and L.D. go out of the field of vision, out of perpetual dying, and into the next place.

SAVED :: video postcard *and the Black Feminist Avant-Garde*

The production, assembly, performances, editing, and screening involved in SAVED :: *video postcard* all summon erotic power, in the Lordean sense. To call back Audre Lorde's concept from the opening pages of this chapter, erotic knowledge is an empowering force that we can use to scrutinize every facet of our existence.⁷⁵ Kara Lynch and all those who joined her at the 145th Street Bridge in Harlem were marshaling their erotic power to produce a collective synergy that opened a channel for a visitation with Laura Nelson and L.D. to occur. As the testimonies of the participants make clear, this project tapped into a way of knowing that exists outside the scope of dominant power and western standards of time. As noted in the preceding pages, a member of the collective experience remarked, "You could feel the energy and the elements. You felt that you were a part of it. You felt that you were there. You felt that you gave her closure."⁷⁶ The feeling of using erotic power to cut through "dominant corporate, linear time" and make contact with an ancestor who suffers long after death through the repetition of her dying in the lynching photograph is an actualization of M. Jacqui Alexander's conceptualization of the sacred.⁷⁷ To use Alexander's words, SAVED :: video postcard disrupts "the inherited divides of Sacred and secular, the embodied and disembodied" and does in fact stage and visualize an encounter that demands we "take seriously the dimensions of spiritual labor that make the sacred and the disembodied palpably tangible."⁷⁸ Through the performances in SAVED :: video postcard, Lynch initiates the process of creating a ritual that allows a community to mourn, and through the videographic medium, she records the visitation that unfolds. Lynch's video opens up this archive and visualizes the space where the living and the dead can meet. She then uses the visual field of performance and video to agitate the release of Laura and L.D. from the perpetual dying that was burned into the photograph, a photograph that would have one day disintegrated but remains in digital space.

The archive may be a tomb, but even worse, the photographic evidence of a lynching means reliving the terror and helplessness of the victims alongside the glee of both white mob violence and the consumers of the original postcard image. This work does not simply contend with the violence of the archive; it moves beyond mere reflection to provide the reckoning that Laura and L.D. Nelson need to be freed from the photographic purgatory of the lynching photograph. By not showing the lynching photograph as such, by treating the image in a way that removes the rope and the bridge, Laura becomes free in the image. Erotic power and the sacred are the frequencies that enliven the living memorial that is SAVED :: video postcard. Through the visitation that Lynch, and all the performances in the video draw forward, a reckoning has been made possible. With the visual and sonic terrain of the video, Lynch begins to release the photographic hold that binds Laura and L.D. to the catastrophic moment of their deaths. The artist's Black feminist avant-garde aesthetic practice in this video is made manifest in the way that she dilutes the lynching photograph. She overblows the bridge over the North Canadian River in Okemah, Oklahoma, with light, and it fades away. The murderers gawking from above, the rope, everything disappears except Laura floating through space. By overexposing all the figures and objects in the photograph except Laura Nelson, Kara Lynch enables Laura to get free from the image; she begins to pull Laura Nelson out of the archival void. Laura Nelson ascends. She is being disaggregated from the landscape of the photographic image, both visually and affectively. Lynch's SAVED :: *video postcard* contributes to the archive of Laura Nelson, a video that destabilizes images of Black depravity and death that have submerged Laura Nelson for too long.

Lynch uses the moving image to stage and execute a visual reckoning that takes place through the collective mourning and performances at work in SAVED :: *video postcard*. The letting-go ceremony that is the live public installation, the living memorial, and the video postcard all produce and document a rite of passage.[79] This is not a rite of passage that marks a transition of life stages or status but rather a passage from being locked in the moment of one's own murder to an actualization of release. Because the lynching photograph is the tool that locks Laura Nelson in the moment of her murder, the visual register becomes an apposite landscape for this crossing. The performances of the gospel choirs, the liturgical dancers, those who march slowly over the bridge dressed in white, and the community members who gather to witness Laura Nelson's suffering all enact for her the rite of passage from death to what comes after. Kara Lynch's video recording of these performances combined with the artist's visual treatment of the lynching photograph, in which she exacts the erasure of the noose, bridge, and lynch mob from the photograph, usher Laura Nelson and her son out of the liminal space of perpetual dying and into a place of freedom. The authority who is called on to confer this rite of passage is Lorde's erotic and Alexander's sacred. These powers are exercised through the performances staged at the Harlem River, the visual treatment of the lynching photograph, and the witnessing that takes place when SAVED :: *video postcard* is screened. Through these processes, Lynch actualizes a methodology of tenderness and induces a reckoning on behalf of Laura and L.D. Nelson. The collective that Lynch creates enacts a reckoning through performance, and both the photographic and videographic measures that liberate them from perpetual liminality.

The visitation that Lynch conjured with Laura Nelson at the 145th Street Bridge bypassed western standards of time as it harnessed the power of the sacred and the erotic to mobilize the haunted photographic/cinematic/videographic medium. The artist joined that complex of forces with the collective energy of the live performances on the riverbank to produce a reckoning for Laura Nelson and her son. Something was done, something happened, and it was a reckoning. Those who participated in the event felt it, commented on it, and through the dissemination of Lynch's video, those who screen *SAVED :: video postcard* can feel it too. The haunted medium allows for the presence of Laura's specter to be felt, an absent presence in need of a reckoning who receives that reckoning as it takes place with each screening of the video; a bit more freedom and letting go happens with each viewing—this is the power of Black feminist avant-garde cinema.

With her living memorial, Kara Lynch intervenes into Laura Nelson's archive of violence. The lynching photograph is an archival object that burdens the memory of Laura and L.D. Nelson, yet with this Black feminist avant-garde piece, Lynch is able to subvert the spectacle and avoid a pornotropic consumption of the image. Lynch stages a spectral encounter with *SAVED :: video postcard* that traverses the space that exists between life and death. When Laura and L.D. are joined by compassionate strangers rather than gawking spectators at the bridge, their reckoning unfolds. Laura and L.D. are given a homegoing ceremony with performances and recordings that have become *SAVED :: video postcard*. As Lynch's video exemplifies, Black feminist avant-garde artists are able to listen, to enter into an archive and produce something that can make absent archival presences legible, and then support them through their passage out of the horror to which they have been relegated and on to a better place.

With the next chapter, we are no longer immersed in the era of jim crow vigilante violence that characterizes the early decades of the twentieth century; we are entering the era of the Stonewall rebellion in New York City. This move brings with it a shift in tone and content. Chapter 3 delves more deeply into the discourse of performance, which was touched upon in this chapter, to explore the relationship between film, trans activism, and performativity as they appear in the cinematic theatrical production *Happy Birthday, Marsha!* This Black feminist avant-garde piece, directed by Tourmaline and Sasha Wortzel, merges film and theatrical performance to conjure a visitation with the iconic trans activist and performer Marsha P. Johnson. In order to contextualize the film and performances in *Happy Birthday, Marsha!*, chapter 3 discusses the tensions, elisions, and wages of violence that are revealed by examining the archives of gay liberation organizations and studying the New Left. The next chapter will focus on the archive of the nascent trans activist group S.T.A.R. to underscore the bold visionary resistance of its founders, Sylvia Rivera and Marsha P. Johnson.

3

CARRYING THE KNOWLEDGE / PERFORMING THE ARCHIVE

An Afternoon with Marsha P. Johnson

On a perfect September afternoon in 2018, we gathered together in the lobby of The Kitchen, a black box theater and performance space in Chelsea, New York City.[1] The small crowd of twenty-something to seventy-something hipsters, activists, artists, musicians, and scholars tried to contain its excitement as the doors opened. When invited, we moved quietly and methodically into a cozy darkened theater. We found a stage framed with silver streams of tinsel that twinkled under the spotlights. Blood-red roses and white candles in clear glass jars were placed delicately at the foot of the stage. The chatter ended when the filmmakers entered the space. Wearing flowing scarlet garments that were distinct but clearly coordinated, Tourmaline and Sasha Wortzel faced each other with microphones in hand. They whispered lovingly in unison into the

FIGURE 3.1 Marsha P. Johnson. Photographer and date unknown.

microphones: "Marsha, Marsha, Marsha, Marsha; Sylvia, Sylvia, Sylvia, Sylvia; S.T.A.R., S.T.A.R., S.T.A.R., S.T.A.R., S.T.A.R."

Ethereal sounds emanated from the collection of keyboards, microphones, and percussion instruments that would be providing live accompaniment for the afternoon.[2] Egyptt LaBeija warmed the stage in a turquoise and indigo peacock feather–patterned gown. She glided effortlessly across the stage, performing Patti LaBelle's "Changed." Once the rousing performance was complete, a screen unfurled at center stage. The film *Happy Birthday, Marsha!* began to play.

The experimental short film *Happy Birthday, Marsha!* juxtaposes black-and-white archival footage of Marsha P. Johnson with lush narrative sequences designed in crimson and gold, set in New York City in 1969. In this segment of the archival footage, Marsha is sitting on a chair wearing her signature crown of flowers, talking to the person behind the camera. Marsha laments with laughter: "I got lost in the music in 1963 at Stonewall.... No, no it was Stonewall—it was 1967 that I got lost. In 19—oh my dear, Stonewall, I got lost at Stonewall. Heard it through the grapevine. 1969. I got lost in the music and I couldn't get out. I still can't get out of the music." With a lilt in her voice and earnestness in her eyes, Marsha remarks that her computer gets all tangled up. The film moves back and forth from this archival footage of Marsha with its pale veneer of videotape to rich narrative sequences of a Stonewall-era drama that centers Marsha, Sylvia Rivera, and their friends. In the narrative portion of the film, we see Marsha, played by Mya Taylor, on a street in the West Village near the Stonewall Inn. Marsha happens upon a nefarious exchange between the police and the managers of the Stonewall Inn; the police are extorting money from the bar in tacit agreement that they will not raid the place later on that night. The police notice Marsha passing by and approach her. They grab her and push her into the brick wall of the Stonewall Inn. The flowers that she is holding and the invitations to her birthday party that she handcrafted fall to the ground. After the police let her go, Marsha collects her things and continues on with her day. She strolls through the village, inviting her friends to her party that evening; it is her birthday. Back at her apartment, Marsha sinks into a bath. As she washes, bubbles in the bath water part revealing bruises and scrapes on her legs. All dressed now, and ready for the party, Marsha ices her cake and then waits. She becomes disappointed as time passes and no one shows up for her party. She calls her friend Sylvia Rivera, played by Eve Lindley, who apologizes for missing her party. They agree to meet and celebrate at the Stonewall Inn. On her way to the bar, Marsha sees a friend, Junior, driving by in a convertible. Marsha hops in along with her other friends and they all head down to the bar.

The film stops midway through and the screen rolls up.

Eve Lindley, in character as Sylvia, appears on stage before the audience. She is steeped in the late 1960s, wearing a slight pompadour hairstyle, cat eyes fashioned with liquid eyeliner, a halter top, a miniskirt, and knee-high boots. The charge, the attitude, the presence of Sylvia Rivera is before us. Sylvia spins a loving tale about Marsha. She was a friend who would give you the shoes off her feet, her last dollar, the coat off her back. Sylvia describes the work she and Marsha did with S.T.A.R. (Street Transvestites Action Revolutionaries), taking care of sex workers and cofounding a community home, S.T.A.R. House, which was located in an apartment they rented in the East Village.[3] Sylvia remembers marching for liberation alongside the Young Lords and how the Black Panthers were in solidarity with S.T.A.R.; they never humiliated her or looked down on her. Sylvia recalls how Marsha discovered that she had syphilis but that it was diagnosed much too late to treat. Sylvia tells us of the pact she and Marsha made that neither one of them would kill themselves and leave the other alone to fight. Marsha went missing in the summer of 1992. When they found her body in the Hudson River, the police ruled Marsha's death a suicide. Because of their pact, Sylvia does not believe that Marsha threw herself into the Hudson; Marsha would not have broken their promise. Sylvia recalls that a group of guys was seen giving Marsha a hard time the day she died. She remembers that during the last days of her life, Marsha started to see her father in the river and wonders if maybe she tried to go out there to find him. Sylvia accepts that Marsha may have drowned but insists that she did not kill herself.

Jimmy Camicia, Marsha's friend and a poet who plays himself in the film, takes the stage after Sylvia. He recites a poem that captures Marsha's sensibility, voice, and humor. Jimmy's poem remembers Marsha as an integral part of the cabaret performance group Hot Peaches, of which Jimmy was the founder. He recounts the ways that Marsha was generous with everything that was in her possession; if you liked her scarf, she would give it to you. She would stand in front of Village Cigars and ask the passersby, "Can you spare any change for a dying queen, darling?" She was beloved, unabashedly herself, generous beyond belief, and full of joy. Jimmy tells the story of the *P* in Marsha P. Johnson's name. One day when Marsha was in court, on the charge of solicitation, the judge asked Marsha what the *P* in her name stands for. Marsha replied, without missing a beat, that the "*P* stands for Pay it no mind, honey." Jimmy exits the stage. The screen unfurls once more and the film resumes.

Marsha and her friends are now inside the Stonewall Inn. Egyptt LaBeija performs on the small stage. The tinsel curtains that frame the stage in the film mirror the curtains that frame the stage at The Kitchen, the theater where this film and performance are unfolding. Marsha and her friends order drinks from the bar and begin to celebrate Marsha on her birthday. It seems that as soon as the celebration begins, it comes to a crashing end—the police raid the bar. The bartenders hide the cash from the till before the police can snatch it. The police begin to beat everyone up and the melee ensues. The Stonewall rebellion has begun. The film ends. The screen rolls up.

The quiet, almost solemn space inside The Kitchen gave way to glamour and fabulosity when Egyptt LaBeija appeared on the stage performing Gloria Gaynor's "I Will Survive." Mya Taylor, the actor who portrayed Marsha in the film, did not appear in the stage production of this event. We saw cinematic representations of Marsha but she did not enter the proscenium, as did Sylvia Rivera, Egyptt LaBeija, and Jimmy Camicia. There was a way that Egyptt LaBeija's performance of "I Will Survive" channeled Marsha and filled the room with Marsha's love of singing and performance. The absent presence of Marsha settled into the space. While we were remembering and honoring Marsha's life, her loss became palpable; the loss of Marsha was alive in this performance. The film, the performances, the opening incantation, and the audience all conspired to usher in a visitation with Marsha and Sylvia that took place at The Kitchen on September 22, 2018.[4]

In the analysis of *Happy Birthday, Marsha!* that follows, I discuss the ways that performance complements Black feminist avant-garde film as a method of contending with an archive of violence and the violence of the archive itself. I examine the presence of archival material in the theatrical performance and avant-garde film that are brought together in this production. I am interested in the way that knowledge is transmitted through performances steeped in the archive and consider the performativity of the archival document that is the S.T.A.R. Manifesto. In my analysis of the relationship between archival violence, theatrical performance, and narrative film in *Happy Birthday, Marsha!*, I discuss Tourmaline's relationship to this archive and examine what is revealed at the juncture of performance and film that enables occluded archival documentation to emerge through this meeting. I consider the contradictions and moments of convergence that occur when archival exploration rubs up against performance and the cinematic. The cinematic archival intervention that Tourmaline and Wortzel issue with this film demonstrates the inherent value of trans women of color, which is a hallmark of the Black feminist avant-garde. The filmmakers' integration of avant-garde film with live performance in *Happy Birthday, Marsha!* ratchets up the stakes of the Black feminist avant-garde. The friction between their experiments with the historical film genre, archival documentation, and performance make immediate the relationship between western epistemology, cinematic temporality, and embodied knowledge. Tourmaline and Wortzel's performative cinematic experience becomes an event that represents and riffs on the archival documentation of Marsha P. Johnson and Sylvia Rivera's lives together. The film *Happy Birthday, Marsha!* also serves as a visual and performative text that contributes to the archival documentation of Marsha P. Johnson's life. By focusing on Marsha's life through a film that captures a moment in her life, by bringing her friends to the stage, both alive and passed on, to offer beautiful testimonials about their relationship, this production conjures up a visitation with Marsha P. Johnson that enlivens her archival corpus.

Tourmaline and Wortzel's presentation of *Happy Birthday, Marsha!* at The Kitchen upends the staid film-screening convention of a film programmer introducing the film and filmmakers, screening the film for an audience, then hosting a Q&A with the filmmakers after the film ends. The filmmakers eschew the traditional mode of introduction and open the stage with an incantation that invites the presence of the ancestors whose lives are being represented on stage and screen; this ceremonial opening makes room for a visitation to unfold in the theatrical space. Because they immerse their film within a stage performance, the work of cinema takes on a performative role. The filmmakers decenter their film, and it becomes an element in a production that channels the presence of Marsha P. Johnson. Their presentation of *Happy Birthday, Marsha!* weaves together theatrical performance, cinematic narrative, archival documentation, musical accompaniment, and a calling in of the ancestors that honors Marsha, Sylvia, and S.T.A.R. and lifts up their legacies in our contemporary place in LGBTQ history. The defiance of convention and innovation of form, the use of performance to connect with Marsha, and the centrality of the archive in all these facets of *Happy Birthday, Marsha!* exemplify the political imperatives and complex aesthetics of the Black feminist avant-garde.

Tourmaline's extensive archival research of Marsha P. Johnson's activism, her friendship with Sylvia Rivera, and their strategies for survival are made salient in this Black feminist avant-garde piece. The film and theatrical production lay bare the affective and archival labor that Tourmaline has exerted over the past decade to bring Marsha P. Johnson out of the shadows of LGBTQ history and into the prominence that she deserves. Aside from being a filmmaker and archivist, Tourmaline is also an activist and a scholar.[5] She held the position of Activist in Residence at the Barnard Center for Research on Women from 2014 to 2016. Tourmaline's archival research, interviews, and publications have broken new ground in recording the legacies of Marsha P. Johnson and Sylvia Rivera and have brought these figures into the foreground of contemporary conversations about trans, queer, and/or LGBTQ activism. Tourmaline's archival labor, which includes scouring newspapers, periodicals, and archival collections for documentation of Marsha P. Johnson, has played a fundamental role in bringing Marsha P. Johnson's life and legacy into the current discussion of LGBTQ history. Tourmaline freely shares this archival material on her website and has done so since 2012.[6] Her website is an archive itself, hosting interviews in which she discusses prison abolition, archival records of Marsha P. Johnson's activism, and Johnson's work with Sylvia Rivera and S.T.A.R. As a scholar, Tourmaline has made a hefty contribution as coeditor of the visionary and vital anthology *Trap Door: Trans Cultural Production and the Politics of Visibility* with Eric A. Stanley and Johanna Burton. As a filmmaker, Tourmaline is both lauded and accomplished.

Happy Birthday, Marsha! was included in the Brooklyn Museum's 2019 show that commemorated the fiftieth anniversary of the Stonewall rebellion, *No-*

body Promised You Tomorrow. The Brooklyn Museum and High Line Art co-commissioned a film by Tourmaline, *Salacia: Ill of Fame*, which was featured in *Nobody Promised You Tomorrow* and was the first film commissioned as a High Line original. In addition to the Brooklyn Museum, the High Line, and The Kitchen, Tourmaline's work has been presented at the Museum of Modern Art, PS1, BFI Flare, the New Museum, the Whitney Museum, the Studio Museum in Harlem, and the Venice Biennale. Tourmaline's body of cinematic work, which also includes *Atlantic Is a Sea of Bones*, *The Personal Things*, and *Lost in the Music*, all lyrically and vibrantly contends with Black trans and queer life in a way that both spans epochs and dislocates time.[7] Tourmaline's extensive and groundbreaking archival research of Marsha P. Johnson, Sylvia Rivera, and S.T.A.R. has been a driving force in centering Marsha and Sylvia in our memory of the Stonewall rebellion and the history of gay liberation; this labor clearly undergirds this film and buttresses the theatrical cinematic experience of *Happy Birthday, Marsha!*

In an interview archived at the Barnard Center for Research on Women, Tourmaline discusses the fact and the impact of the historical erasure of trans women of color.

> I was trying to connect myself at a time when I didn't feel connected to a history of other trans women of color, and it was really hard. There was the Sylvia Rivera Law Project and I kind of heard a little bit about Marsha P. Johnson. But not anywhere where it is right now. And I felt really disconnected from any kind of past. And I think that made me feel really isolated and increased the levels of isolation that I was having to deal with every day. It was a kind of historical isolation. And I think through doing this kind of archival work, it made me think that that historical erasure is like a form of violence. And, then it really made me feel that doing that work is even more important. Right? Because trans communities, our legacies and our work is so often erased. So, I just wanted to find out as much as possible.[8]

As Tourmaline documents in her interview, historical erasure is a kind of violence. She describes an archival violence that not only happens through an institutional devaluing of archival documentation of trans women of color but raises to the surface the impact of that historical erasure on trans people who become isolated in their estrangement from their elders and ancestors by this violent archival process.

The archive of Marsha P. Johnson, Sylvia Rivera, and S.T.A.R. is composed of interviews with Marsha and Sylvia recorded on audio and video, newspaper articles, flyers for events and meetings, their open letters to the community, the S.T.A.R. Manifesto, and photographs of these activists at protests and marches. Marsha P. Johnson, Sylvia Rivera, and S.T.A.R. have a substantial archival presence, yet the photographs, audio and video recordings, and written material are located in several archival collections that are held across the New York Public Library (NYPL), the Lesbian Herstory Archives, the LGBT National History Archives, and in private collections. That the archival documentation of their activism has been preserved is fortunate. The dispersal of these records, however, makes accessing the archive much more difficult; this element of the Johnson/Rivera/S.T.A.R. archive contributes to the kind of violence through estrangement to which Tourmaline was referring. Tourmaline's archival research, her labor and generosity, has brought together many of these archival elements and made them available on her website. The historical isolation that Tourmaline felt, as documented in her interview, had to be countered through her own archival labor, and she offered up that labor to her community to help assuage that sense of isolation for other trans people of color looking for their history. Tourmaline's research, her archival and affective labor, courses through the film and the theatrical presentation of *Happy Birthday, Marsha!* In an effort to historically situate the archival footage, narrative sequences, and stage performances in Tourmaline and Wortzel's *Happy Birthday, Marsha!*, I will offer a discussion of the Stonewall rebellion that draws together the dispersed archive of Marsha, Sylvia, and S.T.A.R.

What Happened at the Stonewall Inn?

The uprising at the Stonewall Inn erupted around 1:00 a.m. on June 28, 1969.[9] In a 1989 interview with Eric Marcus, Sylvia Rivera recounts what happened at the Stonewall Inn the night of the rebellion.[10] As she explains: "The Stonewall wasn't a bar for drag queens. Everybody keeps saying it was. So this is where I get into arguments with people. They say, 'Oh, no, it was always a drag queen bar and it was a Black bar.' No, Washington Square Bar was the drag queen bar. Okay, you could get into the Stonewall if they knew you and there were only a certain amount of drag queens that were allowed into the Stonewall at that time."[11]

Sylvia Rivera recounts in her interview with Marcus that nickels, dimes, and quarters started flying and hitting the police when the uprising broke out. She believed that throwing these coins was a symbol of resistance to police brutality and corruption, that this act of hurling coins was a statement about the practice of police extorting gay bars. Sylvia remembers that the effeminate men and butch women would get the brunt of the police punishment and that they were tired of being in the closet. They were not going to get back in that closet! The gay patrons and the drag queens who were at the Stonewall Inn that night did not go quietly into the paddy wagons as they had done before. The police panicked when the patrons of the Stonewall Inn resisted; they did not expect the resistance, and the resistance grew.[12]

In the documentary film about her life, *Major!* (2015), trans activist, prison abolitionist, and elder Miss Major Griffin-Gracy offers an oral history of the Stonewall rebellion and the role that trans women played in the uprising. Miss Major was at the Stonewall Inn on the night of the rebellion. She describes the moment when the rebellion ignited:

> And what happened was, that night it was just a matter of they used to do that to us all the time. Just come into the bar and the lights would go on and everybody would just stream out. Nothing ever really had to get said because you knew that's what had to happen. You knew that's what the routine was. And it was just a night that it simply wasn't going to happen. You know it's just It's a feeling you get when you all go to the movies and see something together and everybody "ah" and gasps at the same time. That's the feeling. You just knew. Everyone just looked at one another and said, Enough. Not leaving. Not going anywhere.

This rebellion certainly was a flashpoint in the lineage of gay liberation and gender self-determination. Marsha P. Johnson was there, Sylvia Rivera was there, Miss Major Griffin-Gracy was there; three iconic historical figures of the gay, lesbian, and trans movement were present for the moment when the queers fought back in a collective and sustained way. The archival presence of these three iconic trans leaders is concretized through the documentary films and interviews recorded of them, which offer a measure of archival reversal for the historical erasure of trans women from the gay liberation movement.[13] Their memory of the night of the Stonewall rebellion situates them at the center of this moment of collective resistance. Upon further examination, it becomes clear that the Stonewall rebellion may have happened spontaneously, but it did not happen out of nowhere. The problem with locating the beginning of the gay liberation movement at the Stonewall rebellion is that it obfuscates the work of trans women in liberation movements before Stonewall and overlooks gay activists who were active in other liberation groups. In order to understand the many facets of liberation that helped ignite the Stonewall rebellion, it is necessary to discuss the liberatory movement-building work that was taking place before the uprising at the Stonewall Inn.

The Stonewall rebellion and the gay liberation movement happened during an era of political upheaval in which resistance to the Vietnam War, police brutality, racism, and class warfare was being waged by groups like Students for a Democratic Society (SDS), the Student Non-Violent Coordinating Committee (SNCC), the Black Panther Party for Self-Defense (BPP), and the Young Lord's Party, which were all part of the New Left.[14] New Left groups demonstrated, boycotted, and issued their critiques of capitalist exploitation, racial oppression, and US militarization within and outside the United States. They organized to fight imperialism and end racial and class oppression. New Left organizations recognized how their distinct experiences of oppression were tied together, yet they were not immune to overlooking or reinforcing oppression. While these groups had Marxist critiques of capitalism and deep anti-imperial commitments, their approach to destabilizing dominant power elided gender and sexuality. Feminists and women-of-color activists of the New Left critiqued the ways that these groups held patriarchal beliefs about women and fixed women in supportive roles rather than in positions of leadership. Even though gay and lesbian activists were participating fully in these liberation groups, the groups did not overtly fight for gay civil rights, and some group members harbored homophobic beliefs.[15] Feminist organizations, like the National Organization for Women, focused on middle-class white women's issues and were rightly critiqued for not addressing issues important to working-class women of color. Women in the SDS and the BPP were often silenced or expected to serve the men in those movements; masculinist attitudes and homophobic rhetoric were wielded by some men in these groups to shore up and display the patriarchal power of these movements.[16] The word *faggot* was used as a virulent metaphor to describe the power that the state had over men, a power that the revolution would reinstate to the people.[17]

During the 1950s and pre-Stonewall 1960s, groups in the homophile movement did focus their attention on gay and lesbian rights but did not have the radical edge of the New Left. Homophile groups such as the Los Angeles–based Mattachine Society focused on gay men's issues, and the Daughters of Bilitis, out of San Francisco, focused on issues that lesbians faced. Mattachine and Daughters of Bilitis, under the threat of criminalization because of anti-sodomy laws, worked to combat isolation by secretly connecting gays and lesbians. Even though the Mattachine Society's founders had communist political beliefs, this was not a politically radical organization like those in the New Left. These groups did not make themselves visible as radical gay activist organizations in the larger public forum; they were covert groups that connected gay men and brought lesbians together through newsletters and local gatherings.[18] Both

Mattachine and Daughters of Bilitis were committed to proving that homosexuals were respectable and not pathological. Their public efforts were used to resist the image of gay and lesbian promiscuity and make gay and lesbian people more palatable to the mainstream. It is important to note that during the era in which Mattachine and Daughters of Bilitis operated, being out of the closet was a terrifying prospect: people caught committing homosexual acts could be arrested and jailed, lose their families or their jobs, or be involuntarily hospitalized and lobotomized. In 1962 Illinois was the first state to decriminalize homosexuality, and it was not until 2003 that the Supreme Court decision *Lawrence v. Texas* struck down anti-sodomy laws in Texas and the remaining thirteen states that still kept these laws on the books.

After the Stonewall rebellion in 1969, several gay liberation groups emerged that shed the confines of the closet and demanded gay liberation in public. The Gay Liberation Front (GLF), a New York–based gay political organization, formed immediately after the Stonewall rebellion.[19] The GLF was committed to radical change; GLF members were not interested in assimilation or respectability but were dedicated to fighting for radical systemic change. By 1970 the GLF had chapters across the country.[20] Some members of the GLF were committed to ending oppression of all kinds, while other members wanted to focus their attention solely on issues of sexuality; this distinction caused a defining rift in GLF when some members wanted to donate five hundred dollars to the Black Panther Party.[21] Given the heterosexism that circulated in New Left movement groups, it came as a surprise that the leader of the Black Panther Party for Self-Defense, Huey P. Newton, publicly supported the Gay Liberation Front in a statement released in 1970.[22] Frustration with the leaderless style of the GLF, its decision to monetarily support the BPP, and its choice to use its resources to combat multiple forms of oppression—and not exclusively fight for gay rights—led some members to leave the GLF. In the winter of 1969, members of the GLF broke off and formed the Gay Activists Alliance (GAA).[23]

The momentum for gay liberation kept building during the months following the Stonewall rebellion. In the summer of 1970, the GAA organized a series of dances at New York University's Weinstein Hall to raise money for legal, medical, and housing expenses for people in the gay community. Two dances had been held earlier that summer without incident. The administration balked at the third dance but eventually allowed it to proceed. The fourth dance was canceled, and the university forbade any events that were centered on gay issues until a panel of medical professionals and clergy convened and made a decision about the morality of homosexuality. The NYU student organization Gay Student Liberation organized a protest and asked the GLF for support. Sylvia Rivera and Marsha P. Johnson were some of the GLF members who showed up to occupy Weinstein Hall in protest of NYU's anti-gay policy.[24] The occupation lasted for five days and ended with New York City's Tactical Squad demanding that students leave the premises. Sylvia Rivera refused to leave and was subsequently arrested.[25]

In an interview with Leslie Feinberg, Sylvia Rivera recounts that S.T.A.R. emerged out of the action at Weinstein Hall.[26] Sylvia tells Feinberg:

> S.T.A.R. was for the street gay people, the street homeless people and anybody that needed help at that time. Marsha and I had always sneaked people into our hotel rooms. Marsha and I decided to get a building. We were trying to get away from the Mafia's control at the bars.
>
> We got a building at 213 East 2nd Street. Marsha and I just decided it was time to help each other and help out other kids. We fed people and clothed people. We kept the building going. We went out and hustled the streets. We paid the rent.
>
> We didn't want the kids out in the streets hustling. They would go out and rip off food. There was always food in the house and everyone had fun. It lasted for two or three years.
>
> We would sit there and ask, "Why do we suffer?" As we got more involved into the movements, we said, "Why do we always got to take the brunt of this shit?"[27]

Sylvia Rivera and Marsha P. Johnson began organizing as Street Transvestites for Gay Power after the Weinstein Hall event. In the fall of 1970, they augmented the name and emerged as Street Transvestites Action Revolutionaries (S.T.A.R.). Sylvia and Marsha produced a manifesto that outlined a nine-point plan for gender self-determination, the end of job discrimination, the end of police harassment and exploitation by doctors, the ability to have one's gender listed correctly on one's identification, and free education, health care, clothing, food, and housing for trans people, gay people, and all people. They wanted access to all areas of society and full participation in liberation struggles.

In her interview with Feinberg, Sylvia Rivera enters into the record that the S.T.A.R. banner was first carried publicly at a demonstration in 1970 to protest police violence and remembers that members of the Young Lord's Party showed them respect as human beings; Sylvia became a member of the Young Lord's Party. She also describes meeting Huey Newton in Philadelphia in 1971; he recognized S.T.A.R. as a part of the revolution. Sylvia and Marsha, as founders of S.T.A.R., were revolutionary leaders of their movement committed to fighting for gay power. Their presence as members of the gay community forced gay and lesbian organizations like GAA to confront their own oppressive conceptions about gender.²⁸

A painful and elucidatory example of the contempt for trans women in the gay liberation movement was on full display in 1973, after the Christopher Street Liberation Day March held on June 24 (see figure 3.2). In the rally at Washington Square Park, where the march culminated, S.T.A.R. had not been given the opportunity to address the crowd. Sylvia demanded that she be given a chance to speak and worked her way onto the stage. As she began her speech, lesbian separatists and gay men heckled her. The audience booed her at first but Sylvia pushed on (see figure 3.3).

> Y'all better quiet down. I've been trying to get up here all day for your gay brothers and your gay sisters, in jail, that write me every motherfucking week and ask for your help. And you all don't do a goddamn thing for them.
>
> Have you ever been beaten up and raped in jail? Now think about it. They've been beaten up and raped after they've had to spend much of their money in jail to get their hormones, and try to get their sex changes. The women have tried to fight for their sex changes or to become women. On the women's liberation—and they write S.T.A.R. Not the women's groups. They do not write women. They do not write men. They write S.T.A.R. because we're trying to do something for them.
>
> I have been to jail. I have been raped. And beaten. Many times! By men! Heterosexual men that do not belong in the homosexual shelter. But, do you do anything for them? No. You all tell me to go and hide my tail between my legs. I will no longer put up with this shit. I have been beaten. I have had my nose broken. I have been thrown in jail. I have lost my job. I have lost my apartment for gay liberation and you all treat me this way? What the fuck's wrong with you all? Think about that!
>
> I do not believe in a revolution, but you all do. I believe in the gay power. I believe in us getting our rights, or else I would not be out there fighting for our rights. That's all I wanted to say to y'all people. If you all want to know about the people that are in jail and do not forget Bambi L'amour, and Dora Mark, Kenny Mesner, and other gay people that are in jail, come and see the people at S.T.A.R. House on Twelfth Street on 640 East Twelfth Street between B and C apartment 14.
>
> The people are trying to do something for all of us, and not men and women that belong to a white middle-class white club. And that's what you all belong to!

FIGURE 3.2 *Marsha P. Johnson and Sylvia Rivera, Christopher Street Liberation Day March*, June 24, 1973. Photo by Leonard Fink. Courtesy of LGBT Community Center National History Archive.

FIGURE 3.3 *Sylvia Rivera, "Y'all Better Quiet Down" speech at Christopher Street Liberation Day rally, Washington Square Park, New York City*, June 24, 1973 (video still). Recording by LoveTapesCollective. Courtesy of Lesbian Herstory Archives.

> REVOLUTION NOW!
> Gimme a G! Gimme an A! Gimme a Y! Gimme a P! Gimme an O! Gimme a W! Gimme an E! Gimme an R!
> [*Sylvia begins to cry*]
> Gay power!
> Louder!
> GAY POWER![29]

The crowd joined in with Sylvia in her chant; they gave her a "G.A.Y. P.O.W.E.R." when she asked for it from the stage. Sylvia challenged the crowd's resistance, withstood their virulence, and eventually won the audience over. This is a heartbreaking moment to witness for Sylvia, who had dedicated herself to fighting for the rights of the very people who were booing her.

After Sylvia left the stage, Jean O'Leary, a former member of GAA who left the group to start Lesbian Feminist Liberation, gave a speech that critiqued men who dressed in drag for entertainment purposes, and in her critique, she conflated trans women, drag queens, and cross-dressers. This conflation became abundantly clear when she denounced the presence of Sylvia Rivera on the stage and with seething vitriol referred to Sylvia as a man wearing women's clothes.[30] The refusal to acknowledge trans women in O'Leary's speech reveals a hostile entrenchment within the lesbian feminist organizing communities.

In his 1989 interview with Sylvia Rivera, Eric Marcus asks about her activism and political work; the betrayal that she experienced from the gay community rises to the surface.

SYLVIA: And the gay rights bill, as far as I'm concerned, you know, to me, the gay rights bill and the people that I worked with on the gay rights bill and when I did all the petitioning and whatnot, when the bill was passed ... that bill was mine as far as I'm concerned. I helped word it and I worked very hard for it. And that's why I get upset when I give interviews and whatever, because the fucking community has no respect for the people that really did it. Drag queens did it. We did it. We did it for our own brothers and sisters. But, damn it, don't keep shoving us in the fuckin' back and stabbing us in the back and that's ... And that's what really hurts. And it is very upsetting.

ERIC: Not only do you get beaten up by the straights, you get beaten up by the gays.

SYLVIA: You get beaten up by your own and that's what hurts.

Marsha and I fought a lot for the liberation of our people. We did a lot back then. Marsha and I had a building on Second Street, which is called STAR House. And when we asked the community to help us, there was nobody to help us. We were nothing. We were nothing. And now we were taking care of kids that were younger than us. I mean, Marsha and I were young and we were taking care of them. And GAA had teachers and lawyers and whatnot and all we asked them was is, well, if you could help us teach our own so we can all become a little bit better. There was nobody there to help us. There was nobody.

ERIC: They left you.

SYLVIA: They left us hanging. There was only one person that came and helped us. Once again is ... Bob Kohler was there. He helped us paint. He helped us put wires together. We didn't know what the fuck we were doin'. I mean, we took a building that was, I mean, a slum building. We tried. We really did. We went out and made that money off the streets to keep these kids off the street.[31]

The multiple forms of oppression that S.T.A.R. was working to combat become apparent in the archived audio and video recordings that document acts of violence that Sylvia, Marsha, and the S.T.A.R. children suffered both within and outside the gay liberation movement. The records of GAA, GLF, the Mattachine Society, and the Daughters of Bilitis are all accessible, cogent collections.

The violence of the archive itself becomes apparent through the disparate archival location and occlusion of S.T.A.R. in narratives of LGBT history and activism. The archival subsumption of S.T.A.R. persisted until quite recently, when Tourmaline's archival research, labor, and publicization of S.T.A.R. lifted the group to the foreground of the history of LGBTQ activism. The archival material, interviews, video footage, photographs, newspaper articles, and oral history of Stonewall all demonstrate that S.T.A.R. was mobilizing a vision of freedom on the vanguard of what has become the contemporary LGBTQ movement. Marsha P. Johnson's place in the archive is less obvious than Sylvia Rivera's but quite evident in the photographs of the marches and protests at NYU and Bellevue (see figures 3.4 and 3.5) and at the Christopher Street Liberation Day March and rally in post-Stonewall New York City.[32]

Because Sylvia Rivera was willing to put herself and her body literally on the line for gay power and trans liberation, her presence in the movement is at the forefront: she has become the voice of S.T.A.R. and trans justice during the Stonewall era. Marsha P. Johnson was less vocal than Sylvia Rivera, but as can be seen in photographs of Sylvia at the rallies and marches in the early days of gay liberation, Marsha was right by her side. Marsha's role in the movement is less evident because the archival record of her activism is scattered, but when an intrepid exploration to find Marsha P. Johnson in the archive is undertaken—as exemplified by Tourmaline's extensive work in the archives and the research that I undertook for this chapter—Marsha's archival trace can be found. The archival labor that Tourmaline has exerted is a response to the violent erasure of trans women in the archive, and for trans women of color, the archives of violence are deep and pervasive. The suspicion, exclusion, and hostility that trans women suffered during this monumental era in lesbian and gay history haunt queer and feminist liberation struggles in the new millennium. Trans liberation is not a foregone conclusion in contemporary LGBTQ activism. Transphobia has a stronghold in some quarters, and trans-exclusionary radical feminists do still exist. The lethal violence that trans women like Sylvia and Marsha struggled to survive, and too often succumbed to, persists into our contemporary moment. There is a direct historical connection between the violence that trans women suffered in 1969 and the violence that trans women suffer today. By 2019, fifty years after the Stonewall rebellion, digital space and social media platforms had become an archive for the murders of trans women; this digital space had become a social media graveyard, vigil, and memorial. With Tourmaline and Wortzel's *Happy Birthday, Marsha!*, a pause has been initiated, and in the abeyance created with their piece, these filmmakers offer a cinematic and performative event that is as rooted in archival concerns as it is in the avant-

FIGURE 3.4 *Marsha P. Johnson hands out flyers for support of gay students at N.Y.U.*, 1970. Photo by Diana Davies. Manuscripts and Archives Division, New York Public Library, Digital Collections, https://digitalcollections.nypl.org/items/510d47e3-57b0-a3d9-e040-e00a18064a99.

garde, is as dedicated to archival recovery as it is to defying any conception of historical accuracy, is as much a film as it is a performance as it is a mediation as it is a séance.

Performance, the Archive, and the Black Feminist Avant-Garde

The theatrical event *Happy Birthday, Marsha!* builds on the performativity that was raised in the second chapter's analysis of Kara Lynch's SAVED :: *video postcard*. Both pieces draw issues of performance and performativity into my conception of the Black feminist avant-garde; the incorporation of performance adds temporal multiplicity to the cinematic space carved out in these projects. The archival embodiments and connections that unfold in SAVED :: *video postcard* and the archival conjuring that takes place in *Happy Birthday, Marsha!* are activated through the performances staged in each work of art. The political stakes and aesthetic imperatives of avant-garde cinema that trouble the visual, destabilize the spectator, and upend conventions of time are amplified

FIGURE 3.5 *Marsha P. Johnson pickets Bellevue Hospital to protest treatment of street people and gays*, ca. 1968–75. Photo by Diana Davies. Manuscripts and Archives Division, New York Public Library, Digital Collections, https://digitalcollections.nypl.org/items/510d47e3-5fa8-a3d9-e040-e00a18064a99.

through engagements with performance in Black feminist avant-garde films. The film *Happy Birthday, Marsha!*, I argue, actually takes on a performative quality as it is woven into the performance and staging of *Happy Birthday, Marsha!* at The Kitchen. Both the film and the theatrical performances in *Happy Birthday, Marsha!* intervene in the archive of the Stonewall rebellion and gay liberation by centering Marsha P. Johnson and disrupting the epistemological power of an archive that subsumes her. The relationship between issues of the archive and performativity in performance studies scholarship has been an uneasy one that is embedded in the foundation of the field. When this relationship is explored, it exposes the hierarchy of western systems of knowledge production that emerge out of histories of conquest and have produced and continue to instantiate racial and gender stratification. The archival process of amassing, cataloging, and storing records enacts a privileging of the written word and visual evidence. Through documentation, hierarchical categorization, and ease of retrieval, western modes of knowledge production are made more legitimate than that which cannot be collected, stored, and documented on paper, in audio recordings, or on film. The value placed on the written word makes illegible the nonwritten or not impeccably written work, and dehumanizes people and groups of people whose mode of carrying knowledge exceeds the written word or is not recognized as valuable enough to be preserved in the repository.[33]

Western epistemologies that privilege observation, reason, and the empirically proven proclaim that systems of western knowledge production are devoid of bias and subjectivity, yet this premise is deeply duplicitous given that this very method of knowledge production is based on the presumptive historical belief that white, landowning men are the universal subject. This belief produced racial, class, gender, national, and ableist hierarchies that permeate systems of knowledge that continue to structure everyday life. In "Performance Studies: Interventions and Radical Research," Dwight Conquergood refers to the process of devaluing knowledge as epistemic violence and contends that "what gets squeezed out by this epistemic violence is the whole realm of complex, finely nuanced meaning that is embodied, tacit, intoned, gestured, improvised, co-experienced, covert—and all the more deeply meaningful because of its refusal to be spelled out."[34]

The radical intervention of performance studies destabilizes the hierarchy of the written word, by valuing nonwritten expression and recognizing knowledge bases, forms, and modes of expression that have been subjugated by the epistemic violence of western regimes of knowledge production. Performance becomes an interrogative through which text and practice, theory and creation, critique and memory, history and culture interact, struggle, and are then hurtled into question.[35] Conquergood contends: "Performance studies struggles to open the space between analysis and action, and to pull the pin on the binary opposition between theory and practice. This embrace of different ways of knowing is radical because it cuts to the root of how knowledge is organized in the academy."[36]

Performance studies offers methods for understanding performance in ways that expose the intentional and tacit performances of social life. Performance can be understood as a discrete cultural event with players, an audience, a beginning and ending, like a theatrical production or a happening, or it can be concerned with less self-aware social performances like clothing choices, greetings and salutations, and moving through space.[37] Theories of performance have been foundational in excavating the insidiousness of heteronormativity on the production of gender and sexuality. The relevance of the relationship between performativity and gender is made salient when one looks back at the first issue of the premier journal *GLQ: A Journal of Lesbian and Gay Studies*. This inaugural issue opens with Eve Kosofsky Sedgwick's "Queer Performativity: Henry James's *The Art of the Novel*," followed by Judith Butler's "Critically Queer." In tandem, these articles track the history of the term *performativity* from its theatrical consideration to its use in analyzing speech acts, capitalist efficiency, and deconstructive textual analysis, topics that all lead toward understanding the regulatory regime of gender construction and its effect on the subject.[38] The relationship between performance and activism is taken up in Diana Taylor's *Performance*, in which she explores the world-making impetus of performance as it is used in struggles for freedom; her analysis foregrounds the way that the body becomes a crucial performative site in this context.[39] Taylor closes *Performance* with a recognition of the world-making quality of performance:

> As a practice, performance constitutes a means of communication, a doing, and a doing *with* and *to*. As an act of imagination, performance allows us to imagine better scenarios and futurities. José Esteban Muñoz put it eloquently: "Some will say that all we have are the pleasures of this moment, but we must never settle for the minimal transport; we must dream and enact new and better pleasures, other ways of being in the world, and ultimately new worlds."
>
> Performance is world-making. We need to understand it.[40]

The world-making that is performance tracks back to the archive as well. In her earlier published volume *The Archive and the Repertoire: Performing Cultural Memory in the Americas*, Taylor challenges western epistemology by unseating the dominant position that writing holds in the production of knowledge and by recognizing that performance is an "embodied praxis and episteme."[41] Taylor argues that because we have accepted writing as the preeminent way of producing knowledge, the written word has taken the place of embodiment. Taylor contends that when we take "'performance' seriously as a system of learning, storing, and transmitting knowledge, performance studies allows us to expand what we understand by 'knowledge.'"[42] Tourmaline and Wortzel's *Happy Birthday, Marsha!* elicits an examination of the role of performativity in archival documentation, political protest, and trans liberation as they are staged in the theatrical event of which this film was a central part. The archival documentation of Marsha and Sylvia's resistance to gender domination and homophobia, their desire to create a cooperative movement for gay liberation with GAA, and the actualization of gender self-determination and community building with S.T.A.R. House demonstrate the world-making impetus that is a defining feature of performance.[43] What is most compelling for my analysis of *Happy Birthday, Marsha!* is Taylor's insight that "performances function as vital acts of transfer, transmitting social knowledge, memory, and a sense of identity through reiterated, or what Richard Schechner has called 'twice-behaved behavior.'"[44] My analysis of knowledge production and transfer in *Happy Birthday, Marsha!* raises questions about the use of archival material, the incorporation of the document, and the archival impulse at work in the film and theatrical production.

In Michel-Rolph Trouillot's analysis of the archive, as discussed in *Silencing the Past: Power and the Production of History*, he identifies dimensions of power at play within an archive. In his discussion of archival power, Trouillot addresses the inequalities of the archival process that privileges some voices and experiences while silencing others. He then examines the assembly of the archive within an institution and the power exerted in the process of collecting and cataloging archival materials.[45] In an observation that appears axiomatic, Trouillot recognizes that the ability to locate archival material is paramount in the process of archival research and discovery; the power, though, lies in the way that archival access ultimately impacts the production of history.[46] He insists: "Archives assemble. Their assembly work is not limited to a more or less passive act of collecting. Rather, it is an active act of production that prepares facts for historical intelligibility."[47]

The scattering of Marsha P. Johnson's archival materials across collections and institutions reflects both a recognition of her historical relevance and a concomitant diminished value in making cogent and easily accessible the body of archival material she generated in her lifetime. It is clear that archival power inflects archival choices, produces silences, and determines what will be understood as fact and, as a result, as history itself.

The dislocation of Marsha's archive across the archival collections of LGBTQ organizations and individuals means that the assembly of her archive happens in the retrieval process. Without a central location for all the photographs in which Marsha appears, the manifesto she helped draft, the newspaper articles in which she was mentioned, or the film footage and sound recordings that capture her voice in a time and place, her archival presence remains diffuse. Yet Marsha P. Johnson does have an archival presence. This fact of the Marsha P. Johnson archive exemplifies Trouillot's concern with the power of archival retrieval. If the archival documents are not easily found or are few in number, then the knowledge of Marsha P. Johnson will be obscured and her place in LGBTQ history will be lost.

The unevenness of accessibility is made salient when the archival presence of a more dominant gay liberation group, such as the Gay Activists Alliance, is held in contradistinction. The GAA's archival material is held together at the NYPL; there are eleven linear feet of documents. This archive is fixed, stable, and accessible. Because of the accessibility of this archival material, the GAA can more easily become the focal point of this historical moment, and the work of Marsha, Sylvia, and S.T.A.R. fades into the background. An LGBTQ history told without Marsha, Sylvia, and S.T.A.R. is an incomplete history that subjugates these foundational leaders, who were the vanguard of trans liberation.[48] The challenges in archival retrieval produce a silence and an archival occlusion, even though some documents have been preserved and cataloged. This challenge, in part, enables the mythology of Stonewall to exist as a spontaneous eruption of gay people who were tired of harassment. By overlooking the concerted effort of trans members of the pre-Stonewall community to organize with gay activists, the messy history of gay liberation, which includes vehement contempt for trans women by lesbian and gay organizations, is sidestepped. The archival abundance of the larger organizations like GAA, GLF, the Mattachine Society, and the Daughters of Bilitis overwhelms knowledge of Marsha, Sylvia, and S.T.A.R. and situates the more prominent groups at the helm of gay liberation. The archival dispersal and occlusion of knowledge both reflect and produce Marsha's place in the archive of LGBTQ history and the memory of the Stonewall rebellion.

The oral history that Miss Major offered in the documentary film about her life, *Major!* (2015), documents the ways that trans women have been left out of the legacy of the Stonewall rebellion:

You know the girls, we can put up with some stuff, you know, but I guess it was just like at that time, we were done. Can't take anymore. This has got to stop here. You know. After that, years, you've heard that oh someone threw a shoe. Someone threw a beer bottle or whatever have you. I don't know who threw what and it doesn't matter. All that mattered was, we were bustin' the cops' ass. And when the community at large got involved, all of a sudden it was the white gay guys who had did this and the lesbians. And oh there might have been a drag queen or two there. Really? When we frequented that bar, you know what I mean, and hung out there.

The community at large, to which Miss Major is referring, consisted of the gay activist organizations that were founded after the Stonewall rebellion like GAA and GLF. When discussing the Stonewall community, I would be remiss if I did not mention Stormé DeLarverie, a Stonewall Inn regular who was present when the Stonewall rebellion began. Rumor has it that DeLarverie's retaliatory punch, which laid low the police officer who struck her and bloodied her eye, was the catalyzing event of the uprising. DeLarverie—a butch lesbian, a singer who performed ballads dressed in a tuxedo in the Jewel Box Revue, and an MC— worked to protect the LGBTQ community in public spaces like the Stonewall Inn and, later, at Henrietta Hudson's. Insurgent voices of trans activists like Miss Major and archivist/filmmaker Tourmaline correct the force of dominant history that elides trans people who refused domination at the Stonewall Inn. The oral histories recorded by Eric Marcus and those that appear in documentary films like *Major!* collect firsthand testimonies of trans history that together work to dismantle the production of knowledge that excludes trans people from LGBTQ history and the flashpoint of the Stonewall rebellion. Miss Major's, Sylvia Rivera's, and Marsha P. Johnson's oral histories; Tourmaline and Wortzel's film; Tourmaline's archival research and assembly on her website; and scholarly texts like this one all combine to reassemble the archive with trans women's archival presences as the nexus and connective tissue during this pivotal moment in the history of our contemporary LGBTQ movement/moment.[49]

Another example of trans exclusion from the history of the Stonewall rebellion takes place not inside a repository but in public space. When remarking on the monuments to commemorate Stonewall located in Christopher Park, which sits across the street from the Stonewall Inn in Greenwich Village, Miss Major expresses deep disappointment about there being statues of two gay men and two lesbians.[50] No transgender women are memorialized in the park at all. She asks: "Where are we? We were such a part of this, you know. Where is the respect for the folks that have gone through this? Where is Sylvia Rivera, you know, and Marsha Johnson? . . . There were other people there who had a voice before this happened. You know. Who was trying to make things better. Girls of color. Friends. You know. And they just berated them. And talked about them like they were drug addicts and alcoholics. And in going through this, they pulled this thing away from us."[51]

Members of GLF and GAA such as Jim Fouratt, Arthur Bell, and Arthur Evans have described their experiences of gay life in the village before and after the Stonewall rebellion; it is clear that the Stonewall Inn was not a place they frequented. According to Fouratt, he was walking home from work and happened upon police activity in front of the Stonewall Inn, and because of his work in left politics, he wanted to support the struggle. He described the Stonewall Inn as a dive bar that was "really horrible. And drug den, chicken hawk heaven."[52] Bell and Evans, members of the GLF and founding members of the GAA, did not know of the Stonewall Inn and did not participate in the rebellion, but they were politicized by attending a GLF meeting in the wake of the rebellion in August 1969.[53] It is important to remember that the GAA was formed by members of the GLF who decided to split off from the GLF. As described by GAA founder Arthur Evans, GAA was formed to focus solely on issues of sexuality faced by gays and lesbians and was not committed to building a liberation front to combat the interlocking oppressions of racism, capitalism, homophobia, misogyny, and imperialism, as was GLF's commitment.[54] The issue of gender freedom and transgender liberation was outside the purview of the GAA; the archival footage of the 1973 Christopher Street Liberation Day rally, where Sylvia Rivera was heckled and booed, makes this tension painfully evident. Even though the Stonewall Inn was a bar frequented by trans women and reviled by members of the gay community, somehow in the historical process of commemorating the rebellion at the Stonewall Inn, trans women are erased from the scene. That archival erasure is violent. The archival violence happens with a rewriting of history that displaces the trans women who frequented the Stonewall Inn and replaces them in history with gay and lesbian people who get to centralize themselves at this epochal turning point of LGBTQ history and activism. Miss Major, Marsha P. Johnson, and Sylvia Rivera are not recognized as leaders of this movement. Archival violence compounds the physical violence that trans people withstood during the raids and arrests that led up to this moment of rebellion; the terror they experienced is occluded and devalued through the epistemological violence of archival occlusion and erasure.[55]

S.T.A.R.

One of the most valuable pieces of archival material that can name and counter this violent archival occlusion and epistemological erasure of trans women from LGBTQ history is the S.T.A.R. Manifesto. This document is part of the New

York Public Library's archive, which is the most comprehensive archival collection for S.T.A.R. held by an institution; the file has seventeen documents. The S.T.A.R. Manifesto is performative. It incites action. It captures the feeling of the post-Stonewall historical moment within the gay and lesbian activist community, which excluded trans women. The manifesto demands room for gender self-determination and is working to develop the language with which to name transgender embodiment and politics decades before the theoretical and academic infrastructure for trans studies and queer theory emerged. The S.T.A.R. Manifesto registers the need for resources for the trans community and offers a cogent and brave critique of capitalism and imperialism. The manifesto opens with a statement about the oppression that trans people have to contend with in daily life:

> The oppression against transvestites of either sex arises from sexist values and this oppression is manifested by heterosexuals and homosexuals of both sexes in the form of exploitation, ridicule, harassment, beatings, rapes, murders.
>
> Because of this oppression the majority of transvestites are forced into the streets we have framed [sic] a strong alliance with our gay sisters and brothers of the street. Who we are a part of and represent we are; a part of the revolutionaries armies fighting against the system.

While trans studies has moved away from the term *transvestite* in the intervening years, S.T.A.R. was clearly offering a critique of the violence of heteronormativity and homonormativity that insidiously emanated through exploitation, ridicule, and harassment, and which manifested abominably in the beatings, rapes, and murders of trans people in the 1960s and 1970s; this kind of violence is still being waged against trans people fifty years later.

S.T.A.R.'s nine-point plan begins with a prescient demand for the right to gender self-determination, a call that also includes the right to have identification that matches one's gender identity. The manifesto calls for the end of job discrimination for trans and gay street people and an end of police harassment that is paired with a demand for the release of all gay and trans people from jail, as well as all political prisoners. S.T.A.R.'s critique of exploitive systems of labor that leave trans people vulnerable to police harassment and arrest is met by a critique of the medical industrial complex; S.T.A.R. demands an end to the medical exploitation of trans people by doctors and psychologists. The manifesto calls for equal rights and free education, health care, food, clothing, transportation, and housing for trans people, gay street people, and all oppressed people. The S.T.A.R. Manifesto ends with the following point:

We want a revolutionary peoples' government, where transvestites, street people, women, homosexuals, blacks, puerto ricans, indians, and all oppressed people are free, and not fucked over by this government who treat us like the scum of the earth and kills us off like flies, one by one, and throws us into jail to rot. This government who spends millions of dollars to go to the moon, and lets the poor Americans starve to death.

Power to the People

S.T.A.R.

In this call to action, S.T.A.R. is responding to the interlocking oppressions of homophobia, transphobia, sexism, patriarchy, poverty, ablism, and racism that leave people vulnerable to state violence waged by the police and codified by the prison industrial complex and the medical industrial complex. Before queer theory was canonized, before intersectionality was coined, before the term *trans* was used, S.T.A.R. produced a manifesto that leveraged a critique of capitalism and imperialism while it envisioned a liberatory future for all oppressed people. S.T.A.R. was doing the queer coalitional work that Cathy J. Cohen would later theorize in her immensely important article "Punks, Bulldaggers, and Welfare Queens: The Radical Potential of Queer Politics?" (1997). In this article, Cohen is skeptical about the efficacy of "queer" except as a framework through which the radical potential of queer politics can be harnessed to enact transformative coalition building between differently marginalized groups. Cohen envisions "queer" as that which can activate "a politics where one's relation to power, and not some homogenized identity, is privileged in determining one's political comrades. I'm talking about a politics where the nonnormative and marginal position of punks, bulldaggers, and welfare queens, for example, is the basis for progressive transformative coalition work. Thus, if there is any truly radical potential to be found in the idea of queerness and the practice of queer politics, it would seem to be located in its ability to create a space of opposition to dominant norms, a space where transformational political work can begin."[56]

The S.T.A.R. Manifesto delineates Johnson and Rivera's investment in the radical potential of transformative political work. S.T.A.R. was theorizing and actualizing a transformative queer politics that recognized how all marginalized people were interconnected and was ready to move in solidarity to resist dominant power and end oppression for all people. With their community home, S.T.A.R. House, and in their visionary nine-point platform, Sylvia Rivera and Marsha P. Johnson were using their power to create the political landscape imagined by the GLF, and yet they had to contend with groups like the GAA who were only interested in rallying around the single issue of gay sexuality. The radical potential of queer transformative politics was envisioned in the S.T.A.R. Manifesto and put in practice by S.T.A.R.'s movement-building work. This manifesto offered tools for resisting domination, but it required the willingness to pool resources and engage in resistance activities that did not always yield results for every person's needs at the same time. It required sacrifice—something that Marsha and Sylvia offered willingly. Marsha and Sylvia were marching, sitting-in, and protesting for their gay brothers and sisters, yet when it was time for solidarity with trans women, the support was not returned. The speech that Sylvia had to fight to make at the 1973 Christopher Street Liberation Day rally, where she was met by a chorus of boos by lesbians and gay men in the crowd, is a most salient demonstration of the failure of gays and lesbians to participate in the coalitional world-making project that S.T.A.R. was in the process of actualizing.

Performativity of the Document: The S.T.A.R. Manifesto

The S.T.A.R. Manifesto is a rallying cry meant to forge solidarity across differently marginalized groups and enact coalitional politics that could save the lives and support the well-being of all oppressed people. I am interested in thinking about the performance of the document—what is lost, what has disappeared, what has been saved, what has come to pass. The world-making that S.T.A.R. envisioned, what was being activated in the manifesto and actualized with S.T.A.R. House, exemplifies the world-making drive of performance. The relationship between an archival document and performance is taken up by Rebecca Schneider, who contends with the incongruence between the archive, which is understood as that which remains of history, and performance, which is understood as that which disappears.[57] Schneider interrogates the western conception of knowledge production that places more value on the stability of the document, which in turn undergirds the conception of the total impermanence of performance. This archival process reveals loss and showcases what is missing while leading us to who has disappeared. Schneider argues: "The archive itself becomes a social *performance* of retroaction. The archive performs the institution of disappearance, with object remains as indices of disappearance and with performance as given to disappear."[58] Schneider is pointing to the way that the archive holds in place the document that turns us backward, that gestures toward what has gone and lays bare what remains.

The S.T.A.R. Manifesto holds in time Marsha P. Johnson and Sylvia Rivera's vision for the future as it engenders in us a social performance of retroaction. By turning back with Marsha P. Johnson and Sylvia Rivera through the S.T.A.R. Manifesto, we can tap into both the anger and the possibility that is at work in this document. Marsha and Sylvia are offering theories of complex gender dynamics that capture the urgency of the moment in a document that demonstrates the technology of the past, typewritten words from which the phantom smell of mimeographic ink wafts, and one that captures in tone, language, and imagination the tenor of street life and survival. The misspellings, the crosshatches, the fervor, and the platform of the manifesto itself all reach back in time through this document. The nine-point format is historically, ideologically, and formally linked to the Black Panther Party for Self-Defense's ten-point program.[59] The refusal to conform comes through in the exigency of the message, the clarity of the demands, and the disinterest in producing a perfect document. The S.T.A.R. Manifesto is a work of proto-trans theory, a documentation of gender self-determination that outlines trans concerns about the openly and defiantly hostile gay community; this document demonstrates that Marsha P. Johnson and Sylvia Rivera were actualizing trans theory before trans theory or queer theory existed. The S.T.A.R. Manifesto is a call to action and as such, this document performs—it visualizes a liberatory future and demands actions from the community that will make material that liberatory future in the present moment. The revolutionary moment of the 1970s is being performed in the crispness of the language and the audacity of the demands in this manifesto. Abolition is at work in this document, before the vision of prison abolition took flight. If the gay community at that time could have rallied with S.T.A.R., as opposed to dismissing the group and excluding it because members of the gay community could only see pathology and not brilliance in its presence, they would have been able to shrink the separation between marginalized groups and move closer to liberation for all. What I encounter when I turn back, through this manifesto, is an overwhelming sense of pride in S.T.A.R.'s vision and action as well as a profound sense of loss about what the movement could have been had S.T.A.R. been recognized as the vanguard that it was. The S.T.A.R. Manifesto envisions the transformative potential of radical queer politics just as it captures the loss of having had the chance to begin this work back in 1970. S.T.A.R. was and still is avant-garde.

The S.T.A.R. Manifesto, following Schneider, is the object remains from S.T.A.R.'s movement-building work. While the everyday movement-building actions of revolutionaries, Marsha P. Johnson and Sylvia Rivera, are given to disappear, the manifesto holds a vision of that work in place and the archive keeps this precious document fixed, locatable, and preserved. The social performance of retroaction carries with it the knowledge of the cost of the community failure to build a queer coalition with S.T.A.R. What remains alongside the revolutionary vision of a liberated people captured with this document is the knowledge of the loss of Sylvia, the loss of Marsha, and the short-lived S.T.A.R. House that could still be a home for queer and trans youth today.

While the S.T.A.R. Manifesto, as a performative document, enacts movement and emblazons in memory the pain felt for its authors and a cascade of forsaken possibilities, this document also brings forward the vision of Sylvia and Marsha and the promise of a future in which marginalized people, no matter their differing experiences of oppression, could find common cause, resist domination, and upend power structures meant to strip them of their rights, safety, education, health care, and home. This manifesto is a beautiful, heartbreaking document, something that remains of S.T.A.R., an archival object that viscerally carries forward those who are gone, that which no longer remains, and all that is still possible (see figures 3.6 and 3.7). While we haven't conquered capitalism, imperialism, or the prison industrial complex yet, some of S.T.A.R.'s demands have been actualized. We have trans theory, queer theory, access to trans medical care for many, not all. We recognize gestating parents—not just mothers—and we have gender self-determination on government IDs in some states. Prison abolition and a movement to defund the police have entered the national lexicon, and we have begun to destabilize the gender binary—made most explicit by the discussion of pronouns and the introduction of the singular "they" in institutional and familial spaces. We are living in a world envisioned by the avant-garde of S.T.A.R.

The Archive of Marsha P. Johnson

As this chapter has worked to explicate, the place of trans women in the gay liberation movement of the 1970s has been occluded and through that occlusion the record of Marsha P. Johnson's life as an activist has been overlooked, until recent years, as a vital part of LGBTQ history. Because of her work in gay liberation movements like GLF, GAA, and S.T.A.R., and because of her larger-than-life presence, Marsha P. Johnson has left an archival trace. The documentary films about her life, the photographs of her activism and stage performances, and the audio recordings and newspaper articles that feature her contribute to Marsha P. Johnson's archival presence. The documentary films that chronicle her life tend to mythologize her in their desire to memorialize her legacy, and in one case, the filmmaker capitalizes on the mystery surrounding her death.[60] In the first feature-length documentary film about Marsha, *Pay It No Mind: Marsha P. Johnson* (2012), community members and friends of Marsha offer their first-person testimonies, which are complemented by archival footage of Marsha P. Johnson, and together these elements illuminate her personality and demonstrate the impact that she had on the gay community in the 1970s, 1980s, and 1990s in New York City.⁶¹ Friends such as Randy Wicker, Rich Shupper, Sasha McCaffrey, James Gallagher, and Agosto Machado tell stories about Marsha, remembering that she would spend her last ten dollars on flowers and bedeck herself with a floral crown for the night. In Greenwich Village, she would dress in extravagant handmade gowns and adorn her hair with strings of Christmas lights and ask passersby, "Do you have a dollar for a dying drag queen?" She would sleep in movie theaters when she did not have any other place to go or rest under tables in the flower district surrounded by the fragrant zest of lilies. She was generous with the money she earned and with her joy, of which she seemed to have an abundance. Some of those who knew her thought of her as a saint; others deemed her the mayor of Christopher Street. She had a beautiful, attentive, and kind spirit and was even loving with those in the LGBTQ community who had nothing but disdain for her.

Pay It No Mind culls together a narrative of the Stonewall rebellion that substantiates the mythology of that night and demonstrates how Marsha's mythic role in it began to evolve. David Carter, author of *Stonewall*, declares authoritatively in the documentary film that two "very important figures in the Gay Activist Alliance," Morty Manford and Marty Robinson, reported that Marsha P. Johnson yelled "I got my civil rights" and then threw a shot glass into a mirror, which was the catalyst that kicked off the Stonewall riots. Carter, through a haughty grin, acknowledges that in GAA this became the legendary "shot glass that was heard around the world."⁶² This extraordinary characterization of Marsha is meant to humanize her by mythologizing her, a contradiction that while well-meaning has insidious consequences. In their memories of Marsha, her friends weave together stories that depict her as an outlandish, saintly, magical figure, but this kind of beatification ameliorates the impact that systemic gender, racial, and economic oppression had on her in everyday life. It is clear from the stories shared in *Pay It No Mind*, by friends and famous passersby, that Marsha was loved, and she certainly had charm, charisma, and a style all her own. Yet a tone that is carried across some of these testimonies has within it a kind of surprise that indifferent New Yorkers would embrace Marsha just as she was. This surprise, along with the deification of Marsha, does the work of making her an exceptional "street person" who deserves recognition. While it is undeniable that Marsha was an exceptional human rights activist, fashionista, and survivor of the New York City streets, there is a sense of awe that she could earn this kind of respect.

Agosto Machado very gently and lovingly describes Marsha as follows in *Pay It No Mind*: "Marsha's like a Bodhisattva. Her presence on Sheridan Square. On

STREET TRANSVESTITES ACTION REVOLUTIOARIES

The oppression against transvestite of either sex aries from sexist values and this oppression is manifested by hetrosexuals and homosexual of both sexes in form of exploitation, ridicule, harrassment, beatings, rapes, murders.

Because of this oppression the majority of transvestites are forced into the streets we have have framed a strong alliance with our gay sisters and brothers of the street. Who we are a part of and represent we are; a part of the revolutionaries armies fighting against the system.

1. We want the right to self-determination over the use of our bodies; the right to be gay, anytime, anyplace; the right to free physiological change and modification of sex on demand; the right to free dress and adornment.

2. The end to all job discrimination against transvestites of both sexes and gay street people because of attire.

3. The immediate end of all police harrassment and arrest of transvestites and gay street people, and the release of transvestites and gay street people from all prisons and all other political prisoners.

4. The end to all exploitive practices of doctors and psychiatrists who work in the field of transvestism.

FIGURES 3.6 AND 3.7 "S.T.A.R. Manifesto," 1970. Box 19, Folder IGIC Ephemera, STAR File, Manuscripts and Archives Division, New York Public Library.

5. Transvestites who live as members of the ppposite gender should be able to obtain identification of the opposite gender.

6. Transvestites and gay street people and all oppressed people should have free education, health care, clothing, food, transportation, and housing.

7. Transvestites and gay street people should be granted full and equal rights on alllevels of society, and full voice in the struggle for liberation of all oppressed people.

8. An end to exploitation and discrimination against transvestites within the homosexual world.

9. We want a revolutionary peoples' government, where transvestites, street people, women, homosexuals, blacks, puerto ricans, indians, and all oppressed people are free, and not fucked over by this government who treat us like the scum of the earth and kills us off like flied, one by one, and throws us into jail to rot. This government who spends millions of dollars to go to the moon, and lets the poor Americans strave to death.

                  POWER TO THE PEOPLE
                      S. T. A. R.

Christopher Street, or wherever she stopped and asked for spare change or chatted with people. It was a religious or holy experience. And all of us who did drag, or partial drag, always admired her."[63] Machado's memory of Marsha is glowing, but I am wary of the need to make her more than human in our memory of her and the subsequent archival documentation. I worry that the impulse to deify Marsha will get in the way of remembering her as a human being, an elder, an activist, a sex worker who struggled with being housed and with her mental health, who was a fierce advocate and a loving human being. The superhuman mythos about Marsha makes the real-world violence that she suffered less apparent because what also circulates within that mythos is the dehumanization and precarity with which trans women—pre-Stonewall, post-Stonewall, and in the new millennium—have to contend. These interviews also show that members of the gay community who were active during the Stonewall era have made strides in recognizing that trans women are important members of the queer community, but the notes of tolerance coupled with the mythologization of Marsha exposes a remaining difficulty in simply beholding and loving trans women in their humanity.

The presence of disdain wrapped in reverence for Marsha shows up in an interview that Eric Marcus conducted with gay activist and GAA member Randy Wicker, which was later broadcast on Marcus's podcast, *Making Gay History*.[64] Because Marsha was a close friend and roommate of Randy, her oral history was recorded in this interview, but she was not the archival figure Marcus was initially interested in interviewing. Marcus acknowledges that he set out to interview Randy alone but Randy insisted that Marsha be part of the interview. When they met at Randy's Hoboken apartment in 1989, Marsha was there. Marcus was then able to document Marsha P. Johnson's oral history about what happened at the Stonewall Inn on the infamous first night of the rebellion. This accidental interview exemplifies the historical occlusion of Marsha's role in gay liberation that this chapter is working to address, but through a fortunate coincidence her oral history was recorded and now exists in Marcus's archive. Marcus's short interview is precious in that it captures Marsha's memory of Stonewall, her voice, her cadence, and her relationship with Randy Wicker, with whom she lived during the last twelve years of her life. It is clear that Randy has grown to love Marsha, even though he admits that he was skeptical of her when they first met because she was a "transvestite" sex worker. Marsha was a Stonewall regular before the rebellion and in the interview with Marcus, she offers a little history of the Stonewall Inn: "At first it was just a gay men's bar and they didn't allow no women in. And then they started allowing women in. And then they let the drag queens in. I was one of the first drag queens to go to that place. . . . And then they had these drag queens working there. They never arrested anybody at the Stonewall. All they did was line us up and tell us to get out."[65]

In his interview in *Pay It No Mind*, Tommy Lanigan-Schmidt describes the clientele of the Stonewall Inn: "We were all runaways. Some were like fourteen years old. Some people had scalding water thrown on them by their parents. People that couldn't go back home no matter what. Couldn't go back to school no matter what. And that group of people was the catalyst in the riots. It was the street kids who had nothing to lose that were the force that got it going."

In the Marcus interview, Marsha offers details of her experience of the events of the night of the rebellion; it becomes clear that contrary to the legend, Marsha P. Johnson was not the "drag queen" who started the rebellion by throwing a shot glass into the bar room mirror and shouting "I got my civil rights" because she arrived after the conflict had already begun.[66] She describes the events of the night of the rebellion as follows:

> The way I winded up at Stonewall that night, I was having a party uptown and we were all out there and then Sylvia Rivera and them were over in the park having a cocktail. I was uptown and I didn't get downtown 'til about two o'clock. 'Cause when I got downtown the place was already on fire. It was a raid already. The riots had already started. And they said police went in there and set the place on fire. They said the police set it on fire. Because they originally wanted the Stonewall to close so they had several raids. The night before the Stonewall Riots started before they closed the bar we were all there and we all had to line up against the wall and they were all searching us. They searched every single body that came there because the place was supposed to be closed and they opened anyway. 'Cause every time the police came what they would do is they would take the money from the coat check room and take the money from the bar. So if they heard the police were coming they would take all the money and hide it up under the bar in these boxes, out of the register. And you know and sometimes they would hide it like under the floor or something. So when the police got in all they got were the bartender's tips.[67]

When asked by Randy Wicker, with whom she is being interviewed by Eric Marcus, if she was one of the people standing in the chorus line kicking up her heels at the police, Marsha laughed and said, "No. No. We were too busy turning over cars and screaming in the middle of the street. Because we were so upset because they closed that place."[68]

Carrying the Knowledge 133

The legendary tales of the Stonewall riots may have been created in the aftermath of the rebellion, but for Marsha her very real politicization began that night. The interview with Marsha in *Pay It No Mind*, recorded just days before she died, is a vital piece of archival film footage. Here we see and hear her in time and space offer pieces of her own story, which is a formative complement to the testimonies about her recorded after her death. She shares that in "1969 when the Stonewall Riots started, that's when I started my little riot. I have been in gay liberation ever since it first started in 1969. I was in the Stonewall Riots."[69]

She describes her early commitment to the movement in her work with Alternate U, before S.T.A.R. was founded.

> I was one of the first drag queens to try and help the drag queens and other people have food, at the Alternate U. Alternate U was one of the places that we first tried to help college queens open their drawers to gay liberation. When I started getting in the newspapers, on TVs at the gay pride parade, I was one of the queens who helped feed the queens that were hungry. And I started S.T.A.R. House. I didn't actually start the S.T.A.R. House, Sylvia Rivera started the S.T.A.R. House and I was just one of the queens that was behind her, like the Vice President of S.T.A.R.[70]

In his memory of S.T.A.R., Randy's dismissal of Marsha and Sylvia's revolutionary movement, and the shelter they provided for trans youth, is made quite evident.[71] He describes S.T.A.R. House as follows: "It was a bunch of flakey, fucked up transvestites living in a hovel and a slum somewhere calling themselves revolutionaries. That's what it was in my opinion. Now Marsha has a different idea."

Thankfully, Eric Marcus requests input about S.T.A.R. from Marsha, who describes the liberation group differently, lovingly.

> It was a group for transvestites, men and women and transvestites. . . . Street Transvestites Action Revolutionaries started out as a very good group. It was after Stonewall, they started, they started at GAA. Mama Jean DeVente, who used to be the marshal for all the parades. She was the one that talked Sylvia Rivera into leaving GAA, 'cause Sylvia Rivera who was the president of S.T.A.R. was a member of GAA, and started a group of her own. And so she started Street Transvestites Action Revolutionaries. And she asked me would I come be the Vice President of that organization.[72]

Even though Eric Marcus did not set out to record an interview with Marsha P. Johnson, he was lucky enough to happen upon this chance. His expertise as an interviewer shone through and he was able to capture a moment in time with Marsha that has become an invaluable contribution to her archive.

The care that emerges in this interview is quite distinct from the tenor of the Netflix documentary *The Death and Life of Marsha P. Johnson*. The scandal of this film is not only that the filmmakers use the true crime convention to drive the narrative of this documentary that is centered on Marsha's unsolved murder but that the archival labor of a Black trans woman, Tourmaline, was blatantly and despicably exploited in the process.[73] Tourmaline made a social media post about the filmmaker, David France, stealing her archival labor, and news stories about this theft were published in the *Los Angeles Times* and *Teen Vogue*, quoting her social media posts: "This week while I'm borrowing money to pay rent, david france is releasing his multimillion dollar netflix deal on marsha p johnson. i'm still lost in the music trying to #pay_it_no_mind and reeling on how this movie came to be and make so much $ off our lives and ideas. . . . This kind of extraction/excavation of Black life, disabled life, poor life, trans life is so old and so deeply connected to the violence Marsha had to deal with throughout her life."[74]

Tourmaline recounts the details of how her archival labor was stolen:

> David got inspired to make this film from a grant application video that @sashawortzel and I made and sent to Kalamazoo/Arcus Foundation social justice center while he was visiting. He told the people who worked there—I sh/*t you not—that he should be the one to do this film, got a grant from Sundance/Arcus using language and research about STAR, got Vimeo to remove my video of Sylvia's critical "y'all better quiet down" speech, ripped off decades of my archival research that I experienced so much violence to get, had his staff call Sasha up at work to get our contacts, then hired my and Sasha's ADVISOR to our Marsha film Kimberly Reed to be his producer.[75]

The archival violence that Tourmaline documented in her post, as perpetrated by the filmmakers of *The Death and Life of Marsha P. Johnson*, is a perverse yet unsurprising addition to the archival violence of devaluation and occlusion that was exacted upon S.T.A.R., Marsha, and Sylvia. Tourmaline spent the past decade conducting archival research and interviewing Marsha's and Sylvia's friends and peers. Tourmaline has been carrying the archive of Marsha P. Johnson forward. Like Alice Walker did with Zora Neale Hurston, Tourmaline has been committed to collecting the articles and photographs and interviews and archival footage of Marsha so that she may be recognized as a trans activist elder and so trans people who are her legacy know about the work that she did in her time. Since 2012, Tourmaline has made her archival recovery work of Marsha P. Johnson open to the public on her website, where she shares newspaper articles about Marsha, Sylvia, and S.T.A.R.[76] By collecting this archive and making it accessible to the community, by speaking about Marsha, Sylvia, and S.T.A.R. at community events and academic conferences, Tourmaline has been bringing forward this history and connecting the trans community to a historical legacy that has been at times mythologized but most often obfuscated. Tourmaline is intervening in the historicist subsumption of Marsha, Sylvia, and S.T.A.R. after scouring the landscape for buried archival treasure. *Happy Birthday, Marsha!* becomes a part of Marsha's archive as it draws from the documents, photographs, and recordings that chart the legacy of our trans elder Marsha P. Johnson. To then integrate that archival work, while contending with her own epistemic, archival, psychic violation by a member of the LGBTQ community, David France—which replicates the violence that Marsha and Sylvia were documenting during their lifetimes—compounds the affective labor that undergirds this film. Through all of this, Tourmaline and Wortzel were able to produce a short film and showcase it in a stunning, cinematic performative event. Because *Happy Birthday, Marsha!* incorporates archival film footage, includes live performances of monologues and poetry that are rooted in archival events, and represents historical figures on stage and in the film, the relationship between archival documentation and performance becomes inextricable. In what follows, I discuss the way that knowledge is transmitted through *Happy Birthday, Marsha!* in the theatrical performance, the film, and the dialectical relationship that emerges through their juncture.

Black Feminist Avant-Garde and Happy Birthday, Marsha!

Happy Birthday, Marsha! unearths an archive of Marsha P. Johnson's life and visualizes, through narrative reinterpretation, the moment that the Stonewall rebellion erupted. Because Marsha has an archival presence that, though dispersed, can be retrieved, what remains in the archive determines the narrative of Marsha's life. With *Happy Birthday, Marsha!*, Tourmaline and Wortzel are not stymied by the gaps in the archive or burdened by the fragmentation. They use experimental cinematic techniques that produce an affective experience and create a sense of what Marsha may have felt, not simply what she did, during the time of the Stonewall rebellion. Rather than render her a saint on earth or capitalize on the mystery of her death, *Happy Birthday, Marsha!* opens up a field of emotion that gives us time with Marsha. The filmmakers produce an otherworldly feeling with the slowed-down pace of the film that creates an out-of-time, nonlinear sensation. The ethereal nondiegetic soundscape and the kaleidoscoping mandala-like visual treatments sprinkled throughout the film are conduits that transport the viewers into another dimension. With their choice to juxtapose two Marsha P. Johnsons in the film, the filmmakers elicit a direct confrontation with archival preservation, a move that disrupts the solace of historical veracity promised by western epistemological standards. This doubling raises questions about the stability of an archive and offers an opening for creative intervention into the violent terrain of knowledge production.

Marsha was portrayed by Mya Taylor in the narrative portions of *Happy Birthday, Marsha!*, which butt up against archival film footage of Marsha P. Johnson, creating an epistemological friction within the world of the film. I want to return to the opening moments of the film, as it begins with this friction. The sound of a tape being placed into a video camera is heard. Then the first images of the film are revealed; this is a close-up of Marsha P. Johnson in a black-and-white video. She is wearing a headdress of baby's breath and glittering beads that frame her face (see figure 3.8 and 3.9). She looks up and moves closer to the camera and asks: "Oh, is the camera rolling?"

The film switches to a scene shot in sumptuous color. The title card tells us that it is New York City in 1969; a yellow cab and the sartorial design also cue us to this time and place. Mya Taylor, playing Marsha, exits the cab and saunters down the street and into the Stonewall Inn. The sound of Marsha P. Johnson's voice plays over the scene in the Stonewall Inn as Marsha, played by Mya, selects a song on the jukebox and heads to the bar: "In 1963 when I came to Forty-Second Street and I was a butch queen . . ." The film cuts to archival footage of Marsha P. Johnson in a wider shot wearing that bejeweled headdress and sitting on a small stool on a small stage next to a small table (see figure 3.10). Marsha P. Johnson continues, "And I didn't know nothing about wearing dresses or drags or anything." The film cuts back to Mya, playing Marsha, sitting on a bar stool, wearing a blonde Afro wig, a hot-pink sundress, and dramatic eye makeup (see figure 3.11). The camera pushes in toward Mya/Marsha sitting on the bar stool, gazing into the camera. We hear Marsha P. Johnson's voice: "I went there and honey these queens start calling me Marshall. And I was just . . . and they would just call me Marshall. And I was gagging. And then they start calling me Marsha."

The film cuts to a close-up of Marsha/Mya smiling as she gazes into the camera, as Marsha P. Johnson's voice is heard saying with delight: "And I liked it so much. [*Marsha giggles.*] I said that's who I'm gonna be. I'm gonna be Marsha."

FIGURES 3.8–3.11 Tourmaline, *Happy Birthday, Marsha!*, 2018 (film stills).

The film sinks back into the Stonewall Inn with Mya/Marsha wearing a longer blonde curly wig and a glorious floral tiara. She smiles unabashedly as she glides onto the stage.

The doubleness of the cinematic representation of Marsha refuses the archival promise of offering pathways to definitively answer historical queries, yet we hear Marsha's voice sharing the story of how she got her name. The joy in her voice when she says "and I liked it so much" communicates a feeling of belonging that is visceral and penetrative. The cinematic imbrication between narrative drama and archival footage produces a kind of visual and epistemological superimposition that agitates rather than solidifies the archival inquiry. The dreamy, nonlinear cinematic instigation that is *Happy Birthday, Marsha!* exudes layers of meaning with its screening inside the theatrical production staged at The Kitchen, in Chelsea, in 2018.

In her foundational performance studies article "The Ontology of Performance," Peggy Phelan insists that the filmed recording of a performance is no longer a performance.[77] The filmed performances within Tourmaline and Wortzel's short film may not be performances but rather the recording of a performance, yet in the event held at The Kitchen, the film takes on a performative role.[78] The archival footage of Marsha and the cinematic reconstructive representation of Marsha, through Mya Taylor's performance of her in the film, become a part of the theatrical performance by the inclusion of this work of cinema in it. The archival aspects of the theatrical production saturate the stage during *Happy Birthday, Marsha!* When Egyptt LaBeija graces the stage as the chanteuse that she played in the film, the space between the cinematic and the performative shrinks. When Eve Lindley, the actor who plays Sylvia Rivera in the film, appears on stage as Sylvia Rivera, the narrative film bleeds into the live performance; the cinematic becomes a performance. When Marsha's friend Jimmy Camicia, who appeared in the film, comes onto the stage as himself and delivers a poem about the joyful and generous person that Marsha was, the archive is performing.

By following Diana Taylor's notion of repertoire, which "allows for an alternative perspective on historical processes . . . and invites a remapping . . . this time by following traditions of embodied practice," I am able to examine the ways that an archive performs, cinematically and theatrically, in time and space.[79] Taylor's analysis recognizes the term *performance* as "a process, a praxis, an episteme, a mode of transmission, an accomplishment, and a means of intervening in the world, it far exceeds the possibilities of these other words offered in its place."[80]

When the archive is being performed on stage, the tension between that which vanishes and that which is fixed in time bubbles under the surface. The transmission of archival knowledge that happens in a live performance exceeds the document, yet what remains from the archival document or archival video footage in the performative space of the theater is carried with those who were in attendance. The performance vanishes, yes, as Phelan insists, but the performance remains, as Taylor shows us, through the transmission of knowledge. *Happy Birthday, Marsha!* is a performance of unearthing archival documentation; it is immersive and cinematic, musical and archival. This production participates in the expansion of those terms; traditional notions of the archive must expand with this theatrical, cinematic production. Schneider wrestles with Phelan's claim that performance "becomes itself through disappearance" and in turn pushes the notion of disappearance to account for what performance becomes.[81] Schneider writes about "performance as a medium in which disappearance negotiates, perhaps becomes, materiality."[82] If performance is a medium of becoming, and disappearance is not the only achievement of performance—if what remains could become something material—what would that material be? Taylor, I believe, would recognize the transmission of knowledge through performance as something made material. In the immersive, cinematic, theatrical performance of *Happy Birthday, Marsha!*, what becomes, what is made material, is the knowledge that is transmitted both affectively and narratively. The filmmakers' choice to bring Sylvia, Jimmy, and Miss Egyptt LaBeija out of the world of the film and into the proscenium to recite poetry about Marsha, to recount stories about life in the Village, and to perform songs on stage makes material Marsha's heartbreaking absence.

The condition of archival lack is mitigated with the film and the theatrical presentation of *Happy Birthday, Marsha!* The absence of the material body of Marsha P. Johnson in our community is made present through this performance. Through a refusal to produce the surrogate Marsha on stage, the satisfaction of being in proximity to at least one Marsha is foreclosed; the cinematic performs the presence of Marsha, and her absence is made salient in the theatrical production. This cinematic archival performance of Marsha—both Marshas—heightens, amplifies, and intensifies the great loss of her in life, and what emerges through this performance of documentation, surrogation, and absence is a visitation by Marsha P. Johnson.

Happy Birthday, Marsha! engenders a visitation through a cinematic presence that shapes a performance of absence made material by the juxtaposition of theatrical performance, filmic imagination, and archival video footage. By carrying forward the archival remains and transforming them through the cinematic landscape and then recomposing them within the theatrical space, *Happy Birthday, Marsha!* becomes itself and produces a visionary work of the Black feminist avant-garde. By resisting cinematic, archival, performative conventions, and by producing the weight of Marsha's absence without spectacle, without sanctification, Tourmaline and Wortzel conjure up a visitation that can only be felt in the space of the performance. The absences are made material and multiple and carried out by each person in attendance. That absence makes room to experience the loss of Marsha P. Johnson from our community, yet the film, poems, monologues, stage performances, and musical accompaniment also invite Marsha into the space. The knowledge that is transmitted produces an arena in which to commune with and celebrate Marsha as it saturates us with the gravity of our loss. What her presence and absence leave us with—gratitude, joy, heartbreak, kinship, a commitment to community and liberation—is what remains. A visitation with Marsha is what occurs through the archival remains and theatrical performance of *Happy Birthday, Marsha!* Our respect and adoration for an activist, an advocate, a style icon, a trans elder, a Street Transvestites Action Revolutionary who put the community, action, and loving one another before everything else; this is what we are left with when the screen rolls up, the music ends, the lights come on, and the applause rings out. The visit happened and the sensation, the knowing that a visitation with Marsha occurred, is that which remains from Tourmaline and Wortzel's archival, cinematic, theatrical performance of *Happy Birthday, Marsha!*

4

ECSTASY AND THE ARCHIVE

A Black Feminist Phenomenology of Freedom

What does it feel like to live as a Black woman in the afterlife of chattel slavery, to survive, to mourn, to try, to lose, to be made silent, to suffer, to love, to desire, to succeed, to create, to think, to raise children, to bear children, to know that in generations past they could have been sold at auction, to watch our loved ones leave the house, to bury them, to keep going? What does it feel like to live as a Black woman in the afterlife of slavery? This chapter contends with experience through the vector of Black womanhood by drawing together Black feminist texts that theorize, describe, examine, and historicize experiences of Black womanhood. I am engaging with the framework of phenomenology in this analysis, but I am less invested in exploring the theoretical roots of this concept in continental European philosophy and more drawn to the expansive ways that critical phenomenology examines dynamics of power that struc-

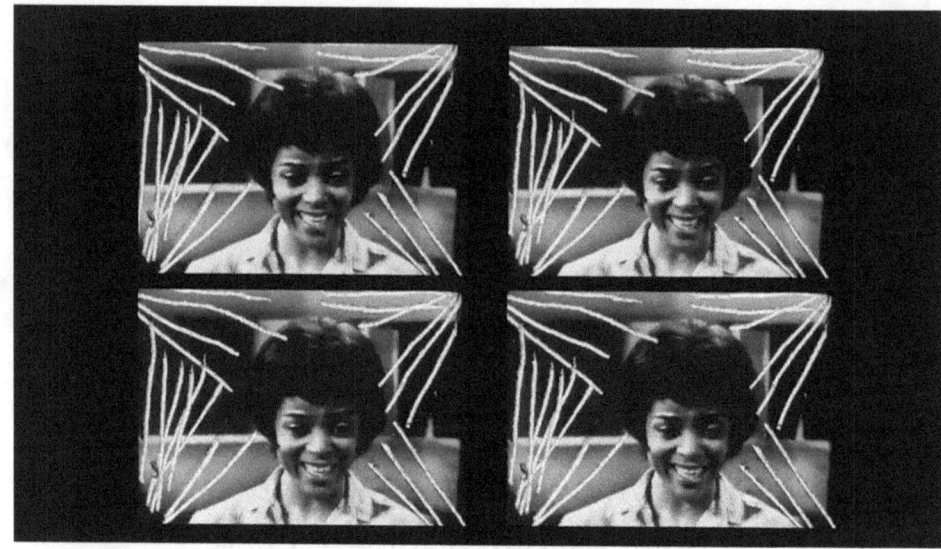

FIGURE 4.1 Ja'Tovia Gary, *An Ecstatic Experience*, 2015 (film still).

ture our experiences of oppression, specifically for Black women, no matter the pathway to, conscription into, or refusal of that category. I will, however, give a brief discussion of phenomenology and critical phenomenology to ground my concept of Black feminist phenomenology.

Phenomenology is a philosophical approach to the study of experience; Edmund Husserl's *Ideas Pertaining to a Pure Phenomenology and to a Phenomenological Philosophy* and later Maurice Merleau-Ponty's *Phenomenology of Perception* are foundational to this branch of philosophy.[1] In his body of work, Husserl developed a method, an intention, to see the world anew by letting go of preconceived notions, habits, and theories that would allow the world to appear as itself before us. In *50 Concepts for a Critical Phenomenology*—an edited volume in which a host of scholars attend to the meaning and relevance of phenomenology and make convincing arguments for the intervention of that body through the framework of critical phenomenology—Lisa Guenther offers a cogent and clear definition of phenomenology: "a philosophical practice of reflecting on the transcendental structures that make the lived experience of consciousness possible and meaningful."[2] In his discussion of Husserl's phenomenological method, Duane H. Davis writes: "Appearances in the phenomenological sense are not psychic constructions. Likewise, the account of appearances-as-they-are does not connote an *objective* account. Appearances in the phenomenological sense are not abstractions bereft of a world. The phenomenological method is not an attempt to purge subjective bias to reveal objective truth—instead it regards the pretense of traditional objectivity as a bias every bit as much as the caprice of subjectivity.... It is helpful to remember that phenomenology seeks to give accounts of appearances as *processes*—of the coming-to-appear."[3]

Within Husserl's effort to shed bias, experience the world anew, and throw into question subjectivity and objectivity, there exists a belief in purity, a sense that the essence of an experience can be achieved. This suggests that if one can successfully filter out biases, then a pure experience can be made salient and ultimately allow for more intentional relationality.[4] Critical phenomenology is an intervention into, or perhaps an application of, phenomenology on structures like race, class, and gender that impact our experiences of the world. Guenther writes: "As a philosophical practice, critical phenomenology suspends commonsense accounts of reality in order to map and describe the structures that make these accounts possible, to analyze the way they function, and to open up new possibilities for reimagining and reclaiming the commons. It is a way of pulling up traces of a history that is not quite or no longer there—that has been rubbed out or consigned to invisibility—but still shapes the emergence of meaning."[5]

Here, critical phenomenology becomes a method for entering an archive, of following the "traces of a history that is not quite or no longer there"; critical phenomenology is a mode of transforming an occluded experience into a legible one.[6] This turn toward a critical phenomenology offers a pathway to address a set of inquiries that excavate some constitutive experiences of Black womanhood. If, as editors Gail Weiss, Ann V. Murphy, and Gayle Salamon argue in their introduction to *50 Concepts for a Critical Phenomenology*, "a critical phenomenology draws attention to the multiple ways in which power moves through bodies and our lives," then I can draw on this method to discuss how power moves through the bodies and lives of Black women and examine how it shapes experiences of Black womanhood in the United States.[7] I can use a critical phenomenological framework to ask: How does an experience of Black womanhood—keeping in mind factors like class, colorism, embodiments of gender, sexuality, ability, region, and size that differently impact that experience—affect the movement through or existence in a place? How does the trace of historic violence that produced Black womanhood emerge through experiences of Black womanhood in the afterlife of slavery? How does an experience of Black womanhood charge time, place, memory, feelings, intimacy, social connection, and community ties? I sort through this set of inquiries about the experience of Black womanhood by bringing together theoretical and creative work by Black women that describe and conceptualize experiences of Black womanhood in the United States from the era of chattel slavery to the contemporary moment.

This approach, my engagement with critical phenomenology, is not a search for a pure experience or an attempt to name a fixed, cohesive, universal experience of Black womanhood but rather a gathering of a set of testimonies about what it feels like to be a Black woman, here, now, there, then. In this effort, I have assembled a collection of Black feminist theories that take the shape of poetry, song lyrics, documentary films, performances, personal essays, and critical scholarship that together produce something like a phenomenology of Black womanhood that has at its core the persistence of grappling with fear, developing strategies for survival, finding joy, forging community, and wresting freedom.

In the movement toward recognizing a Black feminist avant-garde, the previous chapters have explored the power, constraints, and temporality of archival violence and archives of violence as well as the aesthetics, history, and potential of avant-garde cinema; this final chapter will focus on the Black feminist imperatives and theories that undergird my concept of Black feminist avant-garde cinema. The conceptual framework that I offer here will carve out a pathway to analyze Ja'Tovia Gary's experimental short film *An Ecstatic Experience* (see figures 4.1–4.4). This work of Black feminist avant-garde cinema captures a feeling of struggle and produces the sensation of freedom by culling together and repurposing a disparate archive of Black resistance. Gary experiments with the play between celluloid and the cellular, between freedom and bondage, between oppression and resistance. The filmmaker raises the specter of racist science and racist cinema while connecting the machinations of anti-Black terror from chattel slavery to twenty-first-century Black resistance. In my analysis of *An Ecstatic Experience*, I consider the way that Gary collects an archive—through the cinematic—that visualizes experiences of Black women's resistance and sets loose a phenomenology of freedom.

Gathering Black Feminist Phenomenology

In "A Litany for Survival," Audre Lorde grapples with the twin conditions of fear and survival that impose upon experiences of Black womanhood. Fear and survival are conduits that channel the condition of being Black and a woman in the United States. In the second stanza of the poem, Lorde writes:

> For those of us
> who were imprinted with fear
> like a faint line in the center of our foreheads
> learning to be afraid with our mother's milk
> for by this weapon

this illusion of some safety to be found
the heavy-footed hoped to silence us
For all of us
this instant and this triumph
We were never meant to survive.[8]

As Lorde lays bare with this elegiac portrait, fear and survival are qualities of being Black and a woman in the United States—qualities that persist in the afterlife of slavery. Existing in a world that was not designed for our survival scalds and contorts blackness and womanhood into a mold that is distorted and yet remarkable. The condition of once being property is the absent presence that drags like a rudder on a skiff as it creases open water. When describing the torture of plantation life for the enslaved woman who could have been found strung up and bleeding at any moment in time, Hortense Spillers argues: "This materialized scene of unprotected female flesh—of female flesh 'ungendered'—offers a praxis and a theory, a text for living and for dying, and a method for reading both through their diverse mediations."[9]

Until Black feminist historians and theorists began conducting research on chattel slavery that focused on Black women, histories of chattel slavery universalized the experience and made the enslaved man the default figure.[10] In their scholarship, Black feminist theorists and historians acknowledged the ungendering of the "slave" and countered the stultifying abstractions of Black womanhood that emerged in the aftermath of abolition. In its attention to the racialized gender oppression that Black women struggled with during slavery and after abolition, Black feminist discourse contends with the historic and pervasive characterization of Black women as insensitive and negligent mothers, overbearing and castrating wives, lascivious and aggressive lovers, dutiful and vindictive domestic servants, and desexualized wet nurses for white children.

Angela Davis's "Reflections on the Black Woman's Role in the Community of Slaves" was published in 1971 while Davis was being held in prison. This essay was foundational in the scholarly turn that was being made at the time, which recognized the distinct impact that slavery had on women.[11] Davis explained that Black enslaved women did not have the patriarchal "protection" from the depravity of men that white women experienced: "In order to function as slave, the black woman had to be annulled as woman, that is, as woman in her historical stance of wardship under the entire male hierarchy. The sheer force of things rendered her equal to her man."[12]

With her discussion of the Black matriarch, Black women revolutionaries, no-wage laborers, and victims of vicious physical torture and rape in this essay,

Davis was bending the discourse of chattel slavery to recognize Black women's distinct positionality and the confining categorization that plagued Black women's expression of self. Deborah Gray White's intervention emerged in her field-defining text *Ar'n't I a Woman? Female Slaves in the Plantation South*, which assembles a history of the labor, struggles, and strategies for survival that Black enslaved women devised.[13] White expands the history of US chattel slavery that was predominantly universalized through the experiences of Black enslaved men by discussing in detail rape, concubinage, and the sexualized nature of the torture suffered by enslaved Black women at the hands of white enslavers.[14] Building on the foundation laid by Davis and White, whose scholarship made salient the gendered power dynamics that structured Black women's oppression during chattel slavery, Jennifer L. Morgan's *Laboring Women: Reproduction and Gender in New World Slavery* examines US and Caribbean colonial images of enslaved Black women that were used to justify the exploitation of enslaved women's reproductive bodies.

Morgan's research examines the ways that Black women's reproductivity solidified their difference as it unearths the ways that enslavers naturalized the violent extraction of enslaved Black women's reproductive capacity. US chattel slavery depended on an ideology that rationalized enslaving human beings and profiting from slave labor by conceiving of enslaved people as subhuman objects that needed the enslaver's protection and rule to be able to function in the world. The power that the slaveholding class maintained over the reproductive capacity of enslaved women granted them the authority to value, price, bargain over, buy, sell, and pass down their bodies through inheritance. Slave codes and legislation such as the 1662 Virginia code that states that a child's freedom or bondage is determined by the status of their mother supported the practice of enslavers raping enslaved women at will. The children of enslaved Black women would always be enslaved and therefore would not be entitled to a father's name, inheritance, or other benefits of blood.

Morgan uses historical archival documentation, slave records, bills of sale, wills, judgments, letters, and slave ship logs to locate enslaved Black women in the historical record and demonstrate how Black women's reproductive bodies were central to the slave trade. Domestic and field labor as well as reproductive labor were extracted from enslaved women; enslaved women of childbearing age were known as "increasers," which indicates how Black women's reproductivity was valued as potential property and real estate of enslavers and their progeny.[15] Morgan describes the insidiousness of "increase" for Black women and their children.

When planters looked to "increase," they crafted real and imagined legacies. In the absence of living slave children, their own children still inherited the promise of future wealth. Slaveowners whose prospects might have seemed somewhat bleak looked to black women's bodies in search of a promising future for their own progeny. With such demographic expectations also came an articulation of the longevity of the slaveowners' enterprises and a greater certainty of a future in and for the colony. Though clearly there was no guarantee, a planter could imagine that a handful of fertile African women might turn his modest holdings into a substantial legacy. Black women's bodies became vessels in which slaveowners manifested their hopes for the future; they were, in effect, conduits of stability and wealth to the white community.[16]

The contributions of Black women scholars and historians like Davis, White, and Morgan reveal a history hidden from view but one that is not unrecoverable. The knowledge that a significant factor in Black women's suffering during chattel slavery was systemic rape by white men exposes the history of sexually violent predatory behavior of white men who disowned yet possessed children born of this horrific violation. The willful overlooking and erasure from the record of the everyday occurrence of white men raping Black women for profit during chattel slavery at once sanitized the record of violence for white men as it stigmatized enslaved Black women as inherently wanton, a paradigm that in turn justified the systemic rape of Black women. This is an unresolved social violence, the kind that Avery Gordon theorizes in *Ghostly Matters: Haunting and the Sociological Imagination* and that I have described in previous chapters as the specter of miscegenation. The presence of this confounding and convoluted system of violence has permeated experiences of Black womanhood in the afterlife of chattel slavery. The spirit of resistance that is a direct response to this unresolved social violence comes through in Black feminist theory, poetry, and music.

In an interview that appears in the documentary film *A Litany for Survival: The Life and Work of Audre Lorde*, Audre Lorde discusses her experience of Black womanhood, in particular what it meant for her to be a Black feminist. This section of the film homes in on the urgency that Lorde felt around being a Black woman, a lesbian, and a mother, and the struggle that comes at this crossroad. The interviews in this segment are accompanied by an audio track of Nina Simone's "Mississippi Goddam."[17] The romping sound of the upbeat piano in this tune begins, then Simone's voice slowly becomes audible: "Hound dogs on my trail / school children sitting in jail / Black cat cross my path / I think every day is gonna be my last." Audre Lorde's son, Jonathan Rollins, describes the fight that he carried as a son raised by Lorde: "My mother raised my sister and I to fight for what we wanted, to fight for what we believed in, to fight for what we cared about. And she never ever ever let us get away with not fighting. We could lose, but we couldn't not fight."

Simone's voice picks up: "Don't tell me, I'll tell you / me and my people just about due / I've been there so I know / They keep saying 'Go slow.'" Then Lorde appears. She is sitting in a sunlit room wearing a short-sleeve, vibrant, yellow-and-white-striped button-up shirt. Red flowers rest in a vase next to her. This is a combination of color and energy that breathes life and fire into the camera's frame. Lorde explains with fervor: "Let me tell you first about what it was like being a Black woman poet in the sixties. From jump it meant being invisible. It meant being really invisible. It meant being doubly invisible as a Black feminist woman and it meant being triply invisible as a Black lesbian and a feminist."

The politics of visibility for Black women is laden with conscription into regimes of sexualization, labor, vulnerability, and desecration, which all produce an erasure of possibility that seriously impedes the ability of Black women to be recognized outside the purview cast by these obfuscating valences. The foundation of Black feminist history and theory thoroughly examines issues of hypervisibility, dissemblance, and abject characterization that dog experiences of Black womanhood. Though these concepts and arguments about the image and visibility of Black womanhood are so well known that they are now a rudimentary element of the discourse, I am including a discussion of these fundamental critiques here *because* of their pervasiveness; they are so present in the literature and understanding of Black womanhood that they are axiomatic and therefore germane to the phenomenology of Black womanhood.

The research and analysis of historian Darlene Clark Hine tracks the ubiquity of rape in the lives of Black women from chattel slavery through Reconstruction and describes the strategies that Black women used to survive the imminent threat in everyday life. Reconstruction-era Black women reformers developed a culture of dissemblance, which was a technique that drew upon Victorian moral codes—the logic of the time—to dismantle the construction of Black women as immoral and perpetually sexually available.[18] Black women crafted a culture of dissemblance to protect themselves from violence and to improve, to borrow Antonio Gramsci's term, common-sense understandings of Black womanhood as sexually promiscuous, inherently rapable, and truly immoral.[19] A politics of silence and a culture of secrecy developed among Black women around sexuality, alongside the culture of dissemblance, to counter the damaging stereotypes that deemed them overly sexual and wanton, constructions that were used to justify rape during slavery and well as after its abolition.[20]

In "Black (W)holes and the Geometry of Black Women's Sexuality," which I discussed in the introduction, Evelynn Hammonds argues that the strategy of using dissemblance, silence, and secrecy failed because it developed a seemingly open and earnest expression of morality, but this culture actually made Black women's sexuality invisible—the residual effects of which continue to circulate through Black women's sexuality and circumvent Black women's expressions of desire.[21] Hammonds accounts for three historical themes that conspire around Black women's sexuality. The first theme is that Black women are essentially sexual, invisible, and ultimately all that white womanhood should not be. The second is a theme of resistance to the construction of Black womanhood as a hypersexual void and one that recognizes the material effects that negative stereotypes engender. The third theme describes "the evolution of a 'culture of dissemblance' and a 'politics of silence' by Black women on the issue of their sexuality."[22] Hammonds recognizes that the culture of dissemblance and the politics of silence were devised to protect Black women from rape through staunch sexual morality and a negation of their own desire by disaggregating their sexuality from depravity. The consequence, Hammonds argues, has meant that "historically, black women have reacted to this repressive force of the hegemonic discourses on race and sex with silence, secrecy, and a partially self-chosen invisibility."[23] The impact of being persistently threatened with rape and using strategies of survival that involved silence and retreat from sexuality confounded the ability of Black women to experience their sexuality outside the paradigm of hypervisibility and dissemblance.

In *Black Feminist Thought: Knowledge, Consciousness, and the Politics of Empowerment*, Patricia Hill Collins addresses the issue of visibility and Black womanhood with her term *controlling images*, which describes the residue of categorization that saturates the meaning of Black womanhood.[24] The controlling images of the mammy, matriarch, welfare queen, and jezebel project the image of Black womanhood in such a profound way that Black women struggle to not be collapsed back into the confines of one or more of these epistemological and ontological traps.[25] Paradoxically, the overexposure of Black women as lascivious temptresses of moral turpitude subsumes and makes invisible the experiences of Black womanhood that are contrary to this limiting and damaging calculus of racialized gendered embodiment. The controlling images of Black womanhood obfuscate expressions that contravene the expectations of Black womanhood, which cleave to these ontological humiliations. The hypervisible invisibility of Black womanhood is a defining paradoxical quality of the experience.

Collins's description of the four controlling images of Black womanhood elucidates some of the defining features that impose upon the phenomenology of Black womanhood.

Nina Simone's opus *Four Women* wrestles with this pervasive and quartering categorization. In *Four Women*, Simone woefully describes the experiences of four women who were impacted by slavery, colorism, poverty, and exploitation, and who are struggling to survive in the immediate aftermath of the abolition of slavery. Aunt Sarah has Black skin and a back that is strong enough to take the pain again and again; Safronia is caught between two worlds because she is the daughter of a Black woman who was raped by a rich white man; Sweet Thing is beautiful and seductive and makes a living with her inviting hips; and the angry embittered Peaches is ready to kill because her parents were slaves. Simone's rapturous voice and incisive piano strikes capture the spirit of each incarnation of Black womanhood, ringing out the sorrow, the grief, the dislocation, the rage, and the power coursing through each melodic vignette. These four damning categories of Black womanhood haunt expressions of Black women's sexuality, desire, and ability to work, thrive, and move through the world without harm.

These four women linger in the opening lines of "Mama's Baby, Papa's Maybe," in which Hortense Spillers pulls on the thread of the tangle of pathology used to characterize Black women's roles in the so-called Negro problem.[26] She begins with an interrogation of names: "Let's face it. I am a marked woman, but not everybody knows my name. 'Peaches' and 'Brown Sugar,' 'Sapphire' and 'Earth Mother,' 'Aunty,' 'Granny,' God's 'Holy Fool,' a 'Miss Ebony First,' or 'Black Woman at the Podium': I describe a locus of confounded identities, a meeting ground of investments and privations in the national treasury of rhetorical wealth. My country needs me, and if I were not here, I would have to be invented."[27]

The locus of confounding identities that Spillers has delineated spans epochs, generations, and incarnations of Black womanhood—necessity is the connective tissue. No matter the names imposed from the outside, the need persists for Black women to occupy the place of racialized, sexualized subject—a subject who, from time to time, defies expectation and lends haphazard credence to the liberal democratic stranglehold that suffocates the reality of quotidian racial aggression, oppression, and torture by clinging to a belief in possibility, meritocracy, and equality for all. What is more pervasive than the promise of exceeding the confines of these categories with hard work is the routinized pathologization that Spillers identifies as the mechanism of the dominant group. This insidious pathology allows for a defraying of culpability through the naming, categorizing, and problematizing of the other, the Black woman, whose positionality is a necessity, a vital component in the process of producing the hierarchy of human value. Black womanhood provides the distance from white manhood that is needed to make plausible his routine achievement of "greatness," which is achieved in great part by simply not being her.

When discussing the impact and meaning of the Moynihan Report's analysis of "ethnicity" in its examination of the so-called Negro problem, Spillers explains: "Under its hegemony, the human body becomes a defenseless target for rape and veneration, and the body, in its material and abstract phase, a resource for metaphor."[28] The experience of being abstracted into a rapable, salable good that has the reproductive capacity to produce children who will be converted into more salable goods for an enslaver who will sell them away because they are being held as property, is a condition that haunts Black womanhood. The experience of slaughtering your children so that they do not have to experience life as salable, rapable, whippable goods is an ontological, epistemological, spiritual tether that spans generations.[29] The specter of chattel slavery binds the horrors of those years, horrors that defy logic, pervert the imagination, and corrupt any sense of dignity that an enslaved person might covet and any enslaver might imagine they still have.[30] In the afterlife of slavery, the hideous terror of slavery is bound to the skin, to the womb, to the bonds of intimacy that have a secret lever, a quick release that kicks in when you have to let go for good, through no fault of your own—it is just a part of the experience of blackness and womanhood that we are struggling to release in the afterlife of slavery.

In the acceptance speech that Audre Lorde gave after being named the state poet of New York for 1991–93, she asks:

> What does it mean that a Black, lesbian, feminist, warrior, poet, mother is named the state poet of New York? It means that we live in a world full of the most intense contradictions. And we must find ways to use the best we have, ourselves, our work, to bridge those contradictions to learn the lessons that those contradictions teach. And *that* is the work of the poet within each one of us, to envision what has not yet been, and to work with every fiber of who we are to make the reality pursuit of those visions irresistible.[31]

Lorde makes her delivery of the word *irresistible* sound sultry and sweet. By naming herself, by claiming names that feel like home to her, Lorde is countering the effect of the controlling images. She is also bringing our attention to the contradiction that the boldness of her naming engenders and reflects. To name herself produces a friction with the unspoken but always present names and categories, those quadrants of existence that subsume Black womanhood. She defies those phantom quarters that reek of death and rape and grief and shame with her self-description, yet those quarters and their stench hang in the rafters of the space.

Another Black feminist approach to renaming and reclaiming power appears in the Combahee River Collective's "Black Feminist Statement," in which they explicate a set of experiences of Black womanhood that undergird their politics and strategies for survival. Of their politics and their experiences, they insist: "The most general statement of our politics at the present time would be that we are actively committed to struggling against racial, sexual, heterosexual, and class oppression and see as our particular task the development of integrated analysis and practice based upon the fact that the major systems of oppression are interlocking. The synthesis of these oppressions creates the conditions of our lives. As Black women we see Black feminism as the logical political movement to combat the manifold and simultaneous oppressions that all women of color face."[32]

With a commitment to dismantling manifold and simultaneous oppressions, which create the condition of their lives, the Combahee River Collective recounts their difficulty in finding a liberation movement that would address the compounding oppressions that were impacting their lives. The desire to fight patriarchal structures of oppression aligned with some goals of the feminist movement of the 1960s and 1970s, but a commitment to fighting racism and class oppression and heterosexism was not central to a mainstream white feminist platform. Black lesbian feminists were in a position in which they had to choose which element of their lives to elide and which to put their movement-building efforts behind, and this was an unacceptable proposition. In their discussion of the genesis of Black feminism, the Combahee River Collective writes into the record that though Black women were involved in the feminist movements from their inception, the work of Black women activists has been overshadowed and obscured because of racism and elitism in those movements.[33] The statement then addresses the difficulty that Black women face as members of feminist and Black liberation groups: "Although we are feminists and lesbians, we feel solidarity with progressive Black men and do not advocate the fractionalization that white women who are separatists demand. Our situation as Black people necessitates that we have solidarity around the fact of race, which white women of course do not need to have with white men, unless it is their negative solidarity as racial oppressors. We struggle together with Black men against racism, while we also struggle with Black men about sexism."[34]

The Combahee River Collective's clarity of vision and explication of the impossible and inexcusable expectation that Black women pick and choose parts of themselves or parts of their families in order to fight for liberation is a signal, preeminent, and laudatory achievement. Though this explication was clear and concise, the refusal to recognize the manifold oppressions that Black women had to contend with in their everyday lives persisted in liberation movements, in the workplace, and in the court of law.

What emerges through reading for Black feminist phenomenology in Black feminist theory and history is the implicit and explicit expectation that Black women dissect themselves in order to align with a liberation movement. The desire to fight racism was met by Black liberation groups, but as the Combahee River Collective reports, an interest in fighting sexism and homophobia was not integral to this platform. The section of the statement titled "What We Believe" begins as follows:

> Above all else, our politics initially sprang from the shared belief that Black women are inherently valuable, that our liberation is a necessity not as an adjunct to somebody else's but because of our need as human persons for autonomy. This may seem so obvious as to sound simplistic, but it is apparent that no other ostensibly progressive movement has ever considered our specific oppression as a priority or worked seriously for the ending of that oppression. Merely naming the pejorative stereotypes attributed to Black women (e.g. mammy, matriarch, Sapphire, whore, bulldagger), let alone cataloguing the cruel, often murderous, treatment we receive, indicates how little value has been placed upon our lives during four centuries of bondage in the Western hemisphere. We realize that the only people who care enough about us to work consistently for our liberation is us. Our politics evolve from a healthy love for ourselves, our sisters, and our community which allows us to continue our struggle and work.[35]

Here, in the elucidation of their politics and description of their experiences of Black lesbian womanhood, those constricting categories appear once more; the pervasiveness of these overdetermining conscriptions is inescapable. Yet in this same passage, the Combahee River Collective offers an antidote to the specific oppression experienced by Black women. It is self-love that can bring these quarters and halves back together and replenish the rationed-out hope and soothe our deep soul disappointment: self-love.

Nearly a decade after the Black Feminist Statement was written, Kimberlé Crenshaw would coin the term *intersectionality*, which illustrates the absolutely preposterous expectation that Black women who experienced discrimination in the workplace on the basis of race and gender, as Black women, had to choose to align their complaints of workplace discrimination either with white women on the basis of sexism or with Black men on the basis of racism, but to file a workplace discrimination complaint on the basis of the compound oppression of racism and sexism was seen by the court as an overreach, a judicial double dip, if you will.[36] The explication of conditions of oppression, ideological beliefs, mobilizing strategies, consciousness-raising experiences, and struggles within liberation movements that exclude entirely or include with the expectation that Black women divide or quarter ourselves to be able to exist within the space makes the Combahee River Collective's "Black Feminist Statement" and Crenshaw's discourse-turning articles foundational in the archive of Black feminist experience.[37]

Out of this position, through this vector, comes a question that reflects a range of experiences within Black womanhood; a query that taps into the fundamental denial of a place within a socially produced category of gender that impacts and compounds the social production of blackness. The question "Ain't I a woman?" deepens the seminal, perennial query posed by W. E. B. Du Bois, who opens *The Souls of Black Folk* with this problematic:

> Between me and the other world there is ever an unasked question: unasked by some through feelings of delicacy; by others through the difficulty of rightly framing it. All, nevertheless, flutter round it. They approach me in a half-hesitant sort of way, eye me curiously or compassionately, and then, instead of saying directly, How does it feel to be a problem? they say, I know an excellent colored man in my town; or I fought at Mechanicsville; or, Do not these Southern outrages make your blood boil? At these I smile, or am interested, or reduce the boiling to a simmer, as the occasion may require. To the real question, How does it feel to be a problem? I answer seldom a word.[38]

The experience of being a problem, as Du Bois indicates, produces silence within a torrent of questions and provocations meant to demonstrate a sense of empathy between those of the other world and Du Bois. The experience of Black womanhood raises a different question out of a different set of relations than Du Bois is describing. Rather than being implicitly asked *How does it feel to be a problem?* and having seldom a word to speak, the question for Black women is posed by the one who is expected to be silent and dissemble: *Ain't I a woman?* The origin story of the perennial query of Black women has been mythologized, but the question remains potent nevertheless.

Though no audio recordings could have been made, a firsthand account of her speech—an epistolary retelling that Nell Irvin Painter convincingly contends had been edited and altered for effect by its writer, Francis Dana Gage—has circulated widely and has become the archival record of Sojourner Truth's speech.[39] As legend has it, at the Women's Rights Convention held on May 29, 1851, in Akron, Ohio, Sojourner Truth took the stage amidst much contention and gave her impassioned and moving performance. In the most cited portion of the speech, Truth declares:

> That man over there says that women need to be helped into carriages, and lifted over ditches, and to have the best place everywhere. Nobody ever helps me into carriages, or over mud-puddles, or gives me any best place. And ar'n't I a woman? Look at me! Look at my arm! I have plowed and planted and gathered into barns, and no man could head me— And ar'n't I a woman? I could work as much and eat as much as a man, (when I could get it) and bear the lash as well— And ar'n't I a woman? I have borne thirteen children, and seen most all sold off to slavery, and when I cried out with a mother's grief, none but Jesus heard! And ar'n't I a woman?[40]

Though it is clear that Sojourner Truth did not utter these exact words, and I wholeheartedly support and appreciate Painter's correction of the record, I am holding on to the question itself.[41] I am interested in how it names an experience of Black womanhood, an experience that resonates into twentieth-century Black feminist scholarship and historical research, so much so that two volumes bear the name: bell hooks's 1981 volume, *Ain't I a Woman: Black Women and Feminism*; and Deborah Gray White's *Ar'n't I a Woman? Female Slaves in the Plantation South*, published in 1985. This question is raised anew in the twenty-first century when Laverne Cox poses it in her lecture "Ain't I a Woman?"[42] Cox cites Sojourner Truth and bell hooks, and as she does, she deepens the meaning and breadth of this query. In this lecture, Cox shares her life experiences of becoming. She describes how being a Black trans woman has been impacted by the ways Black womanhood is devalued and the ways that some would want to exclude her from the category itself. Drawing on Judith Butler, Cox reminds us that gender is a process, and I would argue that blackness is a process as well. The processes that are gender and blackness—the process of being a Black woman—produce us. Cox expertly weaves together personal narrative and Black feminist and queer theory to convey the understanding that there is no end point, or final arrival to Black womanhood. There is no correct way to be a Black woman, and any attempt to engineer this is unnecessary, violent, exclusionary, and patriarchal.

The Black feminist agitation of feminism and the disheartening reason that intersectionality even needed to be interjected into the judicial process exemplify the stakes of the question. The underlying epistemology of *woman* binds the term to genitalia, reproductivity, heterosexuality, and whiteness, begging the question, do we need to be included in the category or does the category need to be dismantled, reconfigured, destroyed? This is certainly the process of our contemporary moment, disarticulating *woman* from *white* from *vagina* from *womb* from *nurture*. The question is a difficult one because what undergirds this question, at its core, is the patriarchal protection that is afforded white women but costs them autonomy. This patriarchal power ungenders Black women as it disavows trans women, punishes queer women, and refutes trans men. Black women have been brutalized in ways that white women will never ever experience, and the reason they will not ever experience this is because of their relationship to white men. What I think is being annunciated with the question "Ain't I a woman?" is a call to end harm for Black women, a call to recognize that Black women are not simply silent, violatable bodies, whose interlocking oppressions leave us perpetually vulnerable to poverty, violence, and murder. Womanhood, as a category designed for white, heteronormative, cis, non-trans women, is predicated on the exclusion of Black women, trans women, women of color, queer women, and all the overlapping experiences between these identificatory points. I am not making an argument for inclusion into this violent category or imagining that freedom can happen if all marginalized women are regarded as equal to white, heteronormative, cis women but rather insisting that the category of woman be recognized as the violent, limiting, prescriptive structure that it is, for all of us. Which raises the question, what utility does "woman" hold for those of us who are categorically excluded from it? While this is a vital query, one worth examining, the material reality of the violence of the category wages horrors through lived experiences of those concomitantly conscripted and denied full access to "woman." As imperfect as it is, "Ain't I a woman?" brings the experience, the conundrum, the bind of Black womanhood into focus.

Claudia Rankine's *Citizen: An American Lyric*, with its use of personal essays, cultural commentary, and photographs, brings the antebellum provocation attributed to Truth together with Du Bois's query and then pulls it through to the twentieth century and into the twenty-first. Through a series of vignettes, Rankine illustrates, with precision, nearly indescribable moments of quiet violations as well as unabashed racist vituperation that populate the positionality of Black womanhood. Rather than ask "Ain't I a woman?," Rankine exposes the experience of being a Black woman in heartbreaking detail. In *Citizen*, she recounts the experience of public and private encounters in which Black women are belittled, made abject, discounted, made monstrous, humiliated, and expected to participate in their own erasure with pleasure in the course of our everyday lives. She writes:

> When a woman you work with calls you by the name of another woman you work with, it is too much of a cliché not to laugh out loud with the friend beside you who says, oh no she didn't. Still, in the end, so what, who cares? She had a fifty-fifty chance of getting it right.
>
> Yes, and in your mail the apology note appears referring to "our mistake." Apparently your own invisibility is the real problem causing her confusion. This is how the apparatus she propels you into begins to multiply its meaning.
>
> What did you say?[43]

The refrain of invisibility resounds here, in this anecdote. This instance of Black women becoming invisible and indistinguishable from one another makes salient the insulting and insidious Black blurring of distinct human beingness as well as the disappointment that is covered by laughter at the erasure of any hope of friendship and camaraderie between the "woman," "you," and "the friend." This short sketch of casual racism, which contributes to the din of disquiet that amplifies and subsides but never ceases, does a great deal of work. There is a witness who understands because she experiences this too. The laughter is a response to the absurdity of the "mistake," a "mistake" that you both know will not be directly addressed because the caretaking work and the risk involved in addressing the one who made the "mistake" is not worth the satisfaction of making the correction. The satisfaction comes in the shared experience, in the ability to witness the insertion of the shard of violence into one woman, but it is a pain both women feel, and through laughter and "who cares" the shard dissolves. It is not removed; it is absorbed by both women, the witness and the violated. But when the "mistake" is not owned by the one who made it, when the one who is violated is expected to carry the load of being mistaken, the laughter dissipates. The din grows; the sorrow creeps in as the impossibility of recognition sinks in a little bit more.

Rankine is absolutely masterful in her ability to express, in a few words, or in a question posed, the experience of Black womanhood in the United States. She asserts: "To live through the days sometimes you moan like deer. Sometimes you sigh. The world says stop that. Another sigh. Another Stop that. Moaning elicits laughter, sighing upsets. Perhaps each sigh is drawn into existence to pull in, pull under, who knows; truth be told, you could no more control those sighs than that which brings the sighs about."[44]

Whether the pain becomes entertainment or the exasperation causes upset, the experience of being a Black women costs. The experience of sorrow, mourning, or exhaustion produces audible sighs that portend the cascade of spectacle, blurring, and disappointment that must be reconfigured into joy of living, gratitude, and laughter so that something like freedom can be experienced at some point in a day, week, month, year, or life.

This kind of life craft is at work in Alice Walker's *In Search of Our Mothers' Gardens*. She offers a stirring provocation by imagining our mothers and grandmothers as artists. She asks:

> What did it mean for a black woman to be an artist in our grandmother's time? In our great-grandmother's day? It is a question with an answer cruel enough to stop the blood.
>
> Did you have a genius of a great-great-grandmother who died under some ignorant and depraved white overseer's lash? Or was she required to bake biscuits for a lazy backwater tramp, when she cried out in her soul to paint watercolors of sunsets, or the rain falling on the green and peaceful pasturelands? Or was her body broken and forced to bear children (who were more often than not sold away from her)—eight, then, fifteen, twenty children—when her one joy was the thought of modeling heroic figures of rebellion, in stone or clay?[45]

Being crafty and resourceful was certainly the domain of our mothers and grandmothers, but to name them as artists feels foreign in a way that reveals the profound and devastating denial that our mothers and grandmothers suffered, that we inherited, that we are working to dislodge. The kind of resourcefulness needed to survive as an enslaved woman who had children to consider demanded that one's artistic capacity be channeled toward finding freedom, wresting it with some ingenuity. As Toni Morrison's *Beloved* illustrates with Margaret Garner's choice, a mother's love and creativity could be used to kill her children to spare them from the horrors of a life lived in bondage, as property to be bought, sold, beaten, maimed, raped, and made abject by all that they can see and touch but can never have and be.

Ellen Craft, a very light-skinned Black woman who was held in bondage in Macon, Georgia, famously wielded her creativity and knowledge of the slaveocracy to devise and execute a scheme to escape the hideous condition of slavery. She fashioned herself as a sickly slave owner and her husband performed his role as her property so they could escape by train to Canada.[46] They were able to escape chattel slavery using the dual features of white frailty and Black subjugation, modes of being expected by white supremacist public culture, which made their movements in public space not conspicuous at all. The disbelief in or the refusal to acknowledge Black intelligence, as it would undermine the logic of enslaving Black people, carved out the ideological space for Ellen and William Craft to move through the plantation South to a northern land mass in which they were recognized as human and able to live unencumbered by the threat of capture.

Analysis of Black women and the production of space contributes a vital dimension to this discussion of Black feminist phenomenology. Katherine McKittrick's *Demonic Grounds: Black Women and the Cartographies of Struggle* examines the production of space as it organizes metaphorical and material spaces, which privilege and protect white, heterosexual, Eurocentric, imperialist ideologies and positionalities.[47] To illustrate her contentions about Black women and the production of dominant space, McKittrick describes with painstaking detail the exact dimensions of the garret in which Linda Brent / Harriet Jacobs hid herself in order to escape. For seven years, Linda Brent lived in a nine-by-seven-by-three-foot space above her grandmother's house.[48] Brent was able to write her own narrative in her autobiography, *Incidents in the Life of a Slave Girl*, which gives a detailed account of the sexual violence she was subject to by both the husband and the wife who kept her as property.[49] Linda Brent used her mind, her creative faculties, and the resources at her disposal (her grandmother's house, in which she concealed herself, and the love of her grandmother, who provided her with sustenance), and in this suspended state somewhere between enslavement and freedom, Linda lived until she could escape that place. From that space, which was too small to sit up, let alone stand and walk, Linda could hear her children's laughter, hear those who held her in bondage confer about her whereabouts and plot search parties. By focusing on Black women's geographies, McKittrick destabilizes the naturalization of space that builds and maintains a hierarchy of white supremacy and Black estrangement from power. McKittrick explains her approach to the study of space:

> I am emphasizing here that racism and sexism are not simply bodily or identity based; racism and sexism are also spatial acts and illustrate black women's geographic experiences and knowledges as they are made possible through domination. Thus, black women's geographies push up against the seemingly natural spaces and places of subjugation, disclosing, sometimes radically, how geography is socially produced and therefore an available site through which various forms of blackness can be understood and asserted. I do not seek to devalue the ongoing unjustness of racism and sexism by privileging geography; rather I want to stress that if

practices of subjugation are also spatial acts, then the ways in which black women think, write, and negotiate their surroundings are intermingled with place-based critiques, or, respatializations.[50]

By attending to Black women's geographies, McKittrick offers a theory of Black women's experiences of place and subjugation. She asserts that "the category of black woman is intimately connected with past and present spatial organization and that black femininity and black women's humanness are bound up in an ongoing geographic struggle."[51] By considering the struggle of Black women a geographic one, McKittrick adds depth and breadth to the conceptualization of Black women's experiences that I am working to bring together here. A particular kind of confinement, a binding in space, a regime of place, is being defined with McKittrick's analysis of Black women's geography. Naming place as a source of unfreedom denaturalizes space itself. McKittrick's analysis of Black women's geography disrupts dominant ideological conceptions of place that produce place as something inevitable, that happens naturally, that would insist that place is not produced but just is.[52] By accepting place as incidental and innocuous, the subjugation of Black women through the production of space appears inevitable and fixed. The struggle to make obvious a spatial process that is produced to be covert and appear natural is a struggle that indexes the experience of Black womanhood. The naming of the spatial creates a problem for dominant power that exacts itself through the production of space; if the production of space is not made conspicuous, then it appears that everything is running smoothly, as it should, naturally, but lethally for Black women. Naming the issue directly means confronting a system of knowledge production that unfolds, as McKittrick so cogently demonstrates, in the production of the space of a nation that depends on Black women's location as subjugated, confined, invisible, and silenced.

In "The Transformation of Silence into Language and Action," Audre Lorde discusses the ways that silence is an expectation that Black women ingest and refuse at their own peril. In the following quote, Lorde is discussing her recent diagnosis with breast cancer, and in the wake of this news, the issue of silence was brought into sharp relief. She asks:

> What are the words you do not have yet? What do you need to say? What are the tyrannies you swallow day by day and attempt to make your own, until you sicken and die of them, still in silence? Perhaps for some of you here today, I am the face of one of your fears. Because I am woman, because I am Black, because I am lesbian, because I am myself—a Black woman warrior poet doing my work—come to ask you, are you doing yours?

And of course I am afraid, because the transformation of silence into language and action is an act of self-revelation, and that always seems fraught with danger. But my daughter, when I told her of our topic and my difficulty with it, said, "Tell them about how you're never really a whole person if you remain silent, because there's always that one little piece inside you that wants to be spoken out, and if you keep ignoring it, it gets madder and madder and hotter and hotter, and if you don't speak it out one day it will just up and punch you in the mouth from the inside."[53]

The act of speaking, of breaking silence, is an act that makes Black women vulnerable because speaking peels back the veneer of amiability that makes dominant power comfortable with our presence. There is no obfuscation of our difference; we are reminders of injustice, of historical violence, of the profit that dominant power has made off us, wealth that has been compounded and capitalized upon for centuries. The inequity is humiliating for those with a conscience who benefit from a system that exacts racial, hierarchical, economic, and judicial domination on Black women, their children, their relatives, their loves. Our speaking makes those who benefit from this system confront all that they are afforded and connect their largess to our struggle for survival; their freedom to speak and move is in contradistinction to our constraint of voice and mobility. This is dangerous for us; we are expected to apologize for their humiliation with our silence, with our smiles, with our words of comfort—those are the words that we are allowed to speak. This is the condition that Lorde outlines in this essay and this is why she reminds us, alerts us, implores us to remember, "My silences had not protected me. Your silence will not protect you."[54]

What I have just outlined is one possible pathway through Black feminist phenomenology that demonstrates, describes, outlines, and defines experiences of Black womanhood from chattel slavery to the new millennium. Once we could no longer be used as vessels of increase, when our profit-making corporeality ceased to benefit dominant power, the realization that we were never meant to survive becomes clear. After the crisis of the abolition of slavery was ameliorated with a system reconfigured to profit from caging our children and nephews and nieces and siblings and uncles and aunts and cousins and us, our usefulness to the system of domination was restored. The names that categorize us, confine us, silence us, and locate us in a time and place bind us to the limits of vicious, deadly imaginations. This perversion of imagination is even more maddening given that imagination and artistry and creativity are historically and categorically denied Black women, except as entertainers who fit a very particular performative style and sound. When creative exuberance is recognized outside this arena by the dominant power, the anomalousness with which it is received is insidious, insulting, and a betrayal of dignity: being a problem; being a surprise; being a token; being quartered and halved; being made immobile; being able to escape; being made an exception; being palatable; being a threat; smiling to comfort the aggressor; mastering the practice of tongue biting; word swallowing; scream quelling and tear holding, all while inventing pockets of safety for friends and loved ones to luxuriate in; creating sumptuousness out of scraps; defying expectations and rebuffing the insulting implications set by predetermined expectations; living despite the fact that we were not meant to survive, not love and grow and breathe, not us, not our families—this is what Black feminist phenomenology shows us. There is no search for an essence of Black womanhood in this query, no inherent qualities to hypothesize and prove, but rather my mobilization of Black feminist phenomenology offers a space, a clearinghouse of conditions shared by Black women in the United States of which they have written, spoken, performed, and sung.

Black Feminist Phenomenology of Freedom

What becomes clear by following a critical phenomenological line of inquiry, what emerges by studying the structures of power that impact the experiences of Black womanhood in the United States, is the role that freedom plays. Black feminist phenomenology offers a way to contend with freedom, with the desire, need, and practice of wresting freedom out of the kinds of conditions that I just outlined using Black feminist scholarship, prose, documentary film, song lyrics, slave narratives, and poetry. Black feminist poet and theorist June Jordan expertly and painstakingly explores issues of liberation that impact conditions of Black womanhood throughout her body of work. She opens her essay "Freedom Time" as follows:

> A MILLION YEARS AGO, Janis Joplin was singing, "Freedom's just another word for nothing left to lose." I found that puzzling, back then. Or, "white."
>
> To my mind, freedom was an obvious good. It meant looking at an apartment and, if you liked it, being able to put down a deposit and sign a lease. It meant looking for a job and, if you found something for which you qualified—on the basis of education and/or experience—being able to take that position. Freedom had to do with getting into college if your grades were good enough. Freedom meant you could register to vote and live to talk about it.[55]

Charting a critical phenomenology of freedom through a Black feminist framework is quite practical, not necessarily lofty or utopic, at least not something that is outside the realm of quotidian experiences that people, who are not Black women, experience on a daily basis. Freedom means to be able to live, to have choices about school and study, have a home that you like and a career that brings you joy, to participate in politics, to vote, and to "live to talk about it." The lyrics to Beyoncé's "Freedom" capture the feeling of wanting freedom, in this moment in time, in this place when some of those freedoms are granted and some of them are being stripped away. The chorus rings out:

Freedom! Freedom! I can't move
Freedom, cut me loose!
Freedom! Freedom! Where are you?
'Cause I need freedom too!
I break chains all by myself
Won't let my freedom rot in hell
Hey! I'ma keep running
'Cause a winner don't quit on themselves

This cry, this demand for freedom, even as it circulates in mainstream popular culture, is insurgent. It makes salient the reality of contemporary unfreedom while insisting that we are entitled to freedom, that we have a right to freedom, that we will take it, because it will certainly not be given. This bombastic and inviting insistence to snatch freedom out of unfreedom brings to mind Toni Morrison's titular character in *Sula*. In "Unspeakable Things Unspoken," Morrison offers a description of Sula: "I always thought of Sula as quintessentially black, metaphysically black, if you will, which is not melanin and certainly not unquestioning fidelity to the tribe. She is New World Black and New World woman extracting choice from choicelessness, responding inventively to found things. Improvisational. Daring, disruptive, imaginative, modern, out-of-the-house, outlawed, unpolicing, uncontained and uncontainable. And dangerously female."[56] This I read as freedom. This adds to the freedom that Jordan describes; it is quotidian and it has to do with a sense of self that is quickly evacuated from Black girls and is incredibly difficult to cultivate and sustain for Black women. Sula is remarkable; she never rushes, she is never self-conscious, she loves when and who and where she wants. She is beholden to no one. She is free.

In an interview with Audre Lorde, during one of her last days on earth, she looks into the camera and speaks about the feeling when freedom enters. With a scratchy voice that quivers as she speaks, Lorde describes the sensation of freedom and the power that that brings: "When you open and read something that I wrote, the power that you feel from it doesn't come from me. That's a power that you own. The function of the words is to [*snaps fingers*] tick you in, to oh, hey, I can feel like that. And then to go and do the things that make you feel like that more."[57]

She is encouraging us to wrest freedom out of what we have now—to take it; it is ours, she reminds us. Her words, she insists, might open us up to the feeling, and we might want more of that feeling. Good! Her words have done that part of the work, but that freedom, that is something we have already—she is just waking us up to it. Lorde is our guide, a conduit or beacon; her words light the way to our own personal, collective, and dynamic experience of freedom.

An Ecstatic Experience

The Black feminist phenomenological framework that I've brought together offers a theoretical foundation to support my discussion of Ja'Tovia Gary's *An Ecstatic Experience*. Through her use of archival footage of rural Black worship, Ruby Dee's monologue from the 1965 Public Broadcasting Service (PBS) episode "Slavery," an excerpt from Gil Noble's series *Like It Is*, in which he interviews Assata Shakur about her escape from prison, and digital video footage of twenty-first-century Black resistance to state violence, Gary produces a film that captures the sensation of Black resistance and the ecstatic release that wresting freedom brings. Though Gary's film is composed entirely of archival footage, her vision comes together through the juxtaposition of scenes and the experimental visual treatment she adds to the frames, both of which are amplified by a distorted and haunting soundscape that incorporates Alice Coltrane's fourth studio album, *Journey in Satchidananda*.[58]

The film opens with black-and-white footage of a big white house that sits back away from the road, alone, on top of a grassy hill. The sound of a tinny bass guitar is met by a flourish of harp strings, and together they stir up the silence. This is Sunday morning in a rural community. Black women in Sunday dresses, hats, and jewelry and Black men donning suits and ties talk with one another as they move about a plot of grass where the cars are parked. The fashion and the style of automobiles indicate that this footage is from the mid-twentieth century. A white cross stands atop the gable of a modest church that has hand-painted letters on it. The vertical plank reads "Jesus He Is Not Dead" and the horizontal plank reads "He Is Alive Again." A woman with large, round white earrings and a white hat, jacket, and gloves moves purposefully across the frame. Strips of pinkish-yellow translucent material fill the frame and dance back and forth. The sound of the bass intensifies. The deficiencies in celluloid's ability to capture the image of blackness are pronounced in this footage. The contours of the children's faces as they doze off on the church benches are muted and blurred. Another selection of images enters the frame; glassy blue material with small black specks speeds across the frame. The scene of a preacher at the pulpit, sweating, exalting, is met by shots of those pinkish-yellow translucent strips, and then scenes of congregants in the pews holding babies, sweating, fanning themselves, praying, and rocking side to side fill the frame. The screen breaks in half, then in quarters. The minister arches back with his hands in his pockets in emphatic proclamation. The image of the minister stutters and a saxophone peal adds a mournful glint to the bass line. The footage of the minister and what appears to be frenetically moving turquoise and fuchsia microbial matter and microscopic cellular processes bounce into quadrants and then alternately fill the screen (see figure 4.2). Soft drums and symbols join the bass and the saxophone. Black-and-white footage of a young Ruby Dee standing on a soundstage flickers into the frame. The silky ethereal jazz tune builds to a climax and then subsides. The images of Ruby Dee are juxtaposed with the minister at the pulpit and sheets of red plasmatic matter with octagonal black flecks of differing sizes gliding through it.

Audio crackling breaks the silence. A close-up of Ruby Dee blinks into the frame. Dancing chalklike white slashes create a grid that encircles her face. As Ruby Dee delivers her monologue, white lines move into different configurations, sometimes forming scribbles on her face, or into the shape of lasers shooting out of her eyes, or moving into the outline of a box or triangles or smooth concentric waves around her head (see figure 4.3). Dee tearfully shares the compelling and tragic story of an enslaved daughter who recalls a terrifying moment on the plantation. This daughter remembers the way her mother would pray to the Lord that she and her twelve children would one day be able to get off the plantation and out of slavery. On one afternoon, her mother was plowing in the field and then all of a sudden, she stopped moving and started shouting out loudly. The overseer, Master Jim, saw this, came out immediately, and threatened to whip her if she did not get back to work. The threat of a whipping did not make her work. Rather than pick up the plow, a smile slowly grew across her face. She declared with calm: "The Lord has shown me the way. I ain't gon' grieve no more. No matter how you all treat me and my children. The Lord has shown me the way. And some day, we ain't never gonna be slaves, no more." With this response, the overseer started slashing her mother's back with the bullwhip. Her mother was silent. When it was over, she pulled herself up and went back to the field. She was singing and shouting, "I'm free, I'm free, I'm

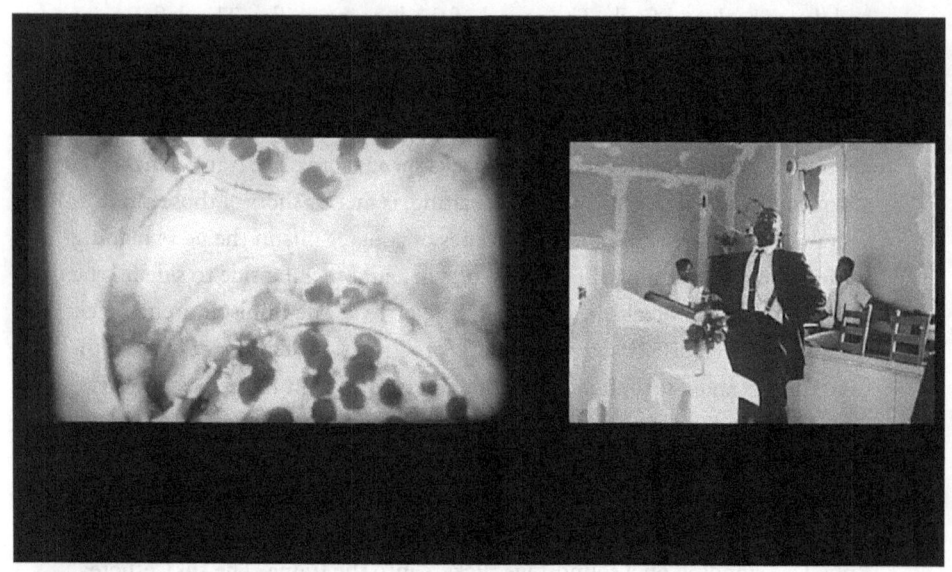

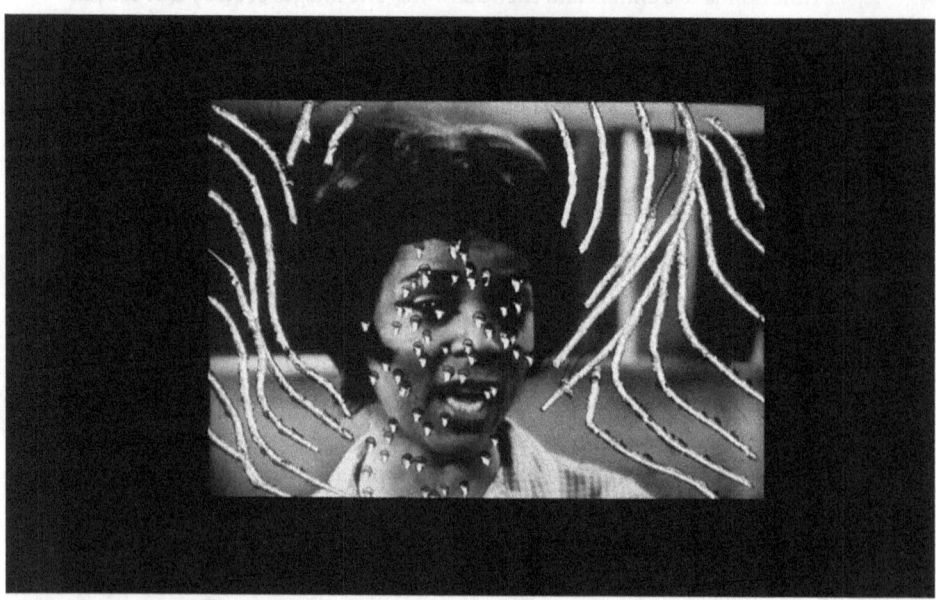

FIGURES 4.2. AND 4.3 Ja'Tovia Gary, *An Ecstatic Experience*, 2015 (film stills).

free, I'm free." With each utterance of "I'm free," the image of Ruby Dee's tear-filled face splits and duplicates, moving into each quadrant of the screen. The camera pulls back into a wide shot of the stage, revealing an ensemble of actors flanking her on all sides, facing her with empathy and grief. The screen goes black and sound drops out.

Then a close-up of Assata Shakur sitting outside at sunset appears on the screen. She looks toward the interviewer, who is positioned outside the frame. She stares at him intently and says frankly with a smile, "I decided." The interviewer replies, "You decided?" She smiles and continues, "It was time." The interviewer repeats, "It was time?" Then he adds, "To?" The smile snaps off Assata Shakur's face and she declares, "To escape. To try to escape." Ruby Dee's face delivering the monologue with chalky striations wiggling around her head flashes in the frame. Then Assata's face reappears. She is looking and remembering, it seems, and continues: "And that's what I did. It was a clean escape. No one was hurt. I planned it as well as I could plan it. And that's all I got to say about it." She blinks repeatedly, holding the gravity of what she just said. The interviewer is silent. Quiet enters the space. The scene of Ruby Dee and the ensemble of actors on the soundstage fills the screen again. A woman, with a somber voice, begins singing the "Battle Hymn of the Republic": "Mine eyes have seen the glory of the coming of the Lord." Static infiltrates the sound of her voice that stretches and distorts the audio track; purple splotches spread over the black-and-white scene of actors with heads bowed (see figure 4.4). It appears as if the celluloid is burning or decaying.

This scene of Ruby Dee in *Slavery* begins to give way to twenty-first-century digital video footage of rows and rows of police marching forward in riot gear and some on horseback (see figure 4.5). The "Battle Hymn of the Republic" continues to play. Quick shots of the decaying image of the ensemble with Ruby Dee on stage are interspersed with the police marching forward. "He is trampling out the vintage where the grapes of wrath are stored." A flash of the ensemble swelling into harmony appears on screen. "He hath loosed the fateful lightning of His terrible swift sword." Everyone in the ensemble has their heads raised as they sing. The sound begins to twist as digital footage of two cars on fire in the middle of the street enters the frame (see figure 4.6). The footage of Black resistance is spliced between the decomposing celluloid of the ensemble singing on stage. "His truth is marching on. Glory! Glory Hallelujah!" Their voices swell and the sonic atmosphere crackles as the digital video footage shows someone throwing a trash can at the onslaught of police in riot gear marching toward protesters. "Glory! Glory Hallelujah!" Someone breaks a car window with a traffic cone. "Glory! Glory Hallelujah!" A car is engulfed in

FIGURES 4.4–4.6 Ja'Tovia Gary, *An Ecstatic Experience*, 2015 (film stills).

flames in the middle of the street. "Glory! Glory Hallelujah!" People jump on top of a car. "Glory! Glory Hallelujah! His truth is marching on." The black-and-white footage shows members of the ensemble leave the stage one by one. Someone throws a trash can into the back window of a police car. The remaining members of the ensemble hum the tune while they stand behind Ruby Dee, who sits on the stage, wiping tears from her eyes. She slowly stands and begins to move toward the camera. A smile cracks through the tears and she is about to take a step forward, but before her foot touches the ground and before her mouth can reach the full extent of a smile, the scene cuts to a black frame that interrupts the motion and the resolution. The film ends.

An Ecstatic Experience is a work of Black feminist avant-garde cinema that offers a provocation about Black experiences of freedom and produces what I am calling a Black feminist phenomenology of freedom. By opening this film with silent, black-and-white footage of mid-twentieth-century Black worship, Gary raises questions about the relationship between Black religious practices and the experience of ecstasy. The visual cues indicate that this is Sunday morning in a southern rural community during either the throes of jim crow–segregation or the years of actively fighting to dismantle this system and install civil rights for Black citizens. This footage is a visualization of what Dr. Martin Luther

King Jr. called the most segregated hour. In a 1960 interview on *Meet the Press*, Dr. King proclaims: "I think it is one of the tragedies of our nation, one of the shameful tragedies that eleven o'clock on Sunday morning is one of the most segregated hours, if not the most segregated hours in Christian America."⁵⁹

The centrality of the Black church in the civil rights movement has long been recognized through the organizing work of Dr. King, the Southern Christian Leadership Conference (SCLC), and the work of activists like Ella Baker. Black churches provided the space, the people, and the enthusiasm with which to meet, organize, and mobilize what became the civil rights movement.⁶⁰ While Black churches afforded the civil rights movement the mobilization through which to foment and catalyze change, there is credence in the critique that religious dogma has the effect of diffusing the fervor for social and political action. While Black churches are sites of resistance, religious doctrine has also been used to dominate and mislead the oppressed into accepting inequality now, in exchange for a place in the promised land later. This is perhaps why Karl Marx famously declared, "Religion is the sigh of the oppressed creature, the heart of a heartless world, and the soul of soulless conditions. It is the opium of the people."[61] Through her avant-garde approach to editing and her use of digital etching on celluloid, Gary is leveraging a critique and an agitation of the ways that ecstasy, religion, domination, and Black resistance commingle. Gary brings together images of religiosity that could quell or excite political action, with images of discord and the defiant concerted effort needed in the dynamic quest to wrangle freedom out of abjection.

By entering her cinematic excavation of an ecstatic experience with scenes in and around a Black church on Sunday morning at a time when the struggle for civil rights was underway, or soon to be, Gary is drawing our attention to the role of religion and the Black church in freedom struggles. The film stages a visual catechism that poses an urgent question: should freedom be reserved as a reward in the afterlife for those who are obedient in this one, or is freedom something that has to be snatched back in the here and now? The ecstatic experiences that surface in this short Black feminist avant-garde film bring images of ecclesiastical devotion, in contact with a corridor of bright-pink pigment and abstracted images of cellular processes, which are interspersed with the recitation of a slave narrative that rests next to the testimony of a successful twentieth-century escape and ends with moments of riotous twenty-first-century defiance, civil disobedience, and protest. Together these images of ecstatic experiences produce a sensation of release that is laden with imminent danger, with the threat of violence, with the perversion of abject domination, with a choice between now or never.

Gary's visualization of translucent material that appears to be strips of overexposed celluloid film stock and microscopic cellular matter speeding about the frame brings together two issues that permeate experiences of modern Black life—visual representation and racist science. Gary's use of raw celluloid juxtaposed with narratives of bondage, freedom, and escape in *An Ecstatic Experience* insists that a connection be made between cinematic possibilities and realities of Black freedom struggles. Histories of Black film and television make clear that these modes of entertainment have been fundamental in producing and reinforcing categorical definitions of blackness that limit freedom for Black people.[62] As Marlon Riggs outlined so beautifully in his documentary film *Ethnic*

Notions, US popular culture emerged through blackface minstrelsy and continues to be the stage on which the meaning of blackness is produced, contested, and struggled over.[63] From mammy figures to degenerate mother characters to castrating and overbearing wives to hypersexualized abstractions, representations of Black womanhood still operate within the realm of those four categories, those four women, those vicious quadrants that impose upon the meaning of Black womanhood.[64] Though more complicated narratives of Black womanhood have emerged in contemporary popular culture, with the advent of more Black women directors and producers at work in the field, the meaning of Black womanhood in popular culture still seems to be magnetically pulled back into the orbit of the pathological.[65] Black women are seen first through familiar and routinized tropes that spill out of the legacy of slavery, the experience of being chattel, of being property. The twin powers of visual representation and racist science that served to reinforce the meaning of blackness as degenerate rub up against one another in Gary's film. The images of ambulatory cellular processes interact with scenes of Black devotion and through their proximity bring to mind the ontological experience of a Black woman whose body was mined for its cells, cells that have now become omnipresent in cellular biological research.

The case of Henrietta Lacks has been expertly discussed by scholars who are committed to examining the medical achievements and ethical violations in which Lacks's life and death are steeped.[66] In "Cells, Genes, and Stories: HeLa's Journey from Labs to Literature," Priscilla Wald tells the story of how Lacks's cancer cells, the cells that caused her death, gave researchers the necessary cellular material to make strides in cell biology that had been previously impossible. Lacks died in a segregated ward of the Johns Hopkins Medical Center in 1951 from aggressive cervical cancer.[67] Lacks did not consent to having her cells taken from her body and used for scientific discovery. Neither Lacks nor her family were informed that her cells, named HeLa, were used to develop an "immortal" cell line, the first of its kind.[68] The provenance of the HeLa cells was kept secret from the family until a member of the Lacks family happened to have a discussion in 1975 with a medical researcher who was conducting research using the HeLa cells. Though medical professionals and scientists have profited from the HeLa cells, the Lacks family did not receive remuneration for the use of their relative's biological material. The HeLa cells have been instrumental, vital, to cell biology, and the treatment of Henrietta Lacks, and her family members who also unwittingly contributed their cellular material to this biological project, is indicative of the racist science that devalues and exploits Black life. Gary's use of colorful images of cells and abstractions of shapes that mimic the cellular process raises the specter of racist science as it has affected Black women like Henrietta Lacks. With these kinds of visual cues that nudge blackness, Black womanhood, and microscopic cellular study up to the surface of this film, Gary is issuing an interrogation of western epistemology and the damage, the violence that it has waged on Black women's bodies. Through her editing process, Gary creates an imbrication of colorful, ambulatory images of cells that meet Ruby Dee's performance in the PBS episode "Slavery," which abut sweltering scenes of Black worship. This juxtaposition brings the violations of racist science and the stultifying dogma of Christianity together with the quotidian horror of chattel slavery. Gary's incorporation of the filmed stage production "Slavery" calls our attention to the experience of chattel slavery for Black women and to the televised performances of Works Progress Administration (WPA) narratives, which aired the year following the passage of the Civil Rights Act of 1964 and the same year in which the Voting Rights Act of 1965 was signed into law.

In 1965 National Education Television, which was later replaced by the Public Broadcasting Service, aired "Slavery" as the third installment of a nine-part miniseries called *History of the Negro People*. Ossie Davis was the host of all nine episodes, each of which had a running time of about thirty minutes. This series covered a wide range of topics: part 1, "Heritage of the Negro," focused on ancient African civilizations; part 2, "The Negro and the South," focused on the history of the South; part 3, "Slavery," was a staged performance of WPA slave narratives; part 4, "Brazil: The Vanishing Negro," examined Brazil as a so-called racial paradise; part 5, "Free at Last," looked at the history of Black people in the United States from emancipation to World War II; part 6, "Omowale: The Child Returns Home," showed author John Williams embarking on a journey to discover his ancestral roots in Nigeria; part 7, "The New Mood," explored the history of the civil rights movement and Black militancy; part 8, "Our Country, Too," focused on the interior world of Black people through interviews and imagery; and the final episode, part 9, "The Future and the Negro," was a panel discussion taped before a live audience at Carnegie Hall with Ossie Davis as the moderator.[69] *History of the Negro People* won a Peabody Award in 1965 and in its description of the program, the Peabody Digest writes that *History of the Negro People* "explores the little known and long neglected history of the Negro. This television effort examines the Negro's heritage, his role in the United States, Latin America and Africa, and his present mood as he struggles for equality and his future."[70] It is striking that the pronouns "he" and "his" are used so unselfconsciously. While this word choice is indicative of the time in which it was written, to me it exemplifies the world in which Black women had to struggle to be recognized as a part of Negro history. That the use of "he" and "his" is startling in this moment in time makes clear to me the strides that Black feminist historians and scholars have made in the intervening decades. Incidentally, Black women have the most prominent role in the series in the episode on slavery, in terms of screen time and with regard to the narrative content.

"Slavery" is also distinct from the other episodes in that this was a televised performance that incorporated the dramatization of WPA slave narratives and choral performances. Ossie Davis and Ruby Dee performed monologues and the company Voices Inc., composed of Bernice Hall, Jo Jackson, Sylvia Jackson, Melba Moore, Jesse Devore, Charles Mitchell, Garrett Saunders, and James Wright, contributed dramatic elements and performed choral arrangements of "Go Down Moses," "Deep River," and "Good News," and of course, the "Battle Hymn of the Republic." "Slavery" begins with an a cappella performance of "Oh Freedom." The chorus of singers harmonizes together on the bare soundstage that is adorned with only a thin fence, four levels of small descending platforms, and an abstraction of trees. Voice-over narration was provided by Chris M. Gampel, a Canadian actor whose quality of voice may have been chosen to call in white members of the viewing public. Gampel sets the stage by announcing: "1619. Jamestown Virginia, a Dutch ship dropped anchor with a cargo of Black men and women for sale." The chorus sings "Oh Freedom," which becomes a refrain that weaves in between the historical narration and the actual testimony of formerly enslaved people performed by Davis and Dee and the ensemble cast. The narratives dramatized in this episode tell the stories of everyday life and toil, suffering and struggle, survival strategies, and family connections. The WPA testimonies that were selected for inclusion in this production all have a theme of resistance. This choice by the writers, of which Davis was one, demonstrates a concerted effort to stage a history of slavery on public television that was being actively kept out of the national discussion. Hearing the resistance narratives of people who were subjugated and brutalized by the system of racial slavery that was trying through every possible avenue to convert them into property and steal their humanity, along with their labor, chips away at the "history of the Negro people" that had been told so often without any of the tales of resistance.[71]

The testimonies that begin "Slavery" are concerned with the church, the conflicting impulses of obedience to God and slave master, and the everyday resistance to domination. One monologue remembers a grandmother who used to be routinely locked in the seed house because she would not go to church. She was not interested in hearing a preacher tell her not to steal meat, or seeds, or anything from the slave master. Another story recalls a white preacher offering a sermon that implicitly encouraged the enslaved to take a little flour or coffee or meat for themselves; the preacher was reportedly hanged for corrupting the morals of the enslaved. The narrator lists some of the slave codes: "no slaves could leave the plantation without written permission, no slave could strike a white person, no slave could be taught to read or write." While the narrator speaks, the chorus sings "Good News Harriet's Coming." Dee and Davis trade sharing everyday tales of laboring on the plantation, the small and large acts of defiance, and the grave incidents of violence that were a fact of life for enslaved people.

The performance of this archive of testimonies given by those who were formerly enslaved takes on another valence in Gary's film. The entire archive of testimonies collected and presented in PBS's "Slavery" does not make an appearance in *An Ecstatic Experience*, just one testimony that Ruby Dee delivers. Her monologue captures the moment when a rupture occurs and freedom emerges out of the crevice. The mother of twelve, who just stopped working in the middle of the field, who was whipped and made to get back to work, experienced freedom. Her body was not free but she found freedom; despite her condition of bondage, she was free. In Gary's film, this ecstatic experience—a rupture out of which freedom emerged for a woman bound in slavery—is linked to the promise of freedom delivered in church on Sunday, to modern-day escape, to the momentary freedom in the eye of a riot when the law recoils. There is pain in this freedom, there are repercussions to this freedom, and there is, paradoxically, bondage in this freedom; so, what is this freedom?

Gary gives us a visual cue with the etchings that she draws on each frame in Ruby Dee's monologue. Gary is gesturing toward an elsewhere, a place where there is freedom, a place where this enslaved mother of twelve who was just beaten with a bullwhip is free. I turn to José Esteban Muñoz's *Cruising Utopia: The Then and There of Queer Futurity* to discuss the elsewhere of freedom that this testimony opens up, an elsewhere that Gary's cinematic intervention is working to index. Muñoz insists:

> Queerness is a structuring and educated mode of desiring that allows us to see and feel beyond the quagmire of the present. The here and now is a prison house. We must strive, in the face of the here and now's totalizing rendering of reality, to think and feel a *then and there*. Some will say that all we have are the pleasures of the moment, but we must never settle for that minimal transport; we must dream and enact new and better pleasures, other ways of being in the world, and ultimately new worlds. Queerness is a longing that propels us onward, beyond romances of the negative and toiling in the present. Queerness is that thing that lets us feel that this world is not enough, that indeed something is missing.[72]

Though Muñoz ties his concept of queer utopia to aesthetics and historically locates the inception of queer utopia around the Stonewall rebellion, his reading of queerness and temporality is instructive for my analysis of the ruptures that occur in *An Ecstatic Experience*. The totalizing rendering of reality would have enslaved people believe their status as slaves, but all the testimonies of small and large acts of resistance that populate "Slavery" indicate the refusal of this version of reality. The narratives shared in this program attest to a then and there, and an elsewhere of freedom that was constantly being reached for, imagined, worked toward, and wrested whenever possible. Gary's treatment of Ruby Dee's "Slavery" monologue in her film homes in on an interior chasm that opens up inside a woman who was being actively converted into property and who could no longer work, not one more step in that condition. Gary's use of the etchings on and around Ruby Dee's face draws our attention to this elsewhere. She is showing us that in the midst of the quagmire of the present, a radical shift occurred in this woman. Something cracked open inside her and freedom entered. She experienced freedom and continued to experience this despite her corporeal condition. She visited an elsewhere, a queer place where she was free. She resides in that place. She is in two places at once, occupying a queer temporality in which she appears as if she is in bondage but she knows that she is free. She knows that the world is not enough. She is more than the world of slavery, and bullwhips, and labor, and babies in bondage, and hacking off of hands and limbs, and shallow graves, and eating out of pig troughs, and rape and blood, and sweat, and suffering. She had enough and she broke open and she found an elsewhere of freedom. This breaking open gave way to an ecstatic experience of freedom. This woman's ecstatic experience is cinematically linked to the breaking open and out that Assata Shakur made with her escape from prison.

Gary connects these two narratives of escape by placing Ruby Dee's narrative next to a snippet of an interview from Gil Noble's series "Like It Is" in which he went to Cuba and interviewed Assata Shakur, who was living there in exile. In this episode, Assata describes her experience of being politicized in college, being shot by the police, being held in prison, and making her escape. Perhaps Assata is enacting the kind of escape that this unnamed woman in the archive of chattel slavery could only attain as an interior respite from the abject subjugation and enslavement of her and her children. A twentieth-century escape, an escape that happened after the abolition of slavery, demands that the condition of freedom in the afterlife of slavery be examined. This small glimpse of Assata's ecstatic experience of escape and freedom is placed next to contemporary images of Black resistance in the era of #BlackLivesMatter. This placement reinforces Gary's provocation of contemporary unfreedom made with Assata Shakur's acknowledgment of her twentieth-century escape. The ecstatic experience of fighting back, of facing police in riot gear, of resisting, disrupting, and refusing to back down is the culminating experience of this film.

Gary's inclusion of contemporary images of Black resistance to state violence recognizes that the present moment belongs in a cinematic treatise that contends with historic experiences of Black subjugation, which precede ecstatic ones. An ecstatic experience emerges out of the pressure of damnation, out of a stripping back of dignity, mobility, and connection and in a condition in which the ability to live without the persistent fear of death or incarceration is absent. The pressure of Black life builds and builds until something cracks, and through that ruptural cavity rushes freedom, a freedom that is as difficult to hold on to as that which gushes through a breach in the edifice of a dam. The experience of ecstasy is the experience of a rupture, of a crack, of a deluge, the end of something and the beginning of something else, somewhere else.

Cinema and the Archive of Black Feminist Phenomenology

An Ecstatic Experience produces a cinematic archive that has at its core a Black feminist phenomenological intervention into dominant narratives of slavery, escape, freedom, and civil disobedience. Each section of Gary's short film uses archival footage and then intervenes in the process of viewing this footage with her Black feminist avant-garde cinematic techniques. Through etching, discoloration, audio distortion, juxtaposition, or manipulating the pace of the moving image, Gary agitates the archive of Black struggle and liberation. There is a temporal component to Gary's cinematic intervention; with this film, she reaches back in time and unsettles a "history of the Negro people." The cinematic intervention that Gary makes with her repurposing of archival footage visualizes Toni Morrison's contention, which I raised in the introduction to this book but will reiterate here. Morrison asks us to consider the possibility that "the past is not done and it is not over, it's still in process, which is another way of saying that when it's critiqued, analyzed, it yields new information about itself. The past is already changing as it is being reexamined, as it is being listened to for deeper resonances. Actually it can be more liberating than any imagined future if you are willing to identify its evasions, its distortions, its lies, and are willing to unleash its secrets."[73]

Gary reexamines the past with her use of archival footage that activates a Black feminist imperative to pursue an unrelenting focus on the stories of Black women in the archive. This approach agitates to the surface stories of triumph and escape, stories that emerge from a historical landscape laden with devastating loss, systemic rape and torture, inconsolable grief, and categorical defeat. From the future, Gary collects together archival pieces, and with her vision and her cinematic, editorial, inscriptive interjection, she trains our focus on the experiences of Black women. Gary visualizes a phenomenology of Black womanhood in which freedom is the goal, and freedom is attained. I am interested in the futurity that courses through this film and I look to cinema scholar Kara Keeling, whose work on film as poetry from the future is instructive.

In "Looking for M—: Queer Temporality, Black Political Possibility, and Poetry from the Future," Keeling theorizes futurity, social revolution, and Black visuality. Keeling works through Frantz Fanon's engagement with Marx's conception of "poetry from the future" and describes this idea as that which "remains a viable formulation of what is required to effect a radical break with the past—a rupture from within history that also breaks from history."[74] With this notion of poetry from the future, I would like to consider Gary's cinematic intervention into the past as poetry from the future, a cinematic elegy that uses the visual to disrupt the stability of the archive of Black suffering. By wielding her cinematic poetry from the future, which enlivens a visual archive and produces new meanings through their proximity along with her creative flourishes, Gary disrupts a past that seems settled and articulates a continuum of experiences of Black women wresting freedom out of a social, political, epistemological, archival abyss. Film studies scholarship that contends with phenomenology adds to this temporal analysis.

Following Vivian Sobchack's discussion of the utility of phenomenology for cinema studies, I am also not compelled by the phenomenological objective to find an essence of human experience as Edmund Husserl's work strove to do but rather work through film analysis to discuss particularities of experiences.[75] Sobchack is interested in investigating phenomenology through vision: "vision as it is embodied, vision as it is performed, vision as it signifies, vision as it radically entails a world of subjects and objects to make sense of them and of itself as it is lived."[76] Sobchack's conception of phenomenology through vision, that the cinematic makes immediate, is connected to Keeling's discussion of affect in "Looking for M—." Keeling brings our attention to the surplus that the cinematic produces, a surplus that actually exceeds vision and exists in the realm of that which is felt.[77] In this article, Keeling draws upon and extends Marcia Landy's notion of affectivity, a move that is generative for the affective-phenomenological analysis that I am constructing here. Keeling writes:

> I follow Marcia Landy's use of *affectivity* to mark "a form of labor expended in the consumption of cinematic images, in the enterprise of vol-

untarily offering up our lives as 'free contributions to capitalist power,'" and I expand that term to define a form of labor that sentient bodies use to constitute themselves as such through interactions with other phenomena. Insofar as affectivity accesses our individual past experiences and the forms of common sense we have forged over time (even when it breaks the sensory-motor link that chains us to the past), it has both subjective and collective elements to it.[78]

Keeling's expansion of Landy's *affectivity* engages with the phenomenological and indexes subjective and collective experiences that impact the affective labor one must exert to exist in the world. Rather than focus on experiences of consuming cinematic images or being visualized through the cinematic, my discussion of the cinematic focuses on labor and looks once more to the theoretical advancements made by Keeling.

In her volume *The Witch's Flight: The Cinematic, the Black Femme, and the Image of Common Sense*, Keeling draws Gilles Deleuze's theory of the cinematic process together with Landy's affectivity to mobilize her theory of "cinematic reality," which addresses the affective labor of the cinematic process, a process that is not confined to the experience of watching a film: "Because cinematic perception is employed not only when consuming film's images but often when interacting with other of the images that comprise the material world (I call this world 'cinematic reality' following my reading of Deleuze and Bergson), affectivity must be understood as designating a form of labor necessary to survive in that reality and integral to that reality's (re)production. As such, affectivity names a form of labor that is a 'natural condition of the producer's existence.'"[79] I would like to work through Keeling's conceptual framework of affective labor and cinematic reality to draw to a close my discussion of Black feminist avant-garde film and the phenomenology of Black women.

The affective labor of the filmmaker, whose vision takes shape through her experimental treatment of archival footage, adds an archival dimension to Keeling's cinematic reality. Gary's cinematic archival examination of Black women's phenomenology visualizes an interrogation of the archive of survival and freedom. *An Ecstatic Experience* engages with the cinematic process of Black womanhood and is a visualization of Keeling's notion of cinematic reality. The multiplicity of cinematic meanings that cohere within Gary's short film excavates and visualizes an archive of cinematic reality in the afterlife of chattel slavery, in which twenty-first-century Black life remains susceptible to white supremacist exsanguination without repercussion. The historical arc from chattel slavery to jim crow to the civil rights era, through the Black Power movement, to the current moment of #BlackLivesMatter that Gary weaves together in this six-minute-and-eleven-second film demands that a phenomenology of Black womanhood be recognized. The affect produced through Gary's assembly of cinematic reality in this short film is a visitation. The visitation occurs in this film through juxtaposition, through resurgence of resistance over time, through the collection of freedom wresting. The archival, historical, and affective labor, Gary insists with this piece, will not be shouldered only by Black women; the experience will be shared and seen and carried by those other sentient beings who exist within this cinematic reality—those who see and participate in the experiences of Black womanhood and who, from a distinct positionality, can look away, step aside, overlook, and misremember. *An Ecstatic Experience*, as a work of Black feminist avant-garde cinema, uses archival footage of Black women who refuse to wait any longer for liberation. I am drawing those women who survived slavery—those escape artists and freedom wresters, together with Black women theorists, singers, activists, and survivors—to visit with us. As I write these words, I am met with the knowing that our brilliant Black feminist guides who now exist outside of the human form—Audre Lorde, June Jordan, Nina Simone, bell hooks, Toni Morrison—are with us here. The words they have written and spoken, the performances they have offered, the voices they have lent provide the space for visitations to unfold in the here and now. In the pages of this chapter, our Black feminist ancestors join with embodied Black feminist creators, agitators, readers, and champions of liberation to listen for deeper resonances from the past and unearth the secrets, lies, and distortions that pass for history. What we find in our excavation we transmute. Together we change the past; we turn foul into fruit and provide the releases that we crave, that we all deserve. These precious, tender visitations remind us that freedom is ours for the taking, that silence will not protect us; we are here to save ourselves and heal each other.

An Ecstatic Experience disrupts cinematic reality with the visualization of cinematic decay that reflects the distortion of vision that subsumes Black women. The images of celluloid decomposition, cellular activity, and archival cinematic evidence that Gary brings together in this film situate Black women's experiences of freedom amid the muck, the heat, the grief, the sorrow songs, the Negro history, the well-hatched escape plans, the exile, the defiance, the rupture. The phenomenology of Black womanhood is not categorical. It is not totalizing, universal, or essential, but what is made clear by seeing and experiencing Gary's cinematic rendering of the phenomenology of Black womanhood is the persistent, reverberating chord of freedom that rings, sometimes quietly and sometimes with alarm, but nevertheless, it rings.

CODA

On Tenderness

The sensual, archival visitations that unfold through Black feminist avant-garde films can only take place through a relationship achieved between cinema, the archive, and tenderness. Black feminist avant-garde cinema visualizes visitations and, in this volume, I have studied those visitations as they have unfolded before the camera. Tenderness is the sensation that opens the channel to be graced by the presence of a disembodied loved one, ancestor, unknown but familiar spirit. Tenderness is the method. It is through tenderness that Black feminist avant-garde filmmakers enter their respective archives, tap into the void, and create the space for visitations to occur through their cinematic engagements. Kara Walker used tenderness to share an interior landscape of young Amanda Willis. Kara Lynch summoned tenderness on a massive collective scale to gather all her participants together at the 145th Street Bridge to bring about a reckoning for Laura Nelson and her son. It was through her tenderness that Tourmaline compiled and shared her archival research on Marsha P. Johnson and brought her image and spirit, with Sasha Wortzel, to the black box theater at The Kitchen. Tenderness is the connective tissue that binds scenes of resistance and calls up the absent presences that generate Ja'Tovia Gary's ecstatic experience. Tenderness is the power of Black feminist avant-garde cinema. The tenderness used by Black feminist avant-garde filmmakers in their projects opens but one way to reach our ancestors. The visitations conjured by these filmmakers needed the visual, required the aesthetics of resistance specific to Black feminist avant-garde cinema to materialize, and, still, the tenderness can exceed the medium. Tenderness, like any solid methodology, can be applied in creative and sustainable ways. The visitations that occurred through Black feminist avant-garde films were made possible through the archival investigations of the filmmakers; these kinds of visitations could only take place through the specificity of the cinematic medium, but Black feminist connections between embodied and disembodied Black women can happen through other mediums as well.

Tenderness and the presences of our ancestors can be sung. The entirety of Solange's fourth studio album, *When I Get Home* (2019), is an incantation.[1] The refrain "I saw things I imagined" opens the sonic space. She repeats the phrase throughout the song in such a way that one wonders if the things that she imagined have been made material. She ends the track with a harmonic chorus of the line "taking on the light." The light of imagination, the divine chasm, the space of the absent present is before her. With these words, I hear Solange invoking a sonic visitation. The track "Down with the Clique" calls up the presence of gone-too-soon, beautiful Aaliyah, who made popular a song of that same name in 1994.[2] The repetition in each track, the harmonics, and the enchanting discord work together to call in a visitation, or many visitations. "You've gotta know. You've gotta know. You've gotta know. You've gotta know. You've gotta know," as Solange reminds us in her "Time (Is)," which appears halfway through the album.[3] Esperanza Spalding ushers in visitations with her *12 Little Spells*, which she casts with her 2018 album of that name. Esperanza Spalding's upright bass guides us to the other side, just as Alice Coltrane's harp has the magnetizing ability to draw in visitations.[4] Visitations can be touched on through the tenderness of visual art as much as they can circulate through music. I'm thinking of the sculptural work of Simone Leigh.

Simone Leigh's sixteen-foot bronze bust, *Brick House*, which appeared as a beacon above New York City's Tenth Avenue, shocked the cityscape with the looming, haunting presence of Black womanhood (see figure C.1).[5] Rather than

FIGURE C.1 Simone Leigh's *Brick House* on a New York City overpass. Photo by Timothy Schenck.

through moving imagery, the visitation comes through in the stillness, in the texture of hair, the braids, the countenance, the expression that Leigh produces with this piece. The visitation comes through in the placement, the eyeless face, the constant reminder that Black women have a presence in this place. Another time and another place are called in with Leigh's work of public art. A visitation happened with *Brick House* for the entirety of its installation on the High Line from June 2019 to May 2021. The place is forever changed; even with the sculpture removed, her presence is still felt.

A visitation can be conjured through dance as much as Black feminist public art and music. Judith Jamison's 1972 performance of Alvin Ailey's *Cry* calls up all the Black mothers whose labor and tears have been poured into families, their own and those who have extracted their labor over the generations.[6] Interestingly, this performance is accompanied by the sounds of Alice Coltrane's avant-garde harp. In the iconic 1972 performance, Jamison wears a flowing white skirt over her long-sleeved white leotard. She dances with a large swathe of white cloth that becomes a scrub brush, a head scarf, a river. There is grief here, there is release here, and there is connection in the movement. The feelings that emanate through the choreography and movement and music take on new mean-

On Tenderness 185

ing when, in the spring of 2020, former and current Alvin Ailey dancers videotaped their own performances of *Cry* in their homes and outdoor spaces during the COVID-19 pandemic.[7] This collage of performances conjures up the original Jamison performance and also taps into the spirit of the unnamed mothers invoked by Ailey's choreography. Through the juxtaposition of different dancers, different spaces, different lighting, and different times, the feeling of cross-generational, temporality-defying connection comes through. All of these dancers produce visitations with their bodies, their movement, their breath. Through the tenderness of movement, their bodies become vessels for visitations to occur, and we are witnesses.

The method of tenderness is ours. The space for a visitation to occur can be created through the visual, through the musical, through the sculptural, and through dance. What I am writing here, with these closing thoughts, is an invitation to welcome tenderness and to follow it to the knowing that connects us, that heals us, that breathes without a body—through us; a tenderness that ticks us in, with an Audre Lorde snap. What we can offer ourselves, as Black women, if not freedom from suffering, is a tender witnessing.

I would like to end this book with the incantation that closes out Solange's *When I Get Home*. In her final track on that album, "I'm a Witness," she recognizes herself as a witness and shares a tender spell of her own that can draw in a visitation. With these words, she also offers us a way to recognize ourselves as witnesses and usher in our own visitations. In this beautiful, elegant, otherworldly invocation, she calls out:

> You can work through me
> You can say what you need in my mind
> I'll be your vessel
> I'll do it every time
> And I won't stop 'til I get it right
> Good night
> Takin' on the, takin' on the light
> And I won't stop 'til I get it right
> Good night (Good night)
> Takin' on the, takin' on the light
> Takin' on the light
> Takin' on the light[8]

My wish for me/you/us is that we can take on the light. That we can serve as vessels for our loved ones and that we do not stop until we get it right.

Notes

INTRODUCTION

1   Alexander, *Pedagogies of Crossing*, 7
2   Alexander, *Pedagogies of Crossing*, 309.
3   I am purposefully not capitalizing jim crow, even though it is a proper name, in order to counter any form of reverence being produced with this name.
4   I am using *study* here as Kevin Quashie discusses the term in his book *Black Aliveness, or A Poetics of Being*. Quashie describes this kind of study as a human undertaking that "invites us to pursue intelligence by giving attention to what troubles and what intrigues" (112).
5   My understanding of the exclusions shared by Black cis or non-trans women and trans women of many racialized experiences has benefited greatly from conversations with trans scholar and philosopher Talia Mae Bettcher.
6   Gordon, *Ghostly Matters*, xvi.
7   Beginning with Hortense Spillers's "Mama's Baby, Papa's Maybe" and moving through the work of Saidiya Hartman in *Lose Your Mother* and Alexander Weheliye in *Habeas Viscus*, discussions of pornotropy are used to describe the pleasure derived from reading about, watching, or otherwise recounting in painstaking detail incidents in which Black people, especially Black women, are subject to dehumanizing acts of violence.
8   In "The Circuitous Route of Presenting Black Butch: The Travels of Dee Rees's *Pariah*," which includes my analysis of Dee Rees's short and feature-film versions of *Pariah*, I discuss how the short-film form offers freedom to representations of Black womanhood that can be foreclosed in feature-length films.
9   The term *avant-garde* is a French military term used to denote an advance guard or the soldiers who were on the front lines of a military force. See Rabinovitz, *Points of Resistance*, 14. See also Rees, *History of Experimental Film and Video*, 2, which offers a military history of the term. The avant-garde film movement of the 1960s and early 1970s maintained a deep resistance to the film industry's commodification of cinematic vision and reveled in abstractionist film techniques that jarred the viewer and

created the visual space to see differently. In *Points of Resistance*, Rabinovitz argues that to consider avant-garde film a purely aesthetic cinematic concern diminishes that important facet of the avant-garde film movement. In his essay "From Metaphors on Vision," Stan Brakhage describes the potential depths that the cinematic medium could plumb if an interrogation of vision and perception were the catalyst for filmmaking (120).

10   Maya Deren's foundational *Meshes of the Afternoon* (1943) uses film to produce the feeling of being inside a dream and to invoke questions about the relationship between the conscious, subconscious, and unconscious. *Un Chien Andalou* (1929), a surrealist film directed by Luis Buñuel and cowritten by Buñuel and Salvador Dalí, is a groundbreaking work that jars reality and draws us into a nightmare. Stan Brakhage's opus *Dog Star Man* (1961–64) is a series of experimental short films that visualizes mystical experiences of a man who treks up a mountain with his dog. Other important avant-garde films of this era are Chantal Akerman's *Jeanne Dielman, 23, quai du commerce, 1080 Bruxelles* (1975); Stan Brakhage's *Mothlight* (1963) and *The Act of Seeing with One's Own Eyes* (1971); Jack Smith's *Flaming Creatures* (1962–63); Yvonne Rainer's *Film about a Woman Who* (1985); and Su Friedrich's *The Ties That Bind* (1984), *Damned If You Don't* (1987), and *Sink or Swim* (1990).

11   I am referring to Chantal Akerman's *La Chambre* (1972) and *Jeanne Dielman, 23, quai du commerce, 1080 Bruxelles*; Laura Mulvey's *Riddles of the Sphinx* (1977); Maya Deren's *Meshes of the Afternoon*; and Barbara Hammer's filmography, including *Dyketactics* (1974) and *Superdyke* (1975). See the commentary in Blaetz, *Women's Experimental Cinema*.

12   The films of Hammer and Friedrich are exemplary of white lesbian avant-garde cinema.

13   Lizzie Borden's *Born in Flames* (1983) is an exception; this film certainly has avant-garde aesthetics and centers Black women as agitators in the struggle for liberation.

14   Stan Brakhage, Maya Deren, Chantal Ackerman, Andy Warhol, Hollis Frampton, Jack Smith, Man Ray, Hans Richter, Salvador Dalí, and Luis Buñuel are some of the filmmakers who are recognized as foundational to avant-garde cinema.

15   The first two feature films by US Black women to garner a national theatrical release are Julie Dash's *Daughters of the Dust* (1991) and Cheryl Dunye's *The Watermelon Woman* (1996). These films use avant-garde cinematic techniques that I will discuss later in this chapter.

16   Petrolle and Wexman, in their introduction to *Women and Experimental Filmmaking*, mention Dash's *Daughters of the Dust* but do not offer analysis of the film, 4–5. Kathleen McHugh's chapter, "History and Falsehood in Experimental Autobiographies," included in that volume, discusses Dunye's *The Watermelon Woman* alongside analysis of work by filmmakers Lourdes Portillo and Rea Tajiri. McHugh also offers a chapter on Dunye's films, "The Experimental 'Dunyementary': A Cinematic Signature Effect" in Blaetz, *Women's Experimental Cinema*. In her introduction Blaetz acknowledges Dash's work in avant-garde cinema but does not include analysis of her films in *Women's Experimental Cinema* because, as she reports, she was not able to find scholars willing or able to write about Dash's films, 6.

17 For more on the feminist avant-garde cinematic intervention taking place during this era, see Blaetz, *Women's Experimental Cinema*; Petrolle and Wexman, *Women and Experimental Filmmaking*; and Rabinovitz, *Points of Resistance*.
18 Black avant-garde literature and visual art have been recognized as such from the New Negro movement into the Black Arts movement. Some key works from the New Negro movement are the poetry of Langston Hughes, the essays and poetry of Jean Toomer, James Van Der Zee's photography, Marita Bonner's plays, and the paintings of Romare Bearden. The poetry of Jayne Cortez, Nikki Giovanni, and Sonia Sanchez, and Amiri Baraka's poetry, essays, and plays are some hallmarks of the Black Arts movement. This is certainly not an exhaustive list, but a start. In her introduction to *Renegade Poetics*, Evie Shockley offers a thorough discussion of Black aesthetics and the Black Arts movement, which was recognized as the aesthetic complement to the Black Power movement.
19 The L.A. Rebellion School of filmmakers included Black filmmakers trained at the University of California, Los Angeles (UCLA) during the late 1960s through the 1980s. The social upheaval of the Watts Rebellion, the civil rights movement, and the war in Vietnam propelled the early group of filmmakers to respond through cinema. Filmmakers such as Charles Burnett, Larry Clark, Julie Dash, Zeinabu irene Davis, Haile Gerima, and Billy Woodbury are some of the most prominent filmmakers from the L.A. Rebellion School.
20 These are but a few examples of Black avant-garde cinema: Barbara McCullough's *Water Ritual #1: An Urban Rite of Purification* (1979), Julie Dash's *Four Women* (1975), Zeinabu irene Davis's *Cycle* (1989) and *Compensation* (1999), and Charles Burnett's *Killer of Sheep* (1978).
21 Moten, *In the Break*, 32–33.
22 McMillan, *Embodied Avatars*, 7.
23 Dash's *Daughters of the Dust* is credited as the first feature film to be directed by a Black woman. A reading of this film is necessary in a book on Black feminist avant-garde film.
24 Dash, *Daughters of the Dust*, 27–68.
25 Dash, *Daughters of the Dust*, 31–32.
26 Dash, *Daughters of the Dust*, 33–34.
27 I learned this detail in a postscreening conversation that I had with producer Alex Juhasz, director Cheryl Dunye, and actress Guin Turner, who assembled as a panel to discuss the film at the Outfest on the Road Film Festival that I organized and programmed at Smith College in 2016, in celebration of the 20th anniversary of *The Watermelon Woman*'s release.
28 Hartman, "Venus in Two Acts," 7–10.
29 Hartman, "Venus in Two Acts," 2.
30 Hartman, "Venus in Two Acts," 2.
31 Hartman, "Venus in Two Acts," 4–5. Inside this quote, Hartman is referring to the question that she posed in her book *Lose Your Mother*.
32 Hartman, "Venus in Two Acts," 11.
33 Hartman, "Venus in Two Acts," 11–12.

34 Hartman defines the afterlife of slavery as a condition of being in which "black lives are still imperiled and devalued by a racial calculus and a political arithmetic that were entrenched centuries ago" (*Lose Your Mother*, 6).
35 Spillers, "Mama's Baby, Papa's Maybe," 206.
36 Hammonds, "Black (W)holes."
37 Hammonds, "Black (W)holes," 139.
38 Lorde, "Transformation of Silence," 42.
39 In "Black (W)holes," Hammonds looks to Lorde's "Transformation of Silence" to discuss the invisible/hypervisible paradox of Black womanhood.
40 This postproduction process is called ADR, automated dialogue replacement.
41 Mitchell, *Seeing through Race*, 13–14.
42 Fields, "Slavery, Race and Ideology," 97–101.
43 The Combahee River Collective's "A Black Feminist Statement" details these sentiments as fundamental imperatives of Black feminist politics.
44 See Lorde, "The Master's Tools Will Never Dismantle the Master's House," in *Sister Outsider*, 110–13; Spillers, "Mama's Baby, Papa's Maybe"; White, *Ar'n't I a Woman?*; A. Davis, "Reflections on the Black Woman's Role," 7; hooks, *Ain't I a Woman*; Hartman, *Scenes of Subjection*; J. L. Morgan, *Laboring Women*; and Garza, "Herstory."
45 See Snorton, *Black on Both Sides*; Bey, "Black Fugitivity Un/gendered,"; Gumbs, *Undrowned*; Nash, *Black Feminism Reimagined*; Sharpe, *In the Wake*; Brooks, *Liner Notes for the Revolution*; and J. Brown, *Black Utopias*.
46 Kara Walker is an acclaimed multimedia installation artist who received her MFA from the Rhode Island School of Design in 1994. Walker is a painter and printmaker; she produces large-scale silhouettes and sculptures, and creates short films, soundscapes, and puppet shows that make visceral the intimate, grotesque, and violent history of blackness and whiteness in the United States. The artist pays special attention to the positionality of Black womanhood throughout her body of work. Walker was a recipient of the prestigious John D. and Catherine T. MacArthur Foundation Achievement Award in 1997, which officially registers her as a genius in the annals of art history. In 2014 Walker erected a gargantuan monument of a Mammy/Sphynx figure out of sugar at the defunct Domino Sugar plant in Williamsburg, Brooklyn, that drew in enormous crowds: *A Subtlety: Or the Marvelous Sugar Baby, an Homage to the unpaid and overworked Artisans who have refined our Sweet tastes from the cane fields to the Kitchens of the New World on the Occasion of the demolition of the Domino Sugar Refining Plant*.
47 The Bureau of Refugees, Freedmen, and Abandoned Lands records are held at the National Archives in Washington, DC. These records, made primarily of letters, affidavits, and testimonies, chronicle some of the horrors newly emancipated people had to contend with in the aftermath of the Civil War, during the brief period of Reconstruction (1865–77).
48 Kara Lynch lives in the Bronx, New York. She received her MFA in Visual Arts from the University of California, San Diego, and is associate professor emerita of video and critical studies at Hampshire College. In 2001 Lynch made a feature-length documentary called *Black Russians*, and over the span of four years, between

1998 and 2002, she made a video travelogue called *The Outing*. Since 2003 the artist has been producing site-specific work in different geographic locations across the United States for the episodic, visual/sonic installation project *Invisible*, of which SAVED :: *video postcard* is a part. Lynch's work has been exhibited in galleries and museums across the United States as well as in Germany, Zimbabwe, Kenya, Palestine, the UK, and Lebanon. Most recently Kara coedited the anthology *We Travel the SpaceWays: Black Imagination, Fragments and Diffractions*, which was published by Transcript in 2019. Kara Lynch's work is defiantly queer and feminist and eloquently attends to the amorphous sensations that accumulate over generations of racialization, gender oppression, state violence, and class warfare.

49 Tourmaline is a coeditor (credited as Reina Gossett) of the anthology *Trap Door: Trans Cultural Production and the Politics of Visibility*. She held the position of activist in residence at Barnard College from 2014 to 2018. The Brooklyn Museum and High Line Art co-commissioned a film by Tourmaline, *Salacia*, which was featured in *Nobody Promised You Tomorrow* and was the first film commissioned as a High Line original. In addition to the Brooklyn Museum, the High Line, and The Kitchen, Tourmaline's work has been presented at the Museum of Modern Art (MoMa), PS1, BFI Flare, the New Museum, the Whitney Museum, the Studio Museum in Harlem, and the Venice Biennale. Tourmaline's body of cinematic work, which includes *Mary Ill of Fame, Atlantic Is a Sea of Bones, The Personal Things*, and *Lost in the Music*, lyrically and vibrantly contends with Black trans and queer life in a way that both spans epochs and dislocates time. Sasha Wortzel is a filmmaker and installation artist living in Brooklyn and Miami whose short film *We Have Always Been Here* was included in *Nobody Promised You Tomorrow*. Her films have been exhibited at the Museum of Modern Art, the New Museum, and Berlinale, and have garnered the support of the Sundance Institute and Art Matters. She has been awarded artist fellowships and residencies across the country, including the Artists in Residence in the Everglades, Abrons Arts Residency for Visual Artists, and the Watermill Center. Wortzel has films in the permanent collections of the Brooklyn Museum and the Leslie Lohman Museum of Art. Tourmaline and Wortzel are both accomplished filmmakers who have produced bodies of work outside their collaboration in *Happy Birthday, Marsha!* A testament to the importance of Tourmaline and Wortzel's work is made clear by the Brooklyn Museum's inclusion of other films that each artist made, in addition to the collaborative piece for *Nobody Promised You Tomorrow*.

50 Ja'Tovia Gary is a Brooklyn-based filmmaker and artist whose work has been exhibited at the Whitney Museum, Galarie Frank Elbaz, David Zwirner, Brown University, and The Kitchen. Her films have screened at the London Short Film Festival; the Anthology Film Archives; the Furora Film Festival in Berlin; the Institute for Contemporary Art in Virginia and Philadelphia; the AFI Fest; Filmforum at the Museum of Contemporary Art, Los Angeles (MOCA); the Museum of Contemporary Art in Chicago; the BlackStar Film Festival; Art Basel; the Toronto Film Festival; and the Smithsonian African American Film Festival. She received her MFA in social documentary filmmaking from the School of Visual Arts in New York City,

and her work has been supported by the Sundance Institute. She was a Radcliffe Fellow at Harvard University during the 2018–19 academic year. She was the recipient of a Creative Capital award and a Field of Vision award in 2019.

51 In 1982 Kathleen Collins made the first feature-length film directed by a US-based Black woman, *Losing Ground*. Because Collins did not have a national theatrical release for the film, it is not recorded in cinema history as the first feature film to be directed by a Black US-based woman. It would take nine more years for that honor to be bestowed on Julie Dash for *Daughters of the Dust*. Barbara McCullough's short film *Water Ritual #1: An Urban Rite of Purification* is exemplary of Black feminist avant-garde cinema, as is Zeinabu irene Davis's *Compensation* and Cauleen Smith's *Dark Matter and Postcard*.

CHAPTER ONE: THE ARCHIVE AND THE SILHOUETTE

1 I use the terms *Black, colored, Negro,* and *mulatto* in response to the language being used in texts that I examine. I work to have parity between the racial term that I employ and the language used in the archival documents with which I engage.
2 The Thirteenth Amendment to the Constitution declares: "Neither slavery nor involuntary servitude, except as a punishment for a crime whereof the party shall have been duly convicted, shall exist within the United States, or any place subject to their jurisdiction."
3 Walker produced work in her *Bureau of Refugees* series between 2007 and 2009.
4 "Outrage" was the term used to describe the rape and sexual assault of a woman in the antebellum and postbellum years. I have placed *outrage* in quotes to amplify the fact that the rape of Black women and girls was not recognized as a crime or an outrage. Black women and girls were routinely subjected to rape, and there was no outrage by the dominant power over this fact of life for Black women.
5 Walker's choice to name this series *Bureau of Refugees* raises questions about the status of the refugee in the United States during the era of Reconstruction. Though the term *refugee* was predominantly used as an assignation for white southerners who were destitute and homeless, I found a few instances in the National Archives Records for the Alabama District of the Bureau of Refugees, 1866, in which the term *colored refugee* was used. The term seems to refer to enslaved men who escaped slavery to serve in the Union army and their family members who are seeking refuge from the Confederacy. The concept of a colored refugee who became a US citizen during this era is a paradox worth investigating, one that I may take up at a later date.
6 Du Bois, *Black Reconstruction in America, 1860–1880*, 489.
7 Alabama was a district in 1866 and was not named a state until February 1868.
8 K. Walker, *Bureau of Refugees*.
9 Arguably Walker's most well-known series was her first major show, *Kara Walker: My Complement, My Enemy, My Oppressor, My Love* (2007). Walker also makes short films that incorporate puppet shows using the silhouette, one of which I had the pleasure to experience in person at the REDCAT in Los Angeles in 2005, *Kara E. Walker's Song*

of the South. The film that was screened at this live performance was *8 Possible Beginnings: Or the Creation of African-America. A Moving Picture by the young, self-taught, Genius of the South K.E. Walker*. Walker made an incredible stir with her 2014 sculpture, "A Subtlety, or the Marvelous Sugar Baby," that was made entirely of sugar and installed in the former Domino Sugar factory in Williamsburg, Brooklyn.

10   The running time for *National Archives Microfilm Publication M999 Roll 34: Bureau of Refugees, Freedmen and Abandoned Lands: Six Miles from Springfield on the Franklin Road* (2009) is 13 mins., 22 secs. *National Archives Microfilm Publication M999 Roll 34: Bureau of Refugees, Freedmen and Abandoned Lands: Lucy of Pulaski* (2009) is the title of the other short film in this series. The running time for *Lucy of Pulaski* is 12 mins., 8 secs.

11   K. Walker, *Bureau of Refugees*, 4. The period of Reconstruction lasted from 1865 to 1877.

12   Lydia Maria Child is credited with creating the tragic mulatto character in her 1842 short story "The Quadroons." The tragic mulatto is a woman, or man, who has white skin but Black parentage and is tortured by the knowledge of their blackness.

13   Literary melodramas such as William Wells Brown's *Clotel; or, The President's Daughter*, Frances E. W. Harper's *Iola Leroy; or, Shadows Uplifted*, Emma Dunham Kelley's *Megda*, and Charles Chesnutt's *The Marrow of Tradition* have protagonists that appear to be white or believe they are white only to discover their lineage has a dark "Negro" past. These texts worked to expose the ills of slavery and white supremacy through creating sympathetic "mulatto" characters.

14   Cid Ricketts Sumner's 1947 novel *Quality* was adapted for the screen in 1949 as Elia Kazan's *Pinky*. Both *Imitation of Life* and *Pinky* tell the story of a Black woman who has white skin and is plagued by her blackness. In *Imitation of Life*, the tragic mulatto character never reconciles with her past; in *Pinky*, the titular character accepts her blackness and takes her place, not unproblematically, among her people.

15   While the term *miscegenation* was not coined until 1864, the laws that made marriage between a "free" Black person and a white person illegal were enacted as early as 1661; Maryland was the first state to legislate the illegality of interracial marriage.

16   Lemire, *Miscegenation*, 51. Elise Lemire offers a genealogy of the term *amalgamation* that was borrowed from the field of metallurgy, which provided the theoretical framework to conceive of race "as a biological trait in the blood and race blood was perceived . . . as a 'mathematical problem of the same class with those mixtures of different liquors or different metals.'"

17   Croly, *Miscegenation*, 16.

18   Croly, *Miscegenation*, 2.

19   Kaplan, "Miscegenation Issue," 283.

20   Kaplan, "Miscegenation Issue," 326.

21   Croly, *Miscegenation*; Kaplan, "Miscegenation Issue." Tavia Nyong'o discusses Croly's hoax in *Amalgamation Waltz*, 28–30.

22   The symbolics of blood have been used to instantiate ideas of racial purity as well as levy moral indictments for sexual "deviance." See Erkkila, *Mixed Bloods and Other Crosses*. Chapter 1, "Blood, Sex, and Other Crosses," and chapter 2, "Mixed Bloods: Jefferson, Revolution, and the Boundaries of America," are both especially helpful on this subject of blood and the making of race in America.

23 The "colored refugee" was made distinct from the refugee in the letters.
24 Morrison, "Be Your Own Story."
25 Lorde, *Transformation of Silence*, 42.
26 See J. L. Morgan, *Laboring Women*, 82–83. Jennifer L. Morgan examines ideologies present in US and Caribbean colonial images of Black women's reproductive bodies. Morgan uses archival documentation, slave records, bills of sale, wills, judgments, letters, and ship logs to locate enslaved Black women in the historical record and demonstrate how Black women's reproductive bodies were central to the slave trade. Domestic and field labor were extracted from enslaved women as well as reproductive labor; those enslaved women of childbearing age were known as "increasers," which indicates how Black women's reproductivity was valued as potential property and real estate of slave owners and their progeny.
27 See Appadurai, "Archive and Aspiration." Arjun Appadurai argues that the archive is better thought of as a project of collective aspiration than a burial site. I agree that an archive is a product of aspiration but one that satisfies the archival desires of a group that is in control of the archive itself, from documentation to collection, preservation, access, and retrieval. For those who exist in the mire, or on the margins, or only appear in historical records as victims of horrific violence, then a tomb would be an appropriate metaphor for an archive.
28 Hartman, "Venus in Two Acts," 5.
29 In the introduction to this volume, I further discuss Hartman's "Venus in Two Acts." In this article, Hartman wrestles with how to handle the violently incomplete archive of Venus, a young enslaved girl who was murdered on a slave shape.
30 Trouillot, *Silencing the Past*, 48–49.
31 Trouillot, *Silencing the Past*, 48–54.
32 Walker created pieces in response to this incident titled "Bureau of Refugees: Black Girl Beaten to Death by Washington and Greene McKinney" (2007) and "Bureau of Refugees: July 16 Black Girl Beaten" (2007). Both are included in her *Bureau of Refugees* series.
33 K. Walker, "Risible Visual."
34 I offer a discussion of Dunye's trickster archive in her film *The Watermelon Woman* (1996) in the introduction of this book.
35 Walker's 2007 exhibition *Kara Walker: My Complement, My Enemy, My Oppressor, My Love* premiered at the Walker Art Center, then traveled to the ARC/Musée d'Art Moderne in Paris, the Whitney Museum in New York, and the Hammer Museum in Los Angeles. See https://walkerart.org/calendar/2007/kara-walker-my-complement-my-enemy-my-oppress.
36 See Pindell, *Kara Walker-no, Kara Walker-yes?*; Sexton, *Amalgamation Schemes*; and Sharpe, *Monstrous Intimacies*.
37 Hartman, *Scenes of Subjection*, 3.
38 Hartman, *Scenes of Subjection*, 3.
39 Moten, *In the Break*, 3–6.
40 Hartman, *Scenes of Subjection*, 4.
41 P. Harper, *Abstractionist Aesthetics*, 2–3.

42　Man Ray's work as a surrealist painter and photographer was part of the Dada movement. Later he expanded his repertoire to include short films. Ferdinand Léger was a formative cubist painter and sculptor who also added cinema to his visual art practice. The famous surrealist painter Salvador Dalí joined Luis Buñuel in making the surrealist film *Un Chien Andalou* (1929). A. L. Rees offers a brief discussion of these artists' incorporation of film into their existing art practice in *A History of Experimental Film and Video*, 8.

43　Stan Brakhage was an experimental filmmaker and is recognized as preeminent in the avant-garde film movement of the 1950s and 1960s. One of his most well-known films is the *Dog Star Man* cycle produced between 1962 and 1965.

44　Brakhage, "From Metaphors on Vision," 120.

45　Avant-garde visual art is recognized as works that push boundaries and movements that revolutionize modes of seeing. Marcel Duchamp's *Fountain* (1917), pop art like Andy Warhol's *Campbell Soup* series made in the 1960s, Jackson Pollack's drip paintings made in the 1950s, and Georges Braque's and Pablo Picasso's cubist paintings made in the first decades of the twentieth century have all been regarded as avant-garde.

46　Affidavit of Amanda Willis: Exhibit A, Tennessee, November 26, 1866, Letters Received, July 1865–October 1867 Record Group 105, Roll M809, National Archives, Washington, DC.

47　Here, the officer has indicated that the (+) plus sign indicates Amanda's mark, by writing "her" above and "mark" below the plus sign. As someone who was newly freed from slavery, Amanda could not write or sign her name to the affidavit. The feeling of that loss, of that violence of slavery, is palpable to me as I read those words.

48　Here again, the name given to the National Archives publication roll, archival locator, is the name of Walker's piece.

49　Excerpt from Henry Willis's affidavit, Letters Received, July 1865–October 1867, Record Group 105, Roll M809, National Archives, Washington, DC.

50　Certeau, *Writing of History*, ix.

51　Hartman, *Lose Your Mother*, 6.

52　Derrida, *Specters of Marx*, xviii.

CHAPTER TWO: RECKONING AT THE BRIDGE

1　Two photographs of Laura Nelson's and L.D. Nelson's murders exist in the archive.

2　"Kara Lynch," STORM PROJECTS, July 29, 2013, https://stormprojects.wordpress.com/biography/kara-lynch/. This was a written interview; as such, Lynch's quote is provided as she wrote her responses in the interview. Laura Nelson's son is listed as both L.W. and L.D. I found L.D. listed on the census records for the Nelson family; for this reason, I will use L.D. throughout the chapter when referring to him. The itinerant photographer's name is G. H. (George Henry) Farnum.

3　"Kara Lynch," STORM PROJECTS, July 29, 2013.

4　"Kara Lynch," STORM PROJECTS, July 29, 2013.

5   See Kathleen Hulser, "Saved: Memories of a Lynching," *New York Almanack*, October 22, 2013, https://newyorkalmanack.com/2013/10/saved-memories-of-a-lynching/. In this interview, Lynch referred to the NAACP Silent March in 1917 as inspiration for the procession in SAVED :: *video postcard*.
6   Lynch's SAVED :: *video postcard* weaves together dance performances by Impact Repertory Theater and choral performances by the choirs from Convent Avenue Baptist Church, First Corinthians Church, and Bethany Baptist Church.
7   Lorde, "Uses of the Erotic: The Erotic as Power," in *Sister Outsider*, 55.
8   Lorde, "Uses of the Erotic," 57.
9   Alexander, *Pedagogies of Crossing*, 7.
10 Alexander, *Pedagogies of Crossing*, 7.
11 See Gordon, *Ghostly Matters*.
12 Gordon, *Ghostly Matters*, xvi–xvii.
13 Gordon, *Ghostly Matters*, xvi–xvii.
14 I am using "colored" here as this was the term used by Black press outlets during this era. Since jim crow segregation was in effect at this time, news outlets were segregated as well.
15 "Woman and Boy Lynched," *The Independent*, May 25, 1911.
16 This bridge is near Paden, Oklahoma, and was home to Claude Littrel, the man whose steer Austin Nelson admitted to stealing. The Nelsons' cabin was located northeast of Paden. See Jones-Sneed, "Gender, Race and the Antilynching Crusade in the United States," 63; "Deputy Sheriff Loney Murdered," *Okemah Ledger*, May 4, 1911; "The Nelsons Have Examination," *The Independent*, May 11, 1911.
17 "Lynchers Avenge the Murder of Geo. Loney," *Okemah Ledger*, May 25, 1911. It is not clear if Laura and L.D. Nelson were cut down at 11:00 a.m. or 11:00 p.m. the next day. As evidenced by the photographs taken by local photographer G. H. Farnum, the murderers and onlookers posed for photos with the hanging corpses.
18 "Deputy Sheriff Killed," *The Independent*, May 4, 1911.
19 "Deputy Sheriff Killed," *The Independent*, May 4, 1911. Crystal Feimster's *Southern Horrors*, 171–74, does not relate the conflicting stories of this case but only reports that Nelson shot and killed the deputy sheriff. On a website that honors police officers killed in the line of duty, Loney is remembered as being shot and killed in Okemah by a fourteen-year-old boy while searching the home for stolen goods. "Deputy Sheriff George H. Loney," *Officer Down Memorial Page*, accessed March 1, 2015, http://www.odmp.org/officer/19605-deputy-sheriff-george-h-loney.
20 "Deputy Sheriff Loney Murdered," *Okemah Ledger*, May 4, 1911. This article reports that the deputy was shot in the leg and died.
21 "Held for Murder in First Degree," *Okemah Ledger*, May 11, 1911.
22 "The Nelsons Have Examination," *The Independent*, May 11, 1911.
23 "A Deputy Sheriff Killed," *The Independent*, May 4, 1911.
24 "Deputy Sheriff Loney Murdered," *Okemah Ledger*, May 4, 1911. See also "The Nelsons Have Examination," *The Independent*, May 11, 1911. Laura and L.D. were reportedly represented by lawyers from the firm Blakely, Maxey and Miley of Shawnee.

25 "Deputy Sheriff Loney Murdered," *Okemah Ledger*, May 4, 1911.
26 "Deputy Sheriff Loney Murdered," *Okemah Ledger*, May 4, 1911. Austin Nelson is misnamed as Oscar Nelson in this article.
27 Du Bois, "Crime," 99–100; Du Bois, "Lynching," 233.
28 In 1911 Carrie and L.D. would be about a year older than they were when the census was taken, but without their birth dates it is difficult to know exactly how old they were on May 25. Newspaper reports of the incident name the son as L.W., but the census records name him as L.D. In the newspaper reports, L.D. is reported to be several different ages, between thirteen and sixteen years old, at the time of his murder.
29 Du Bois, "Crime," 99–100.
30 "Negro Prisoner Gets Unruly," *Okemah Ledger*, May 18, 1911. This report mistakenly refers to Laura as "Mary."
31 "Negro Prisoner Gets Unruly," *Okemah Ledger*, May 18, 1911.
32 "Lynchers Avenge the Murder of Geo. Loney," *Okemah Ledger*, May 25, 1911.
33 Feimster, *Southern Horrors*, 159–60.
34 In *Southern Horrors*, Feimster recounts the years, names, alleged offenses, and states in which Black, white, and Mexican women were lynched between 1837 and 1965. Feimster finds that nearly 200 women were lynched between 1880 and 1930; the majority of these women were Black, with a number of white and Mexican women being lynched throughout that period. A similar list of women lynched can be found in Henrietta Vinton Davis, "Recorded Cases of Black Female Lynching Victims 1886–1957: More on Black Women Who Were Lynched," *Henrietta Vinton Davis's Weblog*, July 22, 2009, https://henriettavintondavis.wordpress.com/2009/07/22/recorded/.
35 Feimster, *Southern Horrors*, 158; "Negress Lynched," *Memphis Appeal*, August 19, 1886; "Eliza Woods Lynched," *Tennessean*, August 19 1886.
36 "Negress Lynched," *Memphis Appeal*, August 19, 1886.
37 "Negress Lynched," *Memphis Appeal*, August 19, 1886.
38 Wells-Barnett, *Southern Horrors*, in *On Lynchings*, 13–14. Ida B. Wells was a turn-of-the-century antilynching advocate and journalist, and a leading figure in the movement to protect Black lives and livelihoods from white supremacist violence. No due process was granted Black men accused of a crime against a white man or woman or child; the mere accusation of a crime committed against a white person was enough to have a Black person tortured and lynched.
39 Wells-Barnett, *On Lynchings*, 29.
40 Wells-Barnett, *On Lynchings*, 30.
41 Wells-Barnett, *On Lynchings*, 30.
42 Wells-Barnett, *A Red Record*, in *On Lynchings*, 146.
43 Wells-Barnett, *Southern Horrors*, in *On Lynchings*, 31.
44 Douglass, *Why Is the Negro Lynched?*, 3.
45 Douglass writes that white men are lynched too. Allen et al., *Without Sanctuary*, includes photos of white men (Italian men) lynched as well.
46 Goldsby, *Spectacular Secret*, 221.

47 I am drawing from Raiford's article "Photography and the Practices of Critical Black Memory" as well as *Imprisoned in a Luminous Glare*. In her article, Raiford forwards a concept of *critical Black memory* by examining the relationship between lynching photography and African American memory through the analysis of visual art that incorporates lynching photography as a way to produce a different narrative about lynching that can disrupt the putative truth with which a photograph can be imbued.

48 Raiford, "Photography and the Practices," 114.

49 As Cedric Robinson discusses in *Forgeries of Memory and Meaning*, 128 and 225–42, comedies, romances, and melodramas were created by Black productions such as the Lincoln Motion Picture Company and the Ebony Film Company using Black writers, directors, and producers.

50 Stewart, *Migrating to the Movies*, 220–22.

51 For more on these films from Black cinema studies scholars, see Robinson, *Forgeries of Memory and Meaning*, 247 and 256–61, where he offers an analysis of Micheaux's cinematic repudiation of Griffith's film. In *Migrating to the Movies*, 189, Jacqueline Najuma Stewart analyzes the cinematic responses to Griffith's *Birth of a Nation* that Micheaux makes with *Within Our Gates*.

52 Benbow, "Birth of a Quotation," 509.

53 Wells, *Crusade for Justice*, 292–94.

54 Raiford, *Imprisoned in a Luminous Glare*, 29–66.

55 Robinson, *Forgeries of Memory and Meaning*, 243.

56 In Robinson's chapter "Resistance and Imitation in Early Black Cinema" in *Forgeries of Memory and Meaning*, he discusses comedies made by Black film companies that reproduce white supremacist violence and Black buffoonery as well as Black film companies that used the medium to usurp racist characterizations and represent Black business, intelligence, and citizenry.

57 See Stewart's *Migrating to the Movies* for more about the cinematic representation of Black people during this era.

58 Robinson, *Forgeries of Memory and Meaning*, 256.

59 In *Migrating to the Movies*, Stewart quotes Toni Cade Bambara's analysis of the rape scene in *Within Our Gates*, stating that Micheaux "set the record straight on who rapes who" (230).

60 In *Migrating to the Movies*, Stewart cites analyses of this title card in *Within Our Gates* made by Jane Gaines in *Fire and Desire* and in Louise Spense and Pearl Bowser's *Writing Himself into History*, in which they each assert that the intertitle attesting to "legitimate marriage" was not in the original print (237).

61 According to Feimster's appendix in *Southern Horrors*, four Black women were lynched for crimes their father, sons, or husband committed. The daughter of J. Hasting was lynched in 1892 in Louisiana because her father was accused of murder, Meta Hicks was lynched in 1906 in Georgia because her husband was accused of murder, Cordelia Stevenson was lynched in 1915 in Mississippi because her son was accused of committing arson, and Mrs. Sarah Williams was lynched in Louisiana in 1924 because her son was accused of murder (235–39). Feimster lists Laura

Nelson's alleged crime as murder (238); though there are conflicting accounts of the murder of Deputy Loney, the report of the case found in Allen et al., *Without Sanctuary*, 179–80, documents that Laura Nelson took responsibility for the crime but states that she did not actually commit the murder.

62 I discuss this topic in more detail in chapter 4. The barbarous term *increase*, used to describe the children born of enslaved women that points to the reproductive violence suffered by enslaved women, is historicized in J. L. Morgan, *Laboring Women*.

63 Goldsby, *Spectacular Secret*, 4–5; Raiford, *Imprisoned in a Luminous Glare*, 15–18.

64 Ida B. Wells-Barnett began writing vociferously against lynching after three of her friends were arrested and lynched when they resisted white supremacist intimidation and mob violence over their business, the People's Grocery Company, which was becoming quite successful. For more about Wells, see Wells-Barnett, *On Lynchings*, a collection of her essays and pamphlets; and Goldsby, "Writing 'Dynamically': Ida B. Wells," in *A Spectacular Secret*, 43–104.

65 There are varying reports about whether these photographs actually circulated as postcards, though the practice of producing and mailing postcards of lynchings was commonplace at the time. It is noted in Allen et al., *Without Sanctuary*, that the word *unmailable* is written on the photograph in the archive.

66 Goldsby's central argument about lynching photography in *A Spectacular Secret* is that though lynching is thought to have been conducted by aberrant, irrational, backward white southerners, the lynch mobs were actually systematic bodies performing a cultural logic that was a defining index of American progress and modernity (6–7, 21–23, 26–27). Amy Louise Wood's article "Lynching Photography and the Visual Reproduction of White Supremacy" examines the use of lynching photographs in local southern communities and in national newspapers to justify the violent barbarous murders of Black men by lynch mobs. Though Wood's article is an attempt to critique the objectivity with which newspapers report lynchings, as they appear to sympathize with white supremacist ideologies, this article often leaves the ridiculous logic and contrived charges used to build a case for lynching a Black person without sufficient interrogation. Wood has published a book since the publication of this article, titled *Lynching and Spectacle*.

67 Digital imagery is not impervious to destruction. A digital image can be lost, or may be inaccessible, but while it exists and is accessible, anyone who knows the search terms and has the means to search for it can retrieve it from digital space.

68 Allen et al., *Without Sanctuary*, is a publication of lynching photographs that catalogs atrocities committed by white lynch mobs. This volume reproduces the photographs and offers some context for these terrible attacks and in so doing serves as an archive of lynching photography as well as a record of white supremacy. The lynching photograph of Laura Nelson is included among the ninety-eight plates in this publication.

69 Barthes, *Camera Lucida*, 5–7.

70 Bazin, "The Ontology of the Photographic Image," in *What Is Cinema?*, 10–11.

71 For more on haunting and cinema, see Leeder, *Cinematic Ghost*.

72 Twenty-four frames per second is the frame rate for cinema. The frame rate for video ranges in speed from twenty-four frames per second for high-definition video

73 Mulvey, *Death 24x a Second*, 18–19, 35–36, 43–47.
74 A video of the pilot performance of SAVED :: *video postcard* on September 29, 2013, is available at https://vimeo.com/132129457.
75 Lorde, "Uses of the Erotic," 57.
76 These are words spoken by a participant in SAVED :: *video postcard* and included in the video.
77 Alexander, *Pedagogies of Crossing*, 7
78 Alexander, *Pedagogies of Crossing*, 7.
79 For more on rites of passage and liminality, see Turner, "Liminality and Communitas."

CHAPTER THREE: CARRYING THE KNOWLEDGE / PERFORMING THE ARCHIVE

1 I attended the matinee showing of *Happy Birthday, Marsha!* at The Kitchen in Chelsea, New York City, on September 22, 2018.
2 Geo Wyeth and his band played the film score that accompanied the screening and live performances of *Happy Birthday, Marsha!* at The Kitchen.
3 While Marsha and Sylvia referred to themselves as transvestites or drag queens, as these were the terms contemporary to their time, I have made the choice to use trans in my analysis throughout this chapter. When I am quoting Marsha and Sylvia or referring to their work with S.T.A.R., I will use their language. The term *gay* was an umbrella term that included gay and lesbian sexuality.
4 Miss Major Griffin-Gracy is a trans activist and elder who fights for prison abolition and the safety of trans women in prison and after their release. She was a member of the audience for the matinee performance and film screening of *Happy Birthday, Marsha!* on September 22, 2018. This production was so popular that the producers needed to add an additional showing during the afternoon and I was lucky enough to get a ticket. After the performance, those in attendance, the author of this book included, clamored to greet her, show respect, and thank her for all that she has done for the community.
5 Tourmaline, formerly Reina Gossett, began using this name after conducting extensive archival research on Marsha P. Johnson, S.T.A.R., and Sylvia Rivera, and producing this film. Tourmaline's previous name is associated with the research that she conducted during that era of her life.
6 See Tourmaline's website, titled Reina Gossett—Activist, Writer, Speaker, accessed March 15, 2019, http://www.reinagossett.com/new-website/.
7 While this chapter focuses on Tourmaline, I do want to recognize the cowriter and codirector of *Happy Birthday, Marsha!*, Sasha Wortzel. See chapter 1 for a detailed biography of Wortzel.
8 "Reina Gossett: Historical Erasure as Violence," Barnard Center for Research on Woman, accessed July 22, 2020, https://bcrw.barnard.edu/videos/reina-gossett

9. -historical-erasure-as-violence/. Tourmaline is the name used by the artist/activist/scholar.
9. As is made evident in the interviews that follow, the details about what exactly took place at the Stonewall Inn, who frequented the bar and who started the "riot," conflict with each other. Though some memories of this time produce a friction, I regard the trans women as authorities on the subject and let each of their accounts of the events fill in the historical picture.
10. Although at the time of the uprising at the Stonewall Inn this was referred to as a riot, in the discussion of these events, the language has shifted, and it is also being referred to as a rebellion. I have decided to refer to this as a rebellion to recognize the concerted effort and deliberate mode of resistance that battled dominant power.
11. Sylvia Rivera was interviewed by Eric Marcus in 1989, who later aired the conversation on his podcast *Making Gay History*. Eric Marcus, "Episode 01—Sylvia Rivera" (part 1) and "Sylvia Rivera—Part 2," *Making Gay History*, recorded December 12, 1989, https://makinggayhistory.com/podcast/episode-1-1/, https://makinggayhistory.com/podcast/sylvia-rivera-part-2/.
12. Marcus, "Episode 01—Sylvia Rivera."
13. Marcus, "Sylvia Rivera"; Kasino and Morrison, *Pay It No Mind*; Ophelian, *Major! OK*
14. For more on these movements, see Gosse, *Rethinking the New Left*. See also Hobson, *Lavender and Red*, for a discussion of gay and lesbian left social movements.
15. The Combahee River Collective's "Black Feminist Statement" details the patriarchy within the Black Power movement and the racism and homophobia rampant in feminist circles. In the documentary film *She's Beautiful When She's Angry*, women who participated in the Students for a Democratic Society describe the patriarchal ideology that was pervasive and pushed women out to start feminist groups.
16. Kissack, "Freaking Fag Revolutionaries," 110–11.
17. Kissack, "Freaking Fag Revolutionaries," 112–13.
18. The Mattachine Society was formed in Los Angeles in 1950 by Harry Hay. The Daughters of Bilitis was a San Francisco–based organization founded in 1955 by Del Martin and Phyllis Lyon. Martin and Lyon were married in 2004, one of the initial marriages performed under the new law allowing gay marriage in California. See also Gosse, *Rethinking the New Left*, 80–81.
19. The Gay Liberation Front was established in July 1969, the month following the Stonewall rebellion. A young activist, Jim Fourrat, met with members of the Mattachine Society in New York in the early days of the GLF, but their distinct approaches to gay liberation made this a short-lived partnership. Fourrat and others formed an ad hoc Action Committee of the Mattachine Society but broke off when they wanted to make an alliance with other New Left groups, some of whom made homophobic remarks. Kissack, "Freaking Fag Revolutionaries," 113–14.
20. Kissack, "Freaking Fag Revolutionaries," 109–10. See also "Gay Liberation Front (GLF)," accessed July 3, 2019, http://web-static.nypl.org/exhibitions/1969/liberation.html.
21. See Kissack, "Freaking Fag Revolutionaries," 107–10.

22 Kissack, "Freaking Fag Revolutionaries," 113. In 1970 Huey P. Newton released a statement that challenged BPP members to reckon with their discomfort with gay and lesbian people.
23 Arthur Evans, "GAA and the Birth of Gay Liberation," Gay Today, accessed July 3, 2020, http://gaytoday.com/garchive/viewpoint/072699vi.htm. In this article, GAA leader Arthur Evans describes GAA emerging out of a rupture in the GLF over its support of the Black Panther Party (BPP). The GLF decided to give the BPP five hundred dollars. Some GAA members wanted to show solidarity with the BPP while others wanted to focus on gay issues exclusively. Those who disagreed with the GLF decision to donate the money to the BPP left the GLF and began the GAA. Evans was among that group.
24 Maggie Schreiner, "An Army of Lovers Cannot Lose: The Occupation of NYU's Weinstein Hall," Researching Greenwich Village History, December 14, 2011, https://greenwichvillagehistory.wordpress.com/2011/12/14/an-army-of-lovers-cannot-lose-the-occupation-of-nyus-weinstein-hall/. See also S. Cohen, "Street Transvestite Action Revolutionaries (S.T.A.R.)," in *The Gay Liberation Youth Movement*, 89–164; and Marcus, "Sylvia Rivera."
25 Schreiner, "Army of Lovers Cannot Lose."
26 Tourmaline, "Sylvia Goes to College and STAR Takes Over NYU," The Spirit Was, February 20, 2012, https://thespiritwas.tumblr.com/post/17984686264/sylvia-goes-to-college-star-takes-over-nyu.
27 Leslie Feinberg, "Interview: Sylvia Rivera," Queer Bible, October 8, 2017, https://www.queerbible.com/queerbible/2017/10/8/interview-sylvia-rivera-by-leslie-feinberg.
28 Feinberg, "Interview."
29 The speech that Sylvia gave was recorded by the L.O.V.E. (Lesbians Organizing for Video Experience) Tapes Collective. See "Y'all Better Quiet Down," Gay Pride Rally, Washington Square Park, New York City, June 24, 1973, https://vimeo.com/234353103. LoveTapesCollective videos are housed at the Lesbian Herstory Archives.
30 Eric Marcus, "Jean O'Leary—Part 1," *Making Gay History*, recorded August 22, 1989, https://makinggayhistory.com/podcast/episode-14-jean-oleary-part-1/. An audio clip of O'Leary's speech from 1973 is included in the recording of Marcus's interview with her. In this interview, O'Leary expresses embarrassment about her transphobia and discusses the way that her understanding of gender and her relationships with trans people have developed since 1973. In 1989, when the interview was recorded, O'Leary no longer believed that trans people should be excluded from the gay and lesbian community.
31 Marcus, "Sylvia Rivera." In this interview, Sylvia mentions Bob Kohler as the only member of GAA or GLF who helped S.T.A.R. Kohler was one of the founders of the Gay Liberation Front. Sylvia also names Marsha P. Johnson, Bambi Lamour, and Endora as some of the original members of S.T.A.R.
32 Photographs of Marsha P. Johnson at the NYU protest at Weinstein Hall in 1970 were taken by Diana Davies and are housed at the NYPL Manuscripts and Archive Division. Photographs of Marsha protesting at Bellevue Hospital in 1970 were taken by Richard C. Wandel and are housed at the Lesbian, Gay, Bisexual and Trans-

gender Community Center. Photographs of Marsha P. Johnson, Sylvia Rivera, and S.T.A.R. taken between 1970 and 1975 by Leonard Fink, including the 1973 Christopher Street Day rally, are held at the Lesbian, Gay, Bisexual and Transgender Community Center.

33 Conquergood, "Performance Studies," 146; Taylor, *Archive and the Repertoire*, 6–7; Schneider, "Archives," 100.
34 Conquergood, "Performance Studies," 146.
35 Conquergood, "Performance Studies," 151.
36 Conquergood, "Performance Studies," 146.
37 Allan Kaprow is distinguished as an artist who was active in the Fluxus movement and coined the term *happening* to describe a mode of performance art that uses dance, painting, sculpture, and music to blur the boundaries of art and everyday life. His discussion of happenings is detailed in Kaprow, *Assemblages, Environments, and Happenings*. See also Turner, *From Ritual to Theatre*, 32–33.
38 Sedgwick, "Queer Performativity," 2; Butler, "Critically Queer," 2–22.
39 Taylor, *Performance*, 147–48.
40 Taylor, *Performance*, 208.
41 Taylor, *Archive and the Repertoire*, 17.
42 Taylor, *Archive and the Repertoire*, 16–17.
43 Taylor, *Performance*, 208.
44 Taylor, *Archive and the Repertoire*, 2–3. See also Schechner, *Between Theater and Anthropology*, 36.
45 Trouillot, *Silencing the Past*, 48–52.
46 Trouillot, *Silencing the Past*, 50–52.
47 Trouillot, *Silencing the Past*, 52.
48 Michel Foucault described his conception of subjugated knowledge as "those blocs of historical knowledge which were present but disguised within the body of functionalist and systematizing theory" (*Power/Knowledge*, 82).
49 For an interview with Stormé DeLarverie in which our elder talks about the Stonewall rebellion, see https://www.youtube.com/watch?v=XgCVNEiOwLs, accessed August 21, 2022. For a history of S.T.A.R. that places it at the center of late 1960s to early 1970s gay liberation, see S. Cohen, "Street Transvestite Action Revolutionaries (S.T.A.R.)."
50 Miss Major discusses this in her documentary film *Major!*
51 In 2020 the East River Park in Brooklyn, New York, was renamed the Marsha P. Johnson State Park.
52 Sarah Schulman, interview with Jim Fouratt, ACT UP Oral History Project, November 28, 2006, Tape II, 15 minutes, https://actuporalhistory.org/numerical-interviews/066-jim-fouratt?rq=Fouratt.
53 Evans, "GAA and the Birth of Gay Liberation."
54 Evans, "GAA and the Birth of Gay Liberation"; Schulman, interview with Jim Fouratt.
55 In 2015 the queer community mobilized an online boycott of Roland Emmerich's *Stonewall*, which dramatized the Stonewall rebellion and placed a fictional white cis gay teen at the center of the story.

56 C. Cohen, "Punks, Bulldaggers, and Welfare Queens," 438.
57 Schneider, "Archives," 100.
58 Schneider, "Archives," 105.
59 See the Black Panther Party for Self Defense Ten Point Program, accessed April 19, 2019, https://www.blackpast.org/african-american-history/primary-documents-african-american-history/black-panther-party-ten-point-program-1966/.
60 France, *Death and Life of Marsha P. Johnson*.
61 Kasino and Morrison, *Pay It No Mind*.
62 Kasino and Morrison, *Pay It No Mind*.
63 Kasino and Morrison, *Pay It No Mind*.
64 Eric Marcus, "Marsha P. Johnson and Randy Wicker," *Making Gay History*, recorded 1989, https://makinggayhistory.com/podcast/episode-11-johnson-wicker/.
65 Marcus, "Marsha P. Johnson and Randy Wicker."
66 Marcus, "Marsha P. Johnson and Randy Wicker."
67 Marcus, "Marsha P. Johnson and Randy Wicker."
68 Marcus, "Marsha P. Johnson and Randy Wicker."
69 Marcus, "Marsha P. Johnson and Randy Wicker."
70 Marcus, "Marsha P. Johnson and Randy Wicker."
71 Marcus, "Marsha P. Johnson and Randy Wicker."
72 Marcus, "Marsha P. Johnson and Randy Wicker."
73 See Tre'vell Anderson, "Trans Filmmaker Reina Gossett Accuses 'The Death and Life of Marsha P. Johnson' Creator of Stealing Work," *Los Angeles Times*, October 9, 2017; Suzannah Weiss, "'The Death and Life of Marsha P. Johnson' Creator Accused of Stealing Work from Filmmaker Tourmaline," *Teen Vogue*, October 8, 2017.
74 Anderson, "Trans Filmmaker Reina Gossett Accuses."
75 Weiss, "Death and Life of Marsha P. Johnson."
76 See Tourmaline, "The Personal Things," 2016, https://www.queer-art.org/tourmaline-2. The video was a Queer|Art|Prize 2017 Recent Work Finalist.
77 Phelan, "The Ontology of Performance," in *Unmarked*, 146.
78 In *The Archive and the Repertoire*, Taylor contends that "the video is part of the archive, what it represents is part of the repertoire" (20).
79 Taylor, *Archive and the Repertoire*, 20.
80 Taylor, *Archive and the Repertoire*, 15.
81 Phelan, "The Ontology of Performance," 146.
82 Schneider, "Archives," 106.

CHAPTER FOUR: ECSTASY AND THE ARCHIVE

1 Husserl, *Ideas*; Merleau-Ponty, *Phenomenology of Perception*.
2 Guenther, "Critical Phenomenology, 11."
3 D. Davis, "Phenomenological Method," 4.
4 D. Davis, "Phenomenological Method," 3–9.
5 Guenther, "Critical Phenomenology," 15.

6   Guenther, "Critical Phenomenology," 15.
7   Weiss, Murphy, and Salamon, introduction to *50 Concepts for a Critical Phenomenology*, xiv.
8   Lorde, "Litany for Survival," 31–32. The full text of Lorde's poem "A Litany for Survival" is available at https://www.poetryfoundation.org/poems/147275/a-litany-for-survival (accessed August 26, 2022).
9   Spillers, "Mama's Baby, Papa's Maybe," 68.
10 See Blassingame, *Slave Community*. See also Genovese, *Roll, Jordan, Roll*.
11 Much of the scholarship that engages with paternalism during chattel slavery responds to Eugene Genovese's analysis of plantation paternalism in *Roll, Jordan, Roll*, which sympathizes with slaveholders by claiming that reciprocal and mutually beneficial relationships existed between the enslaved and slaveholders; this logic is the basis of paternalism itself.
12 A. Davis, "Reflections on the Black Woman's Role," 7.
13 See also J. L. Morgan, *Laboring Women*; Glymph, *Out of the House of Bondage*; Smallwood, *Saltwater Slavery*; Giddings, *When and Where I Enter*; and Fox-Genovese, *Within the Plantation Household*.
14 D. White, *Ar'n't I a Woman?*, 119–23.
15 J. L. Morgan, *Laboring Women*, 82.
16 J. L. Morgan, *Laboring Women*, 83.
17 Nina Simone, "Mississippi Goddam," *Nina Simone in Concert*, Carnegie Hall (Philips Records, 1964).
18 Hine, *Hine Sight*, 37. The concept of "the politics of silence" is also critically engaged by Evelyn Brooks Higginbotham in her article "African-American Women's History and the Metalanguage of Race." Higginbotham also discusses "the politics of respectability" in *Righteous Discontent*.
19 In *Selections from the Prison Notebooks*, Italian theorist Antonio Gramsci outlines key elements of hegemony, which includes the notion of common sense. Common sense is an axiomatic understanding of the way things are or should be that is part of the hegemonic process of coercion and consent that exacts power over subordinate people and communities. This concept is an integral part of Keeling's theoretical framework that supports her discussion of Black lesbian visibility in *The Witch's Flight*.
20 Hine, *Hine Sight*, 41–44.
21 Hammonds, "Black (W)holes," 142–44.
22 Hammonds, "Black (W)holes," 142.
23 Hammonds, "Black (W)holes," 142.
24 Patricia Hill Collins's theory of controlling images is taken up by critical phenomenologists and appears in Weiss, Murphy, and Salamon's *50 Concepts for a Critical Phenomenology*; Collins, "Controlling Images," 77–82.
25 Collins, *Black Feminist Thought*, 76–106.
26 In 1965 Daniel Patrick Moynihan published "The Negro Family: The Case for National Action," commonly referred to as the Moynihan Report. Moynihan, the sociologist turned senator, found that the family structure was the fundamental prob-

lem with the Negro family and the female-headed household was the outstanding culprit. The Moynihan Report shifted the blame off racism, capitalism, and patriarchy and onto the backs of Black women. During the 1960s in the United States, members of the Black Power movement used findings in the Moynihan Report that asserted that Black single working mothers caused the demise of the Black family.

27 Spillers, "Mama's Baby, Papa's Maybe," 65.
28 Spillers, "Mama's Baby, Papa's Maybe," 66.
29 In her novel *Beloved*, Toni Morrison opens with the story of Margaret Garner, who escaped the plantation on which she was being held as a slave. Upon the threat of being returned to the condition of slavery, Garner killed her children rather than see them go back into bondage.
30 In *The Half Has Never Been Told*, Edward Baptist uses the term *enslaver* to refer to those who held people as slaves.
31 Lorde, at 00:02:22 in *A Litany for Survival: The Life and Work of Audre Lorde*, directed by Ada Gay Griffin and Michelle Parkerson (1995).
32 Combahee River Collective, "Black Feminist Statement," 13.
33 Combahee River Collective, "Black Feminist Statement," 14.
34 Combahee River Collective, "Black Feminist Statement," 16.
35 Combahee River Collective, "Black Feminist Statement," 15–16. I included this quote in chapter 3 but I repeat it in the context of this chapter as well because it takes on a different valence here. I want to preserve the integrity of the statement by including the quote and not simply a reference to it.
36 Crenshaw, "Demarginalizing the Intersection," 140–50.
37 See Crenshaw, "Mapping the Margins."
38 Du Bois, *Souls of Black Folk*, 1.
39 Painter, "Representing Truth," 488–92.
40 Nell Irvin Painter includes the letter from Frances Dana Gage, originally published in the *Independent* on April 23, 1863, as appendix II in her article "Representing Truth," 489–92. Gage's letter describes the events surrounding Sojourner Truth's speech at the 1851 Women's Convention in Akron, Ohio. Gage's letter offers a record of the speech that also includes a description of Truth's performance on stage. In my citation of this speech, I only include the words that Truth is reported to have spoken.
41 In *Sojourner Truth: A Life, a Symbol*, Nell Irvin Painter argues that Truth did not actually ask "Ain't I a woman?" in this speech. She contends that Frances Dana Gage created this story to produce more empathy for the plight of enslaved Black women.
42 To read the transcript of Laverne Cox's lecture, see "Ain't I a Woman—Asks Laverne Cox, Actress, Producer and Transgender Advocate," Visual AIDS, April 19, 2013, https://visualaids.org/blog/aint-i-a-woman-asks-laverne-cox-actress-producer-and-transgender-advocate.
43 Rankine, *Citizen*, 43.
44 Rankine, *Citizen*, 59.
45 A. Walker, *In Search of Our Mothers' Gardens*, 233.
46 For an in-depth discussion of Ellen and William Craft, see Snorton, *Black on Both Sides*; and McMillan, *Embodied Avatars*. See also Hunter, *Bound in Wedlock*.

47 McKittrick, *Demonic Grounds*, xiii.
48 McKittrick, *Demonic Grounds*, 37–38.
49 Jacobs, *Incidents in the Life*.
50 McKittrick, *Demonic Grounds*, xviii–xix.
51 McKittrick, *Demonic Grounds*, xviii.
52 McKittrick, *Demonic Grounds*, xv.
53 Lorde, "Transformation of Silence," 41–42.
54 Lorde, "Transformation of Silence," 41.
55 Jordan, "Freedom Time," in *Affirmative Acts*, 59–65. Joplin's lyrics are from Kris Kristofferson and Fred Foster's 1969 song "Me and Bobby McGee," which Joplin covered on her posthumous album *Pearl* (Columbia, 1971).
56 Morrison, "Unspeakable Things Unspoken," 188.
57 Parkerson and Griffin, *Litany for Survival*.
58 Alice Coltrane, *Journey in Satchidananda*, recorded in 1970, Impulse! Records, February 1971, album. Her genre is recognized as avant-garde jazz.
59 "The Most Segregated Hour in America—Martin Luther King Jr.," *Meet the Press*, April 17, 1960, https://www.youtube.com/watch?v=1q88Ig1L_d8.
60 For more on the role of the Black church in the civil rights movement, see Ransby, *Ella Baker and the Black Freedom Movement*. See also Morris, "The SCLC."
61 Marx, "Contribution to the Critique of Hegel's Philosophy of Right," 42.
62 See hooks, *Black Looks*; Robinson, *Forgeries of Memory and Meaning*; Bogle, *Toms, Coons, Mulattoes*; and Everett, *Returning the Gaze*.
63 For more on blackness, representation, and meaning making, see Hall, *Representation*. See also Hall, "What Is This Black in Black Popular Culture?"
64 I am referring to the four categories of Black womanhood that I began this chapter with: Safronia, Sweet Thang, Aunt Sara, and Peaches that Nina Simone sang about in *Four Women*; and Sapphire, Mammy, Jezebel, and Matriarch that Patricia Hill Collins, the Combahee River Collective, and Hortense Spillers each write about in their Black feminist analyses. I am focusing here on Black women, but certainly the image of Black men as dangerous, thieving, violent rapists also proliferates in contemporary popular culture.
65 Ava Duvernay's *Queen Sugar* and Shonda Rhimes's *Scandal* have contributed complex Black women characters to television. Dee Rees's *Pariah* and Lee Daniels's *Empire* have brought Black queer characters to Black popular culture in the contemporary moment. *Pose* on FX has brought Black and Brown trans stories to television.
66 For more on Lacks and the HeLa Cells, see J. Brown, "Being Cellular"; Roberts, *Fatal Invention*; and Holloway, *Private Bodies, Public Texts*. *The Immortal Life of Henrietta Lacks* by Rebecca Skloot is a popular text about Lacks.
67 Wald, "Cells, Genes, and Stories," 247.
68 Wald, "Cells, Genes, and Stories," 247.
69 The panelists for this discussion included the Nigerian ambassador to the United Nations; John Hope Franklin; a representative of the American Society of African Culture; a British African historian and critic; and Antonio Olinto, who was a Brazilian author and critic and a former cultural attaché from Brazil to Lagos, Nigeria.

I want to thank Margaret Odette, research assistant at the Schomburg Center for Research in Black Culture, for her help with researching this series.

70 *Peabody Digest* (1965), quoted by WorldCat, accessed May 19, 2022, https://www.worldcat.org/title/history-of-the-negro-people-no-3-slavery/oclc/42466757.

71 The testimonies of those who were formerly enslaved were gathered under the auspices of the Federal Writer's Project, which was one of the programs within the Works Progress Administration (WPA). It is helpful to remember that the WPA was a part of Franklin D. Roosevelt's New Deal, created in 1935, to combat the desolation and unemployment of the Great Depression. Some WPA jobs were designed to employ workers to build the country's infrastructure, while other programs, like the Federal Writer's Project, were focused on the arts. One Federal Writer's Project initiative was focused on collecting American folklore, but at the outset there was no provision made for collecting the narratives of formerly enslaved people. If a writer was interested in a particular subject, then an interview would be recorded and collected as part of the archive. Black members of the Federal Writer's Project in the southern states started collecting narratives of formerly enslaved people, and as the collection grew, an initiative also formed. In 1936 Zora Neale Hurston was a member of the Federal Writer's Project in Florida that was quite active in collecting the narratives of formerly enslaved people. Once the project became institutionalized, though, more white interviewers began working on the project, and it became clear that formerly enslaved people were less willing to be forthright with white interviewers. With this brief history of the WPA narratives of the formerly enslaved in mind, it is compelling that, still, the theme of resistance courses through so many of the interviews.

72 Muñoz, *Cruising Utopia*, 1.

73 Morrison, "Be Your Own Story."

74 Keeling, "Looking for M—," 566.

75 Sobchack, *Address of the Eye*, xv. See also Husserl, *Ideas*. For more on phenomenology, see Merleau-Ponty, *The Visible and the Invisible*.

76 Sobchack, *Address of the Eye*, xvii.

77 Keeling, "Looking for M—," 566.

78 Keeling, "Looking for M—," 566.

79 Keeling, *Witch's Flight*, 25.

CODA

1 Solange, *When I Get Home*, recorded in 2018, Columbia Records, 2019, album.

2 Solange, "Down with the Clique," recorded in 2018, track 3 on *When I Get Home*, Columbia Records, 2019, album; Aaliyah, "Down with the Clique," recorded in 1993–94, track 5 on *Age Ain't Nothing but a Number*, Blackground, Jive, BMG Records, 1994, album.

3 Solange, "Time (Is)," recorded in 2018, track 10 on *When I Get Home*, Columbia Records, 2019, album.

4 Esperanza Spalding, *12 Little Spells*, recorded in 2018, Concord Records, 2018, album. Alice Coltrane's fourth studio album, *Journey in Satchidananda*, appears in Ja'Tovia Gary's short film *An Ecstatic Experience*, which I discuss in chapter 4. Alice Coltrane,

Journey in Satchidananda, recorded in 1970, Impulse! Records, February 1971, album. For more on Coltrane's music, see J. Brown, *Black Utopias*, especially chapter 2, "Lovely Sky Boat: Alice Coltrane and the Metaphysics of Sound."

5 Leigh's *Brick House* installation was the first commissioned art piece of New York City's High Line Plinth Series. The piece rested above Thirtieth Street and Tenth Avenue and could be visited from June 2019 to May 2021. A version of this sculpture sits at the main entrance of the University of Pennsylvania. It was installed in November 2020. Leigh was the United States representative at the 59th Venice Biennale, held in 2022. Her sculpture, *Brick House*, was one of the works that she presented there. Leigh won the Venice Biennale's top honor, the Golden Lion award, for Best Participant.

6 Judith Jamison, performing *Cry* by Alvin Ailey, City Center, New York City, 1972. See "Alvin Ailey American Dance Theater: Cry," YouTube, 16:01, December 6, 2016, https://www.youtube.com/watch?v=OuTJSbWm2QY.

7 Alvin Ailey American Dance Theater, "Current and Former Ailey Women Dance Cry," YouTube, 6:58, May 6, 2020, https://www.youtube.com/watch?v=m6WK8JKYrLw.

8 Solange, "I'm a Witness," recorded in 2018, track 19 on *When I Get Home*, Columbia Records, 2019, album.

Bibliography

FILMOGRAPHY

Akerman, Chantal, dir. *Jeanne Dielman, 23, quai du commerce, 1080 Bruxelles*. 2017.
Akerman, Chantal, dir. *La Chambre*. 1972.
Brakhage, Stan, dir. *The Act of Seeing with One's Own Eyes*. 1971.
Brakhage, Stan, dir. *Dog Star Man*. 1961–64.
Brakhage, Stan, dir. *Mothlight*. 1963.
Burnett, Charles, dir. *Killer of Sheep*. 1978.
Borden, Lizzie, dir. *Born in Flames*. 1983.
Buñuel, Luis, dir. *Un Chien Andalou*. 1929.
Collins, Kathleen, dir. *Losing Ground*. 1982.
Dash, Julie, dir. *Daughters of the Dust*. 1991.
Dash, Julie, dir. *Four Women*. 1975.
Dash, Julie, dir. *Illusions*. 1982.
Davis, Ossie, et al. *History of the Negro People*. 1965.
Davis, Zeinabu irene, dir. *Compensation*. 1991.
Davis, Zeinabu irene, dir. *Cycle*. 1989.
Deren, Maya, dir. *Meshes of the Afternoon*. 1943.
Dunye, Cheryl, dir. *The Watermelon Woman*. 1996.
France, David, dir. *The Death and Life of Marsha P. Johnson*. 2017.
Friedrich, Su, dir. *Damned If You Don't*. 1987.
Friedrich, Su, dir. *Sink or Swim*. 1990.
Friedrich, Su, dir. *The Ties That Bind*. 1984.
Gary, Ja'Tovia, dir. *An Ecstatic Experience*. 2015.
Griffith, D. W., dir. *Birth of a Nation*. 1915.
Hammer, Barbara, dir. *Dyketactics*. 1974.
Hammer, Barbara, dir. *Superdyke*. 1975.
Kasino, Micahel, and Richard Morrison, dirs. *Pay It No Mind: Marsha P. Johnson*. 2012.
Kazan, Elia, dir. *Gentleman's Agreement*. 1947.
Kazan, Elia, dir. *Pinky*. 1949.

Lynch, Kara, dir. *SAVED :: video postcard*. 2015.
McCullough, Barbara, dir. *Water Ritual #1: An Urban Rite of Purification*. 1979.
Micheaux, Oscar, dir. *Within Our Gates*. 1920.
Mulvey, Laura, dir. *Riddles of the Sphinx*. 1977.
Ophelian, Annalise, dir. *Major!* 2015.
Parkerson, Michelle, and Ada Gay Griffin, dirs. *A Litany for Survival: The Life and Work of Audre Lorde*. 1995.
Rainer, Yvonne, dir. *Film about a Woman Who*. 1985.
Riggs, Marlon, dir. *Ethnic Notions*. 1986.
Sirk, Douglas, dir. *Imitation of Life*. 1959.
Smith, Cauleen, dir. *Dark Matter and Postcard*. 2006.
Smith, Cauleen, dir. *Sojourner*. 2018.
Smith, Jack, dir. *Flaming Creatures*. 1962–63.
Stahl, John M., dir. *Imitation of Life*. 1934.
Tourmaline, and Sasha Wortzel, dirs. *Happy Birthday, Marsha!* 2018.
Walker, Kara, dir. *Six Miles from Springfield on the Franklin Road*. 2009.
Werker, Alfred L., dir. *Lost Boundaries*. 1949.

PUBLISHED WORKS

Alexander, M. Jacqui. *Pedagogies of Crossing: Meditations on Feminism, Sexual Politics, Memory, and the Sacred*. Durham, NC: Duke University Press, 2005.
Allen, James, Hilton Als, John Lewis, and Leon F. Litwack. *Without Sanctuary: Lynching Photography in America*. Santa Fe, NM: Twin Palms Publishers, 2000.
Appadurai, Arjun. "Archive and Aspiration." In *Information Is Alive*, edited by Joke Brouwer and Arjen Mulder, 14–25. Rotterdam: V2/NAI.
Baptist, Edward. *The Half Has Never Been Told: Slavery and the Making of American Capitalism*. New York: Basic Books, 2014.
Barthes, Roland. *Camera Lucida*. Translated by Richard Howard. New York: Hill and Wang, 1981.
Bazin, André. *What Is Cinema?* Vol. 1. Translated by Hugh Gray. Berkeley: University of California Press, 2005.
Benbow, Mark E. "Birth of a Quotation: Woodrow Wilson and 'Like Writing History with Lightning.'" *Journal of the Gilded Age and Progressive Era* 9, no. 4 (2010): 509–33.
Bey, Marquis. "Black Fugitivity Un/gendered." *Black Scholar* 49, no. 1 (2019): 55–62.
Blaetz, Robin, ed. *Women's Experimental Cinema: Critical Frameworks*. Durham, NC: Duke University Press, 2007.
Blassingame, John. *The Slave Community: Plantation Life in the Antebellum South*. New York: Oxford University Press, 1972.
Bogle, Donald. *Toms, Coons, Mulattoes, Mammies, and Bucks: An Interpretive History of Blacks in American Films*. New York: Bloomsbury Academic, 2016.
Brakhage, Stan. "From Metaphors on Vision." In *The Avant-Garde Film: A Reader of Theory and Criticism*, edited by P. Adams Sitney, 120–28. New York: Anthology Film Archives, 1987.

Brooks, Daphne. *Liner Notes for the Revolution: The Intellectual Life of Black Feminist Sound.* Cambridge, MA: Harvard University Press, 2021.

Brown, Jayna. "Being Cellular: Race, the Inhuman, and the Plasticity of Life." *GLQ: A Journal of Lesbian and Gay Studies* 21, nos. 2–3 (2015): 321–41.

Brown, Jayna. *Black Utopias: Speculative Life and the Music of Other Worlds.* Durham, NC: Duke University Press, 2021.

Brown, William Wells. *Clotel; or, The President's Daughter.* New York: Penguin, 2004 [1853].

Butler, Judith. "Critically Queer." *GLQ: A Journal of Lesbian and Gay Studies* 1, no. 1 (1993): 17–32.

Certeau, Michel de. *The Writing of History.* Translated by Tom Conley. New York: Columbia University Press, 1992.

Chesnutt, Charles. *The Marrow of Tradition.* New York: Houghton, Mifflin, 1901.

Child, Lydia Maria. "The Quadroons." In *The Norton Anthology of American Literature*, vol. B, edited by Nina Baym, 180–90. New York: W. W. Norton, 2012.

Cohen, Cathy J. "Punks, Bulldaggers, and Welfare Queens: The Radical Potential of Queer Politics?" *GLQ: A Journal of Lesbian and Gay Studies* 3, no. 4 (1997): 437–65.

Cohen, Stephen. *The Gay Liberation Youth Movement: "An Army of Lovers Cannot Fail."* New York: Routledge, 2008.

Collins, Patricia Hill. *Black Feminist Thought: Knowledge, Consciousness, and the Politics of Empowerment.* New York: Routledge, 1990.

Collins, Patricia Hill. "Controlling Images." In *50 Concepts for a Critical Phenomenology*, edited by Gail Weiss, Ann V. Murphy, and Gayle Salamon, 77–82. Evanston, IL: Northwestern University Press, 2020.

Combahee River Collective. "A Black Feminist Statement." In *All the Women Are White, All the Blacks Are Men, but Some of Us Are Brave*, edited by Gloria T. Hull, Patricia Bell Scott, and Barbara Smith, 13–22. New York: Feminist Press, 1982.

Conquergood, Dwight. "Performance Studies: Interventions and Radical Research." *TDR: The Drama Review* 46 (2002): 145–56.

Crenshaw, Kimberlé. "Demarginalizing the Intersection of Race and Sex: A Black Feminist Critique of Antidiscrimination Doctrine, Feminist Theory and Antiracist Politics." *University of Chicago Legal Forum*, no. 1 (1989): 139–67.

Crenshaw, Kimberlé. "Mapping the Margins: Intersectionality, Identity Politics, and Violence against Women of Color." *Stanford Law Review* 43, no. 6 (1991): 1241–99.

Croly, David Goodman. *Miscegenation: The Theory of the Blending of the Races, Applied to the American White Man and Negro.* New York: Dexter, Hamilton, 1864.

Cvetkovich, Ann. *An Archive of Feelings: Trauma, Sexuality, and Lesbian Public Cultures.* Durham, NC: Duke University Press, 2003.

Dash, Julie. *Daughters of the Dust: The Making of an African American Woman's Film.* New York: New Press, 1994.

Davis, Angela. "Reflections on the Black Woman's Role in the Community of Slaves." *Black Scholar* 3, no. 4 (1971): 2–15.

Davis, Duane H. "The Phenomenological Method." In *50 Concepts for a Critical Phenomenology*, edited by Gail Weiss, Ann V. Murphy, and Gayle Salamon, 3–10. Evanston, IL: Northwestern University Press, 2019.

DeClue, Jennifer. "The Circuitous Route of Presenting Black Butch: The Travels of Dee

Rees's Pariah." In *Sisters in the Life: A History of Out African American Lesbian Media-Making*, edited by Yvonne Welbon and Alex Juhasz, 225-48. Durham, NC: Duke University Press, 2018.

Derrida, Jacques. *Archive Fever: A Freudian Impression*. Translated by Eric Prenowitz. Chicago: University of Chicago Press, 1996.

Derrida, Jacques. *Specters of Marx: The State of the Debt, the Work of Mourning and the New International*. Translated by Peggy Kamuf. New York: Routledge, 2006.

Doane, Mary Ann. *The Emergence of Cinematic Time: Modernity, Contingency, the Archive*. Cambridge, MA: Harvard University Press, 2002.

Douglass, Frederick. *Why Is the Negro Lynched?* Bridgewater: Whitby and Sons, 1895.

Du Bois, W. E. B. *Black Reconstruction in America, 1860-1880*. 1935. Reprint, New York: Free Press, 1998.

Du Bois, W. E. B. "The Concept of Race." In *The Oxford W. E. B. Du Bois Reader*, edited by Eric J. Sundquist, 37-96. 1940. Reprint, New York: Oxford University Press, 1996.

Du Bois, W. E. B. "Crime." *The Crisis: A Record of the Darker Races*, July 1911, 99-100.

Du Bois, W. E. B. "Lynching." *The Crisis: A Record of the Darker Races*, October 1911, 233.

Du Bois, W. E. B. *The Souls of Black Folk*. 1903. Reprint, New York: Dover, 1997.

Du Bois, W. E. B. "The Spawn of Slavery: The Convict Lease System in the South." *Missionary Review of the World* 14 (October 1901): 737-45.

Dunham Kelley, Emma. *Megda*. Boston: James H. Earle, 1891.

Erkkila, Betsy. *Mixed Bloods and Other Crosses: Rethinking American Literature from the Revolution to the Culture Wars*. Philadelphia: University of Pennsylvania Press, 2005.

Eskridge, William N., Jr. *Gay Law: Challenging the Apartheid of the Closet*. Cambridge, MA: President and Fellows of Harvard College, 1999.

Everett, Anna. *Returning the Gaze: A Genealogy of Black Film Criticism, 1909-1949*. Durham, NC: Duke University Press, 2001.

Feimster, Crystal. *Southern Horrors: Women and the Politics of Rape and Lynching*. Cambridge, MA: Harvard University Press, 2009.

Feinberg, Leslie. *Stone Butch Blues*. New York: Firebrand Books, 1993.

Ferguson, Roderick A. *Aberrations in Black: Toward a Queer of Color Critique*. Minneapolis: University of Minnesota Press, 2004.

Fields, Barbara Jeanne. "Slavery, Race and Ideology in the United States of America." *New Left Review* 1, no. 181 (May/June 1990): 95-118.

Foucault, Michel. *Power/Knowledge: Selected Interviews and Other Writings 1972-1977*. New York: Vintage, 1980.

Foucault, Michel. *The Will to Knowledge. The History of Sexuality, Vol. 1*. Translated by Rubert Hurley. New York: Penguin Books, 1998.

Fox-Genovese, Elizabeth. *Within the Plantation Household and Imagined Communities: Reflections on the Origin and Spread of Nationalism*. Chapel Hill: University of North Carolina Press, 1988.

Freeman, Elizabeth. *Time Binds: Queer Temporalities, Queer Histories*. Durham, NC: Duke University Press, 2010.

Gaines, Jane. *Fire and Desire: Mixed Race Movies in the Silent Era*. Chicago: University of Chicago Press, 2001.

Garza, Alicia. "Herstory." Accessed February 15, 2020. blacklivesmatter.com/herstory.
Genovese, Eugene D. *Roll, Jordan, Roll: The World the Slaves Made*. New York: Vintage Books, 1976.
Giddings, Paula. *When and Where I Enter: The Impact of Black Women on Race and Sex in America*. New York: HarperCollins, 1984.
Glymph, Thaviola. *Out of the House of Bondage: The Transformation of the Plantation Household*. Cambridge: Cambridge University Press, 2008.
Goldsby, Jacqueline. *A Spectacular Secret: Lynching in American Life and Literature*. Chicago: University of Chicago Press, 2006.
Gordon, Avery F. *Ghostly Matters: Haunting and the Sociological Imagination*. New ed. Minneapolis: University of Minnesota Press, 2008.
Gordon-Reed, Annette. *The Hemgingses of Monticello: An American Family*. New York: W. W. Norton, 2008.
Gordon-Reed, Annette. *Thomas Jefferson and Sally Hemings: An American Controversy*. Charlottesville: University of Virginia Press, 1997.
Gosse, Van. *Rethinking the New Left*. New York: Palgrave Macmillan, 2005.
Gramsci, Antonio. *Selections from the Prison Notebooks*. Edited and translated by Quintin Hoare and Geoffrey Nowell Smith. New York: International Publishers, 1971.
Guenther, Lisa. "Critical Phenomenology." In *50 Concepts for a Critical Phenomenology*, edited by Gail Weiss, Ann V. Murphy, and Gayle Salamon, 11–16. Evanston, IL: Northwestern University Press, 2019.
Gumbs, Alexis Pauline. *Undrowned: Black Feminist Lessons from Marine Mammals*. Chico, CA: AK Press, 2020.
Halberstam, Jack [Judith]. *The Queer Art of Failure*. Durham, NC: Duke University Press, 2011.
Hall, Stuart. *Representation: Cultural Representations and Signifying Practices*. London: SAGE, 1997.
Hall, Stuart. "What Is This Black in Black Popular Culture?" In *Black Popular Culture*, edited by Gina Dent, 21–33. Seattle: Bay Press, 1992.
Hammonds, Evelynn M. "Black (W)holes and the Geometry of Black Female Sexuality." In *Feminism Meets Queer Theory*, edited by Elizabeth Weed and Naomi Schor, 136–56. Bloomington: Indiana University Press, 1997.
Harper, Frances E. W. *Iola Leroy; or, Shadows Uplifted*. Oxford: Oxford University Press, 1988.
Harper, Phillip Brian. *Abstractionist Aesthetics: Artistic Form and Social Critique in African American Culture*. New York: New York University Press, 2015.
Hartman, Saidiya. *Lose Your Mother: A Journey along the Atlantic Slave Route*. New York: Farrar, Straus and Giroux, 2007.
Hartman, Saidiya. *Scenes of Subjection: Terror Slavery and Self-Making in Nineteenth-Century America*. New York: Oxford University Press, 1997.
Hartman, Saidiya. "Venus in Two Acts." *Small Axe* 12, no. 2 (2008): 1–14.
Higginbotham, Evelyn Brooks. "African-American Women's History and the Metalanguage of Race." *Signs* 17, no. 2 (1992): 251–74.
Higginbotham, Evelyn Brooks. *Righteous Discontent: The Women's Movement in the Black Church, 1880–1920*. Cambridge, MA: Harvard University Press, 1993.

Hine, Darlene Clarke. *Hine Sight: Black Women and the Re-construction of American History.* Brooklyn, NY: Carlson Publishing, 1994.

Hobson, Emily K. *Lavender and Red: Liberation and Solidarity in the Gay and Lesbian Left.* Oakland: University of California Press, 2016.

Holloway, Karla. *Private Bodies, Public Texts: Race, Gender, and Cultural Bioethics.* Durham, NC: Duke University Press, 2011.

hooks, bell. *Ain't I a Woman: Black Women and Feminism.* Boston: South End Press, 1981.

hooks, bell. *Black Looks: Race and Representation.* Boston: South End Press, 1992.

Hull, Gloria T., Patricia Bell Scott, and Barbara Smith, eds. *All the Women Are White, All the Blacks Are Men, but Some of Us Are Brave.* New York: Feminist Press, 1982.

Hunter, Tera. *Bound in Wedlock: Slave and Free Black Marriage in the Nineteenth Century.* Cambridge, MA: Harvard University Press, 2017.

Husserl, Edward. *Ideas Pertaining to a Pure Phenomenology and to a Phenomenological Philosophy.* Translated by Richard Rojcewicz and André Schuwer. Boston: Kluwer Academic Publishers, 1989.

Jacobs, Harriet. *Incidents in the Life of a Slave Girl as Written by Herself.* Cambridge, MA: Harvard University Press, 2000.

Jones-Sneed, Frances. "Gender, Race and the Antilynching Crusade in the United States." *The Mind's Eye: A Liberal Arts Journal* (2011): 59-73.

Jordan, June. "Freedom Time." In *Affirmative Acts: Political Essays*, 59-65. New York: Anchor Books, 1998.

Kaplan, Sidney. "The Miscegenation Issue in the Election of 1864." *Journal of Negro History* 34, no. 3 (1949): 274-343.

Kaprow, Allan. *Assemblages, Environments, and Happenings.* New York: Harry N. Abrams, 1966.

Keeling, Kara. "Looking For M—: Queer Temporality, Black Political Possibility, and Poetry from the Future." *GLQ: A Journal of Lesbian and Gay Studies* 15, no. 4 (2009): 565-82.

Keeling, Kara. *The Witch's Flight: The Cinematic, the Black Femme, and the Image of Common Sense.* Durham, NC: Duke University Press, 2007.

Kissack, Terrance. "Freaking Fag Revolutionaries: New York's Gay Liberation Front, 1969-1971." *Radical History Review* 62 (1995): 104-34.

Larsen, Nella. *"Quicksand" and "Passing."* New York: Anchor Books, 2001.

Leeder, Murray. *Cinematic Ghost: Haunting and Spectrality from Silent Cinema to the Digital Era.* New York: Bloomsbury, 2015.

Leeder, Murray. *The Modern Supernatural and the Beginnings of Cinema.* London: Palgrave Macmillan, 2000.

Lemire, Elise. *Miscegenation: Making Race in America.* Philadelphia: University of Pennsylvania Press, 2002.

Lorde, Audre. "A Litany for Survival." In *The Black Unicorn Poems*, 31-32. New York: W. W. Norton, 1978.

Lorde, Audre. *Sister Outsider: Essays and Speeches by Audre Lorde..* New York: Crossing Press, 2007.

Lorde, Audre. "The Transformation of Silence into Language and Action." In *Sister Outsider*, 40-44.

Lorde, Audre. "Uses of the Erotic: The Erotic as Power." In *Sister Outsider*, 53-59.

Marx, Karl. "Contribution to the Critique of Hegel's Philosophy of Right." In Karl Marx and Friedrich Engels, *On Religion*, 41–58. Mineola, NY: Dover Publications, 2008.

McHugh, Kathleen. "The Experimental 'Dunyementary': A Cinematic Signature Effect." In *Women's Experimental Cinema: Critical Frameworks*, edited by Robin Blaetz, 339–59. Durham, NC: Duke University Press, 2007.

McHugh, Kathleen. "History and Falsehood in Experimental Autobiographies." In *Women and Experimental Filmmaking*, edited by Jean Petrolle and Virginia Wright Wexman, 105–28. Urbana: University of Illinois Press, 2005.

McKittrick, Katherine. *Demonic Grounds: Black Women and the Cartographies of Struggle*. Minneapolis: University of Minnesota Press, 2006.

McMillan, Uri. *Embodied Avatars: Genealogies of Black Feminist Art and Performance*. New York: New York University Press, 2015.

Merleau-Ponty, Maurice. *Phenomenology of Perception*. Translated by Colin Smith. New York: Routledge, 2002.

Merleau-Ponty, Maurice. *The Visible and the Invisible*. Edited by Claude Lefort. Translated by Alphonso Lingus. Evanston, IL: Northwestern University Press, 1968.

Mitchell, W. J. T. *Seeing through Race*. Cambridge, MA: Harvard University Press, 2012.

Morgan, Edmund S. *American Slavery, American Freedom: The Ordeal of Colonial Virginia*. New York: W. W. Norton, 1975.

Morgan, Jennifer L. *Laboring Women: Reproduction and Gender in New World Slavery*. Philadelphia: University of Pennsylvania Press, 2004.

Morris, Aldon. "The SCLC: The Decentralized Arm of the Black Church." In *Disruptive Religion: The Force of Faith in Social Movement Activism*, edited by Christian Smith, 29–46. New York: Routledge, 1996.

Morrison, Toni. *Beloved*. New York: Knopf, 1987.

Morrison, Toni. "Be Your Own Story." Commencement address, Wellesley College, Wellesley, MA, May 28, 2004.

Morrison, Toni. *Sula*. New York: Knopf, 1973.

Morrison, Toni. "Unspeakable Things Unspoken: The Afro-American Presence in American Literature." In *The Source of Self-Regard*, 161–97. New York: Knopf, 2020.

Moten, Fred. *In the Break: The Aesthetics of the Black Radical Tradition*. Minneapolis: University of Minnesota Press, 2003.

Moynihan, Daniel Patrick. "The Negro Family: The Case for National Action." Office of Policy Planning and Research, United States Department of Labor, 1965.

Mulvey, Laura. *Death 24x a Second*. London: Reaktion Books, 2006.

Muñoz, José Esteban. *Cruising Utopia: The Then and There of Queer Futurity*. New York: New York University Press, 2009.

Nash, Jennifer. *Black Feminism Reimagined: After Intersectionality*. Durham, NC: Duke University Press, 2018.

Nyong'o, Tavia. *The Amalgamation Waltz: Race, Performance, and the Ruses of Memory*. Minneapolis: University of Minnesota Press, 2009.

Omi, Michael, and Howard Winant. *Racial Formation in the United States: From the 1960s to the 1990s*. 2nd ed. New York: Routledge, 1994.

Painter, Nell Irvin. "Representing Truth: Sojourner Truth's Knowing and Becoming Known." *Journal of American History* 81, no.2 (1994): 461–92.
Painter, Nell Irvin. *Sojourner Truth: A Life, a Symbol*. New York: W. W. Norton, 1997.
Petrolle, Jean, and Virginia Wright Wexman, eds. *Women and Experimental Filmmaking*. Urbana: University of Illinois Press, 2005.
Phelan, Peggy. *Unmarked: The Politics of Performance*. New York: Routledge, 1993.
Pindell, Howardena. *Kara Walker-no, Kara Walker-yes, Kara Walker-?* New York: Midmarch Arts Press, 2009.
Quashie, Kevin. *Black Aliveness, or A Poetics of Being*. Durham, NC: Duke University Press, 2021.
Rabinovitz, Lauren. *Points of Resistance: Women, Power and Politics in the New York Avant-Garde Cinema, 1943–71*. 2nd ed. Urbana: University of Illinois Press, 2003.
Raiford, Leigh. *Imprisoned in a Luminous Glare: Photography and the African American Freedom Struggle*. Chapel Hill: University of North Carolina Press, 2011.
Raiford, Leigh. "Photography and the Practices of Critical Black Memory." *History and Theory* 48, no. 4 (2009): 112–29.
Rankine, Claudia. *Citizen: An American Lyric*. Minneapolis, MN: Graywolf, 2014.
Ransby, Barbara. *Ella Baker and the Black Freedom Movement: A Radical Democratic Vision*. Chapel Hill: University of North Carolina Press, 2003.
Rees, A. L. *A History of Experimental Film and Video: From the Canonical Avant-Garde to Contemporary British Practice*. 2nd ed. New York: Palgrave Macmillan, 2011.
Ricketts Sumner, Cid. *Quality*. New York: Bantam Books, 1968.
Roach, Joseph. *Cities of the Dead*. New York: Columbia University Press, 1996.
Roberts, Dorothy. *Fatal Invention: How Science, Politics, and Big Business Re-create Race in the Twenty-First Century*. New York: New Press, 2012.
Robinson, Cedric J. *Forgeries of Memory and Meaning: Blacks and the Regimes of Race in American Theater and Film before World War II*. Chapel Hill: University of North Carolina Press, 2007.
Rothman, Joshua D. *Notorious in the Neighborhood: Sex and Families across the Color Line in Virginia, 1787–1861*. Chapel Hill: University of North Carolina Press, 2003.
Schechner, Richard. *Between Theater and Anthropology*. Philadelphia: University of Pennsylvania Press, 1985.
Schneider, Rebecca. "Archives: Performance Remains." *Performance Research: A Journal of the Performing Arts* 6, no. 2 (2001): 100–108.
Sedgwick, Eve Kosofsky. "Queer Performativity: Henry James's *The Art of the Novel*." *GLQ: A Journal of Lesbian and Gay Studies* 1, no. 1 (1993): 1–16.
Sexton, Jared. *Amalgamation Schemes: Antiblackness and the Critique of Multiracialism*. Minneapolis: University of Minnesota Press, 2008.
Sharpe, Christina. *In the Wake: On Blackness and Being*. Durham, NC: Duke University Press, 2016.
Sharpe, Christina. *Monstrous Intimacies: Making Post-Slavery Black Subjects*. Durham, NC: Duke University Press, 2010.
Shockley, Evie. *Renegade Poetics: Black Aesthetics and Formal Innovation in African American Poetry*. Iowa City: University of Iowa Press, 2011.

Skloot, Rebecca. *The Immortal Life of Henrietta Lacks*. New York: Crown, 2010.
Smallwood, Stephanie. *Saltwater Slavery: A Middle Passage from Africa to the African Diaspora*. Cambridge, MA: Harvard University Press, 2007.
Snorton, C. Riley. *Black on Both Sides: A Racial History of Trans Identity*. Minneapolis: University of Minnesota Press, 2017.
Sobchack, Vivian. *The Address of the Eye: A Phenomenology of Film Experience*. Princeton, NJ: Princeton University Press, 1992.
Spense, Louise, and Pearl Bowser. "Writing Himself into History: Oscar Micheaux, His Silent Films, and His Audience." New Brunswick, NJ: Rutgers University Press, 2000.
Spillers, Hortense J. *Black, White, and in Color: Essays on American Literature and Culture*. Chicago: University of Chicago Press, 2003.
Spillers, Hortense J. "Mama's Baby, Papa's Maybe: An American Grammar Book." *Diacritics* 17, no. 2 (1987): 65–81.
Stewart, Jacqueline Najuma. *Migrating to the Movies: Cinema and Black Urban Modernity*. Berkeley: University of California Press, 2005.
Stoler, Ann Laura. *Along the Archival Grain: Epistemic Anxieties and Colonial Common Sense*. Durham, NC: Duke University Press, 1995.
Taylor, Diana. *The Archive and the Repertoire: Performing Cultural Memory in the Americas*. Durham, NC: Duke University Press, 2003.
Taylor, Diana. *Performance*. Durham, NC: Duke University Press, 2016.
Tourmaline [Reina Gossett], Eric A. Stanley, and Johanna Burton, eds. *Trap Door: Trans Cultural Production and the Politics of Visibility*. Cambridge, MA: MIT Press, 2017.
Trouillot, Michel-Rolph. *Silencing the Past: Power and the Production of History*. Boston: Beacon, 1995.
Turner, Victor. *From Ritual to Theatre: The Human Seriousness of Play*. New York: Performing Arts Journal, 1982.
Turner, Victor. "Liminality and Communitas." In *The Performance Studies Reader*, edited by Henry Bial and Sara Brady, 97–104. New York: Routledge, 2016.
Wald, Priscilla. "Cells, Genes, and Stories: HeLa's Journey from Labs to Literature." In *Genetics and the Unsettled Past: The Collision of Race, DNA, and History*, edited by Keith Walloo, Alondra Nelson, and Catherine Lee, 247–65. New Brunswick, NJ: Rutgers University Press, 2012.
Walker, Alice. *In Search of Our Mothers' Gardens*. New York: Harcourt Brace Jovanovich, 1983.
Walker, Kara. *Bureau of Refugees*. New York: Charta, 2008.
Walker, Kara. "The Risible Visual: Humor and Art, Kara Walker Speaks about Her Art." Public lecture, Menil Collection, Houston, TX, March 14, 2011. https://www.youtube.com/watch?v=clvQRQO5x7E.
Weheliye, Alexander. *Habeas Viscus: Racializing Assemblages, Biopolitics, and Black Feminist Theories of the Human*. Durham, NC: Duke University Press, 2014.
Weiss, Gail, Ann V. Murphy, and Gayle Salamon. Introduction to *50 Concepts for a Critical Phenomenology*, edited by Gail Weiss, Ann V. Murphy, Gayle Salamon, xiii–xvi. Evanston, IL: Northwestern University Press, 2019.
Wells, Ida B. *Crusade for Justice: The Autobiography of Ida B. Wells*. Chicago: University of Chicago Press, 1970.

Wells-Barnett, Ida B. *On Lynchings*. 1892. Reprint, Amherst, NY: Humanity Books, 2002.

White, Deborah Gray. *Ar'n't I a Woman? Female Slaves in the Plantation South*. New York: W. W. Norton, 1999.

Wilderson, Frank B., III. *Red, White and Black: Cinema and the Structure of U.S. Antagonism*. Durham, NC: Duke University Press, 2010.

Wood, Amy Louise. *Lynching and Spectacle: Witnessing Racial Violence in America, 1890-1940*. Chapel Hill: University of North Carolina Press, 2009.

Wood, Amy Louise. "Lynching Photography and the Visual Reproduction of White Supremacy." *American Nineteenth Century History* 6, no. 3 (2005): 373-99.

Index

Aberrations in Black (Ferguson), 23
Abstractionist Aesthetics (Harper), 51
Action Committee of the Mattachine Society, 201n19
aesthetics of resistance: in Black avant-garde films, 11–14
affectivity, 179–81
Ailey, Alvin, 185–86
Ain't I a Woman (hooks), 157
Akerman, Chantal, 9, 188nn10–11
Alexander, M. Jacqui, 1–2, 75–77, 95–96
Alternate U, 134
anti-sodomy laws, 108–9
anti-war movement: Stonewall rebellion and, 108
Appadurai, Arjun, 194n27
archival documentation: Black feminist avant-garde films as, 3–4, 29–64; Black feminist phenomenology and, 166–81; conjure work and, 6–7; Freedmen's Bureau and, 38–43; of Laura Nelson's lynching, 77–85; of Marsha P. Johnson, 103–6, 129, 132–36; performance and, 94–97, 103–4, 116–23; of Reconstruction violence, 32–38; of reproductive violence, 194n25; silhouette as, 60–64; violence of, 14–18; Walker's work as, 50–60
Archive and the Repertoire (Taylor), 119–20
"Ar'n't I a woman?" (Truth), 156–57
Ar'n't I a Woman? (White), 148, 157–58
Arthur, Teddy (Mrs.), 82–83
Atlantic Is a Sea of Bones (film), 105
avant-garde films: Black feminists and, 2–4, 23–28, 94–97; cinematic tenderness and aesthetics of resistance in, 11–14; definitions of, 187n9, 195n45; distorted vision of Black womanhood in, 18–22; performance in, 103–4, 116–23; techniques and forms of, 7–11; Walker's work and, 51–60. See also Black feminist avant-garde

Baker, Ella, 171
Baraka, Amiri, 9, 189n18
Barthes, Roland, 93
"Battle Hymn of the Republic" (Howe), 169–70
Bazin, André, 93
Bearden, Romare, 9, 189n18
Bell, Arthur, 123
Beloved (Morrison), 160, 206n29
Bey, Marquis, 23
"Be Your Own Story" (Morrison), 1–2
Birth of a Nation (film), 85–86, 88
Black Arts movement, 9, 189n18
Black church, 171–72
blackface minstrelsy, 50, 86, 173
Black feminist avant-garde: archival intervention and, 41–43, 116–23; cinematic tenderness and, 184–86; disembodiment in, 2; films by, 2–4, 26–28, 94–97; founding principles of, 22–24; Gary's Ecstatic Experience as, 170–72; Tourmaline and Wortzel's Happy Birthday, Marsha! and, 136–42; history of science and, 19–20; performance and, 103–4, 116–23; phenomenology of freedom and, 143–81;

Black feminist avant-garde (*continued*)
  SAVED :: video postcard (Lynch video installation) and, 94–97; *Six Miles from Springfield on the Franklin Road* (Walker short film) and, 53–64; White feminist theory vs., 7–8. *See also* avant-garde films
Black feminist phenomenology: cinema and architecture of, 178–81; evolution of, 146–64; freedom and, 164–81
"Black Feminist Statement" (Combahee River Collective), 154–55, 201n15
Black Feminist Thought (Collins), 151–52
Black film and television, 172–73
"Black (W)holes and the Geometry of Black Women's Sexuality" (Hammonds), 151
"Black (w)hole" theory, 19–22
Black lesbian women: Black feminist theory and, 22–24; in *Daughters of the Dust*, 11–13; in *The Watermelon Woman*, 15–18
Black liberation movement, 23
#BlackLivesMatter, 23, 177–78
Black Panther Party for Self-Defense (BPP), 108–9, 127, 202n23
Black Panthers, 101–2
Black Power movement, 9, 201n15
Black Russian (documentary), 190n48
Black womanhood: in afterlife of slavery, 143–46; archival footage of, 178–81; avant-garde films and, 8–11; controlling images of, 151–52, 155, 173, 207n64; definitions of, 4; distortion of vision and, 18–22; phenomenology of, 147; in popular culture, 173; in Reconstruction era, 41–43; in Walker's *Bureau of Refugees* series, 44–60; in Walker's *Mulatto* image, 33–44
Bonner, Marita, 9, 189n18
Borden, Lizzie, 188n13
Born in Flames (film), 188n13
Brakhage, Stan, 9, 52–53, 187n9–10, 189n10, 195n43
Brent, Linda (Harriet Jacobs), 161–62
Brick House (Leigh sculpture), 184–85, *185*, 209n5
Brooklyn Museum, 26, 104–5, 191n49
Brooks, Daphne, 23
Brown, Jayna, 23
Brown, William Wells, 36
Buñuel, Luis, 188n10, 195n42
Bureau of Refugees, Freedmen, and Abandoned Lands. *See* Freedmen's Bureau

Bureau of Refugees series (Walker), 24, 29–38, *38*, 44–60
Burnett, Charles, 9
Butler, Judith, 119, 157

Camera Lucida (Barthes), 93
Camicia, Jimmy, 102, 140–42
Carter, David, 129
"Cells, Genes, and Stories" (Wald), 173–74
Certeau, Michel de, 62–63
Chesnutt, Charles, 36
Child, Lydia Maria, 193n12
Christopher Street Gay Pride March and Day Rally, 111, 123, 126
cinematic tenderness, 183–86; in Black avant-garde films, 11–14
cinematographic technology, 93–94, 199n72; Black feminist phenomenology and, 178–81
Citizen (Rankine), 158–59
civil rights movement, 171–72
Clansman, The, (Dixon), 85
Clotel (Brown), 36
Cohen, Cathy J., 125
Collins, Kathleen, 27, 192n51, 207n64
Collins, Patricia Hill, 151–52
Coltrane, Alice, 166, 184–86
Combahee River Collective, 22–24, 154–56, 201n15, 207n64
Compensation (film), 27
conjure work, visitation and, 5–7
Cortez, Jayne, 9, 189n18
Cox, Laverne, 157–58
Craft, Ellen, 160–61
Craft, William, 160–61
Crenshaw, Kimberlé, 155–56
Crisis, The (Du Bois), 79–80
"Critically Queer" (Butler), 119
critical phenomenology, 145–46
Cruising Utopia (Muñoz), 175–77
Crusade for Justice (Wells), 85
Cry (Ailey ballet), 185–86

Dada movement, 195n42
Dalí, Salvador, 52, 188n10, 195n42
Daniels, Lee, 207n65
Dark Matter and Postcard (film), 27

Dash, Julie, 8–9, 11–13, 20–22
Daughters of Bilitis, 108–9, 114, 121, 201n18
Daughters of the Dust (film), 11–14, 188n14
Davis, Angela, 23, 147–48
Davis, Duane H., 144–45
Davis, Ossie, 174–75
Davis, Zeinabu irene, 9, 27
Death and Life of Marsha P. Johnson, The, (documentary film), 135–36
Dee, Ruby, 26, 166–69, 174–77
DeLarverie, Stormé, 122, 203n49
Deleuze, Gilles, 180
Demonic Grounds (McKittrick), 161–62
Deren, Maya, 9, 188nn10–11, 188n14
Derrida, Jacques, 63
Devore, Jesse, 175
digital imagery, 199n67
disembodiment: cinematic tenderness and, 94, 183–86; erotic and concept of, 76–77; writers' investigation of, 1–2
District of Alabama List of Murders, Record Group 105 (National Archives), 30–33, *31*
Dixon, Thomas, 85
Dog Star Man (film), 188n10
Douglas, Emory, 84
Douglass, Frederick, 50, 83
Du Bois, W. E. B., 32, 79, 156–58
Dunye, Cheryl, 8, 12, 15–18, 47
Duvernay, Ava, 207n65

Ecstatic Experience, An (Gary), 26–27, *144*, 144–46, 166–81, *168–69*, *171*
Edison, Thomas, 86, 90
Ellington, Duke, 10
Emancipation Proclamation, 29
Embodied Avatars (McMillan), 10–11
Empire (television series), 207n65
erotic space: in *SAVED :: video postcard* (Lynch video installation), 25, 65–69, 66–67, 70, 74–77, 94–97
Ethnic Notions (film), 172–73
Evans, Arthur, 123, 202n23
Evening Scimitar (newspaper), 82

Fanon, Frantz, 179
Federal Writer's Project, 208n71
Feimster, Crystal, 81, 90, 196n19, 198n61
Feinberg, Leslie, 110

feminist movement, 108; Black feminist activism and, 157–58. *See also* Black feminist avant-garde
Ferguson, Roderick, 23
Fields, Barbara Jean, 22
50 Concepts for a Critical Phenomenology (Weiss, Murphy, and Salomon), 145
Forgeries of Memory and Meaning (Robinson), 86, 88, 198n49, 198n56
Fouratt, Jim, 123, 201n19
Four Women (Simone), 152
France, David, 135–36
Franklin, John Hope, 207–8n69
Freedmen's Bureau (Bureau of Refugees, Freedmen, and Abandoned Lands): records of violence and, 24, 29–43, 190n47; refugee terminology of, 192n5
freedom, Black feminist phenomenology of, 143–44, 164–81
Freedom Is a Constant Struggle (Douglas), 84
"Freedom Time" (Jordan), 164
Friedrich, Su, 9
"From Metaphors on Vision" (Brakhage), 52

Gage, Francis Dana, 157, 206nn40–41
Gallagher, James, 129
Gampel, Chris M., 175
Gary, Ja'Tovia, 26–27, 144–46, 166–81, 191n50
Gay Activists Alliance (GAA), 109–14, 120–23, 125, 128–29, 202n23
Gay Liberation Front (GLF), 109–10, 114, 121–23, 125, 128, 201n19, 202n23
gay liberation movement, 25–26; Stonewall rebellion and, 107–16; trans women in, 128–29, 132–36
Gay Student Liberation, 109–10
gender, Black womanhood and, 155–63
Genovese, Eugene, 205n11
Ghostly Matters (Gordon), 5, 149
Giovanni, Nikki, 9, 189n18
GLQ: A Journal of Lesbian and Gay Studies, 119
Goldsby, Jacqueline, 84, 91–92, 199n66
Gordon, Avery, 5, 76–77, 149
Gossett, Reina. *See* Tourmaline (Reina Gossett)
Gramsci, Antonio, 92, 150, 205n19
Griffin-Gracy, Miss Major, 107, 200n4
Griffith, D. W., 85, 90

Index   223

Guenther, Lisa, 144–45
Gumbs, Alexis Pauline, 23

Habeas Viscus (Weheliye), 187n7
Hall, Bernice, 175
Hammonds, Evelynn, 19–21, 151
Happy Birthday, Marsha! (film), 25–26, 97, 100–104, 110, 115–16, 120, 136–42, 191n49
Harper, Frances E. W., 36
Harper, Phillip Brian, 51–52
Hartman, Saidiya, 16–18, 23, 50–51
haunting: Gordon's theory of, 76–77; lynching photography as, 91–94; *SAVED :: video postcard* (Lynch video installation) as, 94–97; visitation and, 5–7
Hay, Harry, 201n18
HeLa cells, 173–74
Hicks, Meta, 198n61
High Line Art, 105, 191n49
Hine, Darlene Clark, 150
History of the Negro People (PBS miniseries), 174–75
Homesteader (film), 85
homophile movement, Stonewall rebellion and, 108–16
hooks, bell, 11–12, 23, 157, 181
Hot Peaches performance group, 102
Hughes, Langston, 9, 189n18
Hurst, Fannie, 36
Hurston, Zora Neale, 135–36, 208n71
Husserl, Edmund, 144–45, 179

Ideas (Husserl), 144
Illusions (1982) (film), 20–21
Image of Life (film), 36, 193n14
Imitation of Life (Hurst), 36
Imprisoned in a Luminous Glare (Raiford), 84
Incidents in the Life of Slave Girl (Jacobs), 161
"increase," Black women defined as, 148–49, 194n25, 199n62
Independent, The (newspaper), 77–79
In Search of Our Mothers' Gardens (Walker), 160
intersectionality, Black feminist research and, 155–56
In the Break (Moten), 10, 50–51
invisibility of Black womanhood, 150, 159–63
Invisible (Lynch installation project), 67–74, 191n48
Iola Leroy (Harper), 36

Jackson, Jo, 175
Jackson, Sylvia, 175
Jacobs, Harriet. *See* Brent, Linda
Jamison, Judith, 185–86
Johnson, Marsha P., 25–26; archival research on, 128–29, 132–36, 184; Black feminist avant-garde and activism of, 136–42; death of, 101, 135–36; gay liberation movement and, 110–11, 115–16; performativity of, 120–23; S.T.A.R. Manifesto and, 125–28; trans activism of, 97, 99–106; Wicker and, 132
Jordan, June, 164–65
Journey in Satchidananda (Coltrane album), 166

Kaprow, Allan, 203n37
Kara Walker: My Complement, My Enemy, My Oppressor, My Love (Walker installation piece), 24, 47, 50–60, 192n9
Kazan, Elia, 36
Keeling, Kara, 23, 179–81
Kelley, Emma Dunham, 36
King, Martin Luther, Jr., 170–72
Kinsman, O. B. (Major), 40–46, 49
Kitchen, The (performance space), 99, 102, 118, 137, 184

L.A. Rebellion School (1960–80), 9, 189n19
LaBeija, Egyptt, 100, 102–3, 140–41
labor: by Black enslaved women, 148–49
Lacks, Henrietta, 173–74
Landy, Marcia, 179–80
Lane, Oscar, 78
Lanigan-Schmidt, Tommy, 133
Larsen, Nella, 36
Lawrence v. Texas, 109
Léger, Ferdinand, 52
Leigh, Simone, 184–85
Lemire, Elise, 193n16
Lesbian Feminist Liberation, 113
Lesbian Herstory Archives, 106
LGBT National History Archives, 106
LGBTQ activism, archival documentation of, 104, 115–16, 121–23, 128–36
"Like It Is" (Noble interview series), 177
Lindley, Eve, 101, 140
"Litany for Survival, A" (Lorde), 146–47, 149–50
Littrell, Claude, 78, 196n16
Loney, George H., 78–81

"Looking for M—" (Keeling), 23, 179
Lorde, Audre, 20, 23, 41, 74–76, 94–96, 146–47, 149–50, 153–54, 162–63, 165–66, 181, 186
Los Angeles Times (newspaper), 135
Lose Your Mother (Hartman), 16–17
Losing Ground (film), 27, 192n51
Lost in the Music (film), 105
Lynch, Kara, 25, 27, 116, 190n48; archival documentation in work of, 77–84; Black feminist avant-garde and work of, 95–97; erotic and sacred space in work of, 74–77; haunted images in work of, 91–94; *SAVED :: video postcard* installation by, 65–74, 94–97; tenderness in work of, 183–84
lynching: of Black women, 79–94, 197n34; cinematic archive of, 85–91; erotic and sacred space in photographs of, 74–77; keepsake photographs of, 91–94; news reports of, 77–84; photographs and videos of, 25, 67–74, 84, 91–94; Wells's anti-lynching advocacy and, 82–85
"Lynching Photography and the Visual Reproduction of White Supremacy" (Wood), 199n66
Lyon, Phyllis, 201n18

Machado, Agosto, 129, 132
Major! (film), 107, 121–22
Making Gay History (Marcus podcast), 132
"Mama's Baby, Papa's Maybe" (Spillers), 18–23, 151–53
Manford, Morty, 129
Man Ray, 52, 195n42
Marcus, Eric, 106, 114, 122, 132–35
Markley, N. B., 46, 48
Marrow of Tradition, The (Chesnutt), 36
Martin, Cliff, 78
Martin, Del, 201n18
Marx, Karl, 172
"Master's Tools Will Never Dismantle the Master's House, The" (Lorde), 23
Mattachine Society, 108–9, 114, 201nn18–19
McCaffrey, Sasha, 129
McCullough, Barbara, 9, 27
McKittrick, Katherine, 161–62
McMillan, Uri, 10–11
medium: photography as, 92–94; race as, 21–22
Meet the Press (television show), 170–72
Megda (Kelley), 36

Merleau-Ponty, Maurice, 144
Meshes of the Afternoon (film), 188n10
Micheaux, Oscar, 36, 85–91
Migrating to the Movies (Stewart), 88–90
miscegenation: sexual violence and, 36–38; terminology of, 193n15
Miscegenation (Croly), 37–38
"Mississippi Goddam" (Simone song), 149–50
Mitchell, Charles, 175
Mitchell, W. J. T., 21–22
Moore, Melba, 175
Morgan, Jennifer L., 23, 148–49, 194n25
Morrison, Toni, 1–2, 20, 22, 41, 62, 160, 165, 178
Moten, Fred, 10, 50–51
Moynihan Report, 153, 205n26
Mulatto hung by a grapevine near road side between Tuscaloosa and Greensboro (Walker), 33–44, 35
mulatto women: in film and literature, 36; literary representations of, 193n13; tragic mulatto figure, 193nn12–13; Walker's images of, 36–38
Mulvey, Laura, 94–95, 188n11, 200n73
Muñoz, José Esteban, 119, 176–77
Murphy, Ann V., 145

NAACP Silent March (1917), 68
Nash, Jennifer, 23
National Archives: District of Alabama List of Murders and, 30–33; documentation of violence and, 38–43, 53–60
National Archives Microfilm Publication M999 Roll 34: Bureau of Refugees, Freedmen and Abandoned Lands: Six Miles from Springfield on the Franklin Road (Walker installation piece), 24, 29–38, 44–50, 55–60
National Organization for Women (NOW), 108
Nelson, Austin, 78–79, 91
Nelson, Laura: as archival documentation, 77–85; cinematic tenderness toward, 184; lynching of, 25, 64–77, 90–91, 198n60; photographs of, 91–97
Nelson, L.D., 66–85, 90–92, 95–97, 197n28
New Left movement, Stonewall rebellion and, 108
New Negro movement, 9, 189n18
Newton, Huey P., 109, 111
New York Public Library (NYPL), 106, 121, 123–24
Noble, Gil, 166, 177

Index 225

Nobody Promised You Tomorrow (Brooklyn Museum exhibit), 26, 104–5, 191n49

Obama, Barack, 39
Okemah Ledger, 77–81
O'Leary, Jean, 113, 202n30
Olinto, Antonio, 207–8n69
"Ontology of Performance, The" (Phelan), 140
Outing, The (film), 191n48

Painter, Nell Irvin, 157, 206nn40–41
Pariah (film), 187n8, 207n65
Passing (Larsen), 36
paternalism, slavery and, 205n11
Pay It No Mind: Marsha P. Johnson (film), 128–29, 132–34
Payne, Lawrence, 80
Peabody Award, 174
Peck, W. M. H. H., 40–43, 46–47, 49
Pedagogies of Crossing (Alexander), 1–2, 75–77
Performance (Taylor), 119
performance and performativity: archive and, 94–97, 103–4, 116–23; in Black feminist avant-garde, 140–42; Black feminist avant-garde and, 116–23; of S.T.A.R. Manifesto, 126–28
Personal Things, The (film), 105
Phelan, Peggy, 140
phenomenology: Black womanhood and, 143–46; cinema studies and, 179–81; of freedom, Black feminist phenomenology of, 164–181
Phenomenology of Perception (Merleau-Ponty), 144
photographs of lynching: erotic and sacred space in, 74–77; haunted roots of, 91–94; in Lynch's videos, 67–74, 84–85; technology of photography and, 93–94
Pinky (film), 36, 193n14
Points of Resistance (Rabinovitz), 187n9
political resistance, avant-garde films and, 7–8
popular culture, Black womanhood in, 151–52, 155, 173, 207n64
pornotropy, 17, 22, 27, 32, 61, 69, 187n7; in Black feminist avant-garde films, 51
Pose (television series), 207n65
postcards of lynching, 67–68, 95–97, 199n65
proto-trans theory, 127
Pryor, James, 46

"Punks, Bulldaggers, and Welfare Queens" (Cohen), 125

"Quadroons, The" (Child), 193n12
Quashie, Kevin, 187n4
Queen Sugar (television series), 207n65
queer-of-color critique, 23
"Queer Performativity" (Sedgwick), 119
queer theory: Black feminist thought and, 23–24; cinematic archive and, 105
Quicksand (Larsen), 36

race and racism, as medium, 21–22
Raiford, Leigh, 84, 86, 91, 198n47
Rainer, Yvonne, 9
Rankine, Claudia, 158–59
rape: Freedmen's Bureau reports on, 30; lynchings and, 79–80; in Micheaux's *Within Our Gates*, 88; miscegenation and, 36–38; during slavery, 90–91; terminology of, 192n4; Walker's visualization of, 41–42, 44, 47, 53–64
Reconstruction: Black womanhood in, 150–51; National Archives' documentation of violence in, 39–43; vigilante violence during, 29–38
Red Record, A (Wells), 82–83
Rees, Dee, 187n8, 207n65
"Reflections on the Black Woman's Role in the Community of Slaves" (Davis), 147–48
refugees: status in Reconstruction, 192n5
refusal of violence, 50–51, 127–28
reproductive violence: archival documentation of, 194n25; Black womanhood and haunting of, 152–53; in *Daughters of the Dust*, 13–14; in film, literature and art, 36–38; slavery and, 148–49
resistance: aesthetics of, in Black avant-garde films, 11–14; political resistance, 7–8
Rhimes, Shonda, 207n65
Riggs, Marlon, 172–73
Rivera, Sylvia, 26, 97, 102–7, 110–16, 122–23, 125–27, 133–34, 140
Robinson, Cedric, 86, 88, 198n49
Robinson, Marty, 129
Rollins, Jonathan, 150
rural Black worship, 166, 170–72

sacred space: in *SAVED :: video postcard* (Lynch video installation), 74–77, 95–97
Salacia (film), 105, 191n49
Salamon, Gayle, 145
Sanchez, Sonia, 9, 189n18
Saunders, Garrett, 175
SAVED :: video postcard (Lynch video installation), 25, 91, 116–23; Black feminist avant-garde and, 94–97, 116; cinematographic technology behind, 94–95; lynching photography and, 65–74; visitation in erotic and sacred space, 74–77, 94–97
Scandal (Rhimes), 207n65
Scenes of Subjection (Hartman), 50
Schneider, Rebecca, 126–27, 141
Sedgwick, Eve Kosofsky, 119
Seeing through Race (W. J. T. Mitchell), 21–22
Selections from the Prison Notebooks (Gramsci), 205n19
sexuality of Black women: Reconstruction-era framing of, 150–52; slavery and, 18–22
sexual violence: Walker's visualization of, 53–60. *See also* reproductive violence
Shakur, Assata, 26, 166, 169, 177–78
Sharpe, Christina, 23
She's Beautiful When She's Angry (film), 201n15
Shipp, Thomas, 84
Shockley, Evie, 189n18
Shupper, Rich, 129
silence: Black womanhood and breaking of, 162–63
Silencing the Past (Trouillot), 45–46
silhouette: archive and, 60–64; in Walker's work, 51–60
Simone, Nina, 149–50, 152
Sirk, Douglas, 36
Six Miles from Springfield on the Franklin Road (film), 24–25, 51–64
slavery: in Black feminist avant-garde films, 26–27; Black feminist research on, 146–64; Black women's sexuality and, 18–22; Federal Writer's Project initiative on, 208n71; Hartman on afterlife of, 16–18; iconography of, 11–13; race as medium and, 21–22; rape and, 90–95
"Slavery" (episode of *History of the Negro People*), 166, 169, 174–77
"Slavery, Race, and Ideology in the United States of America" (Fields), 22

Smith, Abram, 84
Smith, Cauleen, 27
Smith, Jack, 9
Snorton, C. Riley, 23
Sobchack, Vivian, 179
Solange, 184, 186
Souls of Black Folk, The (Du Bois), 32, 156–57
Southern Christian Leadership Conference (SCLS), 171
Southern Horrors (Wells-Barnett), 82, 197n38
Southern Horrors (Feimster), 81, 90, 196n19, 197n34, 198n61
space, Black feminist phenomenology and, 161–63
Spalding, Esperanza, 184
spectacle, of Black suffering, 51
Spectacular Secret, A (Goldsby), 84, 91–92, 199n66
Specters of Marx (Derrida), 63
Spillers, Hortense, 18–23, 147, 152–53, 207n64
spiritual labor, in Lynch's video, 75–76
Stahl, John, 36
S.T.A.R. (Street Transvestites Action Revolutionaries), 97, 101, 103–6, 110–16, 120–28, 134–36
S.T.A.R. House, 126
S.T.A.R. Manifesto, 103, 106, 123–25, 130–31; performativity of, 126–28
Stevenson, Cordelia, 198n61
Stewart, Jacqueline Najuma, 88–90
Stonewall (Carter), 129
Stonewall rebellion, 25–26, 101–16, 118, 121–23; archival documentation of, 129, 132–36; conflicted memories of, 201n9; in *Happy Birthday, Marsha!*, 136–42, 147; terminology about, 201n9–10
Street Transvestites for Gay Power, 110
Student Non-Violent Coordinating Committee (SNCC), 108
Students for a Democratic Society (SDS), 108, 201n15
Sula (Morrison), 165

Taylor, Diana, 119–20, 137–38
Taylor, Mya, 101–2, 137–42
Teen Vogue (magazine), 135
temporality: in Black feminist avant-garde films, 2–4; erotic and, 75–77

Index 227

tenderness, Black feminist avant-garde cinema and, 11–14, 183–86
Thirteenth Amendment, 29, 192n2
Toomer, Jean, 9, 189n18
Tourmaline (Reina Gossett), xi, 25–28, 97, 99–100, 103–6, 115, 120, 122, 135–42, 184, 191n49, 200n5
Trans Exclusionary Radical Feminists, 115
"Transformation of Silence into Language and Action, The" (Lorde), 20, 162–63
transgender theory and identity: in Black feminist avant-garde film, 23, 25–26, 116–23, 191n49; cinematic archive of, 105; S.T.A.R. Manifesto and, 127–28; Stonewall rebellion and, 107–16
Trap Door (Stanley and Burton), 104, 191n49
trickster archive: in Dunye's *The Watermelon Woman*, 15–18, 47; Walker's use of, 47
Trouillot, Michel-Rolph, 45–46, 120
Truth, Sojourner, 157, 206nn40–41
12 Little Spells (Spaulding album), 184

Un Chien Andalou (film), 188n10, 195n42
"Unspeakable Things Unspoken" (Morrison), 165
"Uses of the Erotic" (Lorde), 74–76

Van Der Zee, James, 9, 189n18
"Venus in Two Acts" (Hartman), 16–17
video, Lynch's use of, 67–74
violence: archival violence, 14–18, 38–43, 135–36; in Black feminist avant-garde films, 3–4, 26–27; Black women's sexuality and, 18–22; erotic and sacred space of, 75–77; ghosts of, 93–95; National Archives affidavits as record of, 46–50; Reconstruction era, 29–38; reproductive violence, 13–14; silhouettes as visualization of, 53; visualization of, 50–60
vision: Black womanhood and distortion of, 18–22
visitation: in avant-garde cinema, 52–53; haunting and conjure work and, 5–7; in *SAVED :: video postcard* (Lynch video installation), 74–77; in Walker's work, 62–64

Walker, Alice, 135, 160
Walker, Kara, 24–25, 28, 29–38, 42, 190n46; archival documentation in work of, 47, 60–64; images embraced by, 51; silhouettes in work of, 47, 50–60; tenderness in work of, 183–84
Walsh, Michal, 53–55
Watermelon Woman, The (film), 15–18, 47, 188n14
Water Ritual #1: An Urban Rite of Purification (film), 27
We Have Always Been Here (film), 191n49
Weheliye, Alexander, 187n7
Weiss, Gail, 145
Wells-Barnett, Ida B., 82–85, 197n38, 199n64
western knowledge production: archival documentation and, 126; Black women's bodies and violence of, 174–75; performance and, 118–23
We Travel the Space Ways (Lynch), 190n48
When I Get Home (Solange album), 184, 186
White, Deborah Gray, 23, 148, 157
whiteness, in avant-garde film, 9–10
whiteness, in feminist theory, 7–8, 22–23
Why Is the Negro Lynched? (Douglass), 83
Wicker, Randy, 129, 132–33
Williams, John, 174
Williams, Sarah, 198n61
Willis, Amanda (Mandy), 54–55, 60–63, 183–84
Wilson, Woodrow, 85
Witch's Flight, The (Keeling), 23, 180–81
Within our Gates (film), 36, 85–91
Without Sanctuary (Allen), 199n68
Women's Rights Convention, 157
Wood, Amy Louise, 199n66
Woods, Eliza, 81–82
Wooten, J. P., 81
Works Progress Administration (WPA), slave narratives produced by, 174, 208n71
Wortzel, Sasha, 25–28, 97, 99, 103, 115, 120, 122, 135–42, 184, 191n49
Wright, James, 175
Writing of History, The (de Certeau), 62–63
Wyeth, Geo, 200n2

Young Lord's Party, 107, 110

www.ingramcontent.com/pod-product-compliance
Lightning Source LLC
Chambersburg PA
CBHW050242170426
43202CB00015B/2891